ROYAL
SEX

ABOUT THE AUTHOR

Roger Powell has been a professional genealogist for over forty years and is the co-author of the best-selling book *Royal Bastards: Illegitimate Children of the British Royal Family*. Until his recent retirement he was a senior editor at *Burke's Peerage and Gentry* and Director of *Debretts Ancestry Research*. He is related to the Duke of Monmouth, a bastard son of Charles II and lives in Northamptonshire.

PRAISE FOR ROGER POWELL

Royal Bastards, with Peter Beauclerk-Dewar
'Spicy and enjoyable... an absorbing story'
LITERARY REVIEW
'A great read... the research is excellent'
PROFESSOR RONALD HUTTON
'A delightful and thought-provoking book'
CHARLES BEAUCLERK, AUTHOR OF NELL GWYN
'An important work of historical research... excellent'
FAMILY HISTORY

ROYAL SEX

ROGER POWELL

AMBERLEY

This edition first published 2013

Amberley Publishing
The Hill, Stroud
Gloucestershire, GL5 4EP

www.amberleybooks.com

British Library Cataloguing in Publication Data.
A catalogue record for this book is available from the British Library.

ISBN 978-1-4456-1377-2 (paperback)
ISBN 978-1-4456-1381-9 (ebook)

Typesetting and Origination by Amberley Publishing.
Printed in the UK.

CONTENTS

Contents

1

THE TUDOR PERIOD: THE HOWARD & BOLEYN FAMILIES & THE ENGLISH SUCCESSION

MARY BOLEYN, MISTRESS OF HENRY VIII

In the last decade of the fifteenth century Henry Tudor faced several attempts by rivals to destabilise his kingdom and deprive him of his crown. In quick succession he was faced with the Cornish Rebellion (1496) and the invasion of England by the Scottish King James IV in 1496 and again in 1497 in support of the Yorkist Pretender, Perkin Warbeck. Amongst the men appointed to serve in the King's Army to fight the pretender was Sir William Boleyn and his twenty year old son and heir Thomas, who had recently been appointed one of the King's Esquires of the Body.

The young King of Scots, James IV '... by far the most gifted and balanced of the early Stuart Kings had a flair for languages...; [and was] a true man of the renaissance, [who] cared deeply about literature, painting, music and architecture'. But his support of Warbeck proved an unwise move and when his invasion of England failed he was forced to agree to a seven year truce with Henry VII in September 1497, which eventually led to his marriage with Henry's daughter, the Princess Margaret in 1503. The marriage restored peace between England and Scotland for the next fifteen years and prevented the French King from renewing the 'Ould Alliance' between Scotland and France. Warbeck meanwhile was unceremoniously asked to leave the country and betook himself off to Cornwall in the hope that he could gain support from the uprising there. The result was an ignominious defeat and his capture by the forces of Henry VII.

In the wake of the rebellion Sir William Boleyn successfully negotiated a marriage between his son and heir and the beautiful Lady Elizabeth

Howard, the eldest daughter of Thomas, Earl of Surrey, England's premier Earl. The alliance was a major triumph for the Boleyn family and continued the precedent set by Sir William of taking a bride only from noble stock; Sir William had married a daughter and co-heiress of the Earl of Ormonde, Ireland's premier Earl and head of the famous Butler clan.

Thomas's marriage made him the brother-in-law of the Lady Anne Plantagenet, once the intended bride of Philip 'the Handsome', son of the Emperor Maximilian I and sister of Queen Elizabeth. Eager to make use of this Royal connection, he diligently set about making a career for himself at court. With just an income of £50 per annum to live on during the early years of his marriage it was imperative that he did so as his wife proved to be very fruitful in producing children. As one of the Queen's Ladies in Waiting, the Lady Elizabeth also used her position to further her husband's career.

The eldest surviving child of the family, a daughter Mary, named in honour of the Virgin Mary, was born about 25 March 1498 and she was quickly followed by a sister Anne, named in honour of St Anne, who was born about 26 July 1501. A younger brother George, named in honour of St George, made his appearance about 23 April 1504. Mary arrived in the world at the same time as the Princess Mary, the youngest surviving daughter of Henry VII, whose maid of honour she would become when she married the King of France.

Despite his best efforts, however, Thomas was unable to make the advances in his career that he had confidently expected and was forced to bide his time and perfect his linguistic skills until such time as the Crown decided it had need of his talents. Despite this setback Thomas and his family witnessed at first hand the Crown's continuing attempts to safe guard itself from plots, rebellion and invasion. After the execution of Warbeck and the Earl of Warwick, the last legitimate male Plantagenet, Henry VII was finally able to conclude his negotiations with Ferdinand and Isabella of Spain for the marriage of their daughter Catherine with Prince Arthur. However, just six months after the wedding the Prince died, where upon the Earl of Suffolk, the Queen's cousin, who stood in line to succeed to the crown fled the country for a second time taking his younger brother Richard with him and settled at Aix-La-Chapelle under the protection of the Emperor Maximilian.

Edmund de la Pole, Earl of Suffolk, was the eldest surviving son of John de la Pole, Duke of Suffolk and his wife Elizabeth Plantagenet, sister of Edward IV. His elder brother John, whom Richard III declared his successor, was killed at the Battle of Stoke in 1487, whilst promoting the cause of Lambert Simnel. Described by the chronicler Edward Hall as 'stout and bold of courage, of wit rash and heady', during the Cornish Rebellion he loyally served with Lords Essex and Mountjoy in the King's army. Several years later he fled the country after killing a man but on his return was obliged to undergo a public trial and condemned for his actions. Highly indignant that he had not been tried by his peers Edmund immediately left the country, without permission, and went to the court of his aunt the Duchess of Burgundy. On his father's death he was not allowed to assume the title of Duke of Suffolk and was forced to pay a fine of £5,000, before he could inherit his lands because of his brother Lincoln's rebellion.

Back in England, Sir William Courtenay, husband of the Queen's sister, Edmund's brother William de la Pole and Sir James Tyrell were all imprisoned in the Tower of London. Tyrell was executed in 1502 after confessing that it was he who had murdered the young princes in 1483, whilst Sir William Courtenay remained imprisoned until 1509. William de la Pole, remained a prisoner until his death in 1539.

Despite many attempts by Henry to extricate Edmund from the protection of the Emperor Maximilian the latter refused to co-operate declaring that Aix-La-Chapelle was a free city. However, in the spring of 1504 Edmund fled the city to avoid his debtors but was then detained by the Duke of Gelders and then by Philip, titular King of Castile, Maximilian's son and heir. For two years he remained in Philip's custody but in 1506 Philip was forced by bad weather to land in England whilst on his way to Castile by sea and during his time at the English court he negotiated a treaty with Henry which included the promise that Philip would hand over Edmund in exchange for a written promise by Henry that he would spare his life. Henry kept his promise but Edmund spent the remainder of his life in the Tower of London.

Unlike his brother-in-law Thomas Boleyn, the Earl of Surrey, who was husband of the Queen's sister, prospered during these years. But the sudden death of the Prince of Wales in April 1502 highlighted once again the fragility of the Tudor Succession. Henry VII now had only one surviving son and two daughters, the eldest of whom had just married the King of Scots. Lady Cecily Courtenay's two sons Henry and Edward plus Lord Surrey's son Thomas, were now next in line to succeed to the crown in the event that Henry, Duke of York died before reaching adulthood. But the threat that Edmund de la Pole and his brother Richard might invade England with foreign aid was still very real. Richard who entered the service of Louis XII King of France 'was a colourful prince, fond of women, horses, fine buildings, war and the tournament' and after the death of his brother Edmund would continue to be a thorn in the side of Henry VIII.

With the death of Henry VII and the accession of Henry VIII Thomas Boleyn's career suddenly progressed. At the coronation in 1509, he was made a Knight of the Bath and then appointed one of the King's Esquires of the Body; the following year he was made Sheriff of the county of Kent. But it was his linguistic skills especially his fluency in French that ensured his future advancement. In the mean time he participated in various royal entertainments and tournaments before being appointed, in 1512, an envoy to the court of the Archduchess Margaret, Regent of the Netherlands. Whilst there he impressed the Archduchess with his skills as a negotiator and willingly accepted her offer that his youngest daughter Anne should join her court, which she did in the summer of 1513 as a companion to the grandchildren of the Emperor Maximilian; the following year her sister Mary became a maid of honour to Mary, the King's sister.

Henry VIII's marriage to Catherine of Aragon just six weeks after his accession and the knowledge that she was soon with child created great expectations in England that she would bear a prince. However, the child was a daughter and stillborn. Undaunted she quickly conceived again and much to the nations joy gave birth to a son on New Years day 1511. He lived just fifty-two days and his passing greatly afflicted his parents. Catherine did not conceive again until 1513 but on the 8 October was 'delivered early of a son' who died almost immediately.

The premature death of the King's second son was a great disappointment to Henry but despite this the year did provide him with several reasons to be joyful. In the early part of the year Edmund de la Pole, the attainted Earl of Suffolk, was discovered to be in correspondence with his brother Richard in France and was promptly executed on Tower Hill on 30 April. He left a widow and a young daughter who was placed in a convent to prevent her from marrying and was heard of no more. The removal of de la Pole sent a clear message to all of the King's close relatives that he would brook no opposition or counter claims to his crown. The second event was the total defeat of the army of the King of Scots at Flodden field on 9 September by the King's Army under the command of the Earl of Surrey, Thomas's brother-in-law and the King's uncle. The flower of the Scottish Nobility and their King was destroyed, leaving the country exposed and vulnerable. As a reward for this singular victory Surrey was created Duke of Norfolk and made a Knight of the Garter.

In the wake of this welcome victory and Henry VIII's successful invasion of France in the following June plus the victory at the Battle of the Spurs in August and the capture of Therouanne and Tournai, France, Scotland's ally now sought an alliance with England. The following year the two countries concluded their alliance with the marriage of the Princess Mary with the French King, Louis XII and amongst the Princess's maids of honour was Mary Boleyn, the elder daughter of Thomas and Elizabeth Boleyn. The new Queen took with her some of the greatest ladies in the land, viz: the Duchess of Norfolk, the Countess of Oxford, the Marchioness of Dorset and Lady Monteagle etc but they all returned to England after her marriage except Jane Popincourt, formerly the mistress of the Duc de Longueville, who had been a prisoner at the English court for many years.

However, the marriage was not popular with all of the French King's subjects, according to one, Louis had no need to marry viz: 'For many reasons he had no need to marry nor had he any wish to, but because he saw himself beset on all sides by wars he could not wage without sorely afflicting his people, he sacrificed himself'. But the sacrifice was worth it for the Princess was one of the 'loveliest in English history, very tall, slim, fine boned, with perfect features and wide blue eyes, she was famous for the golden hair which grew down to her waist. Intelligent, sweet natured, she excelled in all the courtly graces, especially conversation and dancing'.

Amusingly the King's performance or lack of it in the royal bed was soon common gossip, leading the heir to the throne, the Comte de Angouleme to comment that 'unless someone has lied to me, it is not possible for the King and Queen to beget children'. The morning after she was married Mary was shocked to learn that all of her English ladies in waiting and her more experienced maids of honour were dismissed but was consoled and amused by the young Comte de Angouleme (the future Francois I) who began to pay her marked attention. So much so that the Seigneur Brantome recalled many years later that an old courtier M. de Grignaux, had warned the Comte thus 'Don't you see, she's a cunning, crafty woman who wants to lead you on till you make her pregnant? And if she does have a child, you'll stay plain Comte d'Angouleme and never be King of France'. Whatever the truth of the matter Mary's marriage did not last very much longer. On 1 January 1515 Louis died of a vomiting fit in the middle of a storm and his widow was free to marry the man of her choice, Charles Brandon, Duke of Suffolk.

The Princess's behaviour could not have made a good impression upon her maids of honour or ladies-in-waiting, including the young Mary Boleyn. But the latter appears to have amused herself any way despite her mistresses situation. Indeed it is rumoured that the new French King, Francois I, took an immense liking to the young maid of honour. This was quite understandable given Francois's nature for he believed 'that the entire ornament of a court lay in its ladies, and wished that his should have more of them than had hitherto been the case. For truly a court without ladies is a garden without beautiful flowers, like that of a Satrap or a Turk, where one never sees any ladies at all'. But Mary's sojourn in France was very brief and she returned to England with her mistress and did not return until her father was appointed Ambassador to France in 1518. She remained for two years and was so liberal with her favours that she acquired a very unsavoury reputation.

As Ambassador to the King of France, Sir Thomas was now able to mix with the good and the great and whilst there he was able to arrange for his younger daughter Anne to be appointed a Maid of Honour to Queen Claude, a post she held until early 1522, when she returned to England. The purpose of his visit was to conclude the negotiations for the marriage of the infant Princess Mary to the French Dauphin but despite his best efforts it did not happen. Instead he supervised the preparations for the meeting between Henry VIII and the French King, known as the Field of the Cloth of Gold. Mary meanwhile returned home to England where a marriage was hastily arranged with Master William Carey, one of the King's Esquires of the Body.

William Carey, was a distant cousin of Henry VIII and a descendant of Edmund Beaufort, 1st Duke of Somerset, uncle of the King's grandmother Margaret Beaufort. Apart from his pedigree there was little to recommend him as a husband except the fact that he was almost always in attendance upon the King in his role as an esquire of the body. As the niece of the newly restored Duke of Norfolk, soon to be England's premier Duke, Mary had every reason to expect to make a much better match.

The Duke of Norfolk was determined to remain as close to the Royal Family as possible despite the death of his first wife the Lady Anne Plantagenet in 1511, without any surviving issue; his subsequently married the daughter of Duke of Buckingham and thus added greatly to the rising status and prestige of the Howard family.

The year before Master Carey's marriage to Mary, the King's mistress Bessie Blount had give birth to his bastard and was with child a second time. After the birth of her second child she was hastily married to Gilbert Tailboys and then had two more sons in rapid succession. During her eight year marriage to William Carey, Mary bore two children, Catherine circa 1523 and Henry, 4 March 1526. Both children appear to have been named in honour the King and Queen and at some point during the marriage Mary became Henry's mistress. William, as an esquire of the body, attended the King during the brief visit of the Emperor Charles V to England at the end of May 1520 and again in early June when Henry met the French King at the Field of the Cloth of Gold. Mary, who accompanied her husband, went as a member of the Queen's retinue and it was almost certainly during these visits that Henry first began to court her.

The benefits of such an affair were not lost on Thomas Boleyn but, as with Bessie Blount, Henry was very discreet in his extra marital activities and not over generous in rewarding his mistresses. Nevertheless Thomas was soon created a Knight of the Garter, an unusual honour for a mere knight but a clear sign that his star was in the ascent. Neither Bessie or Mary received titles in recognition for the service they had performed and the land grants that their husbands received were not such as would raise undue comment. The first major grants of manors and estates to William Carey were in June 1524, after or about the birth of Mary's daughter Catherine and again in February and May 1526, shortly before and after the birth of Mary's son Henry. Some historians believe that the timing of these grants prove they were the King's children but positive proof is lacking.

The grant in May 1526 was for the Manor of Pleasance in the grounds of Greenwich Palace which was reputedly used by Henry for amorous assignations with his mistress. But which mistress? The Manor, its Tower and garden was originally granted in December 1517 to Sir Nicholas Carew, whose wife Elizabeth was a cousin of Mary and Anne Boleyn, thus giving rise to speculation that Elizabeth was also briefly Henry's mistress. However, as she was a very good friend of Bessie Blount it is equally possible that the Tower was used as a rendezvous for Henry and Bessie.

How long the affair with Mary lasted is unclear. Henry was known for quickly tiring of his mistresses but in Cardinal Pole's famous letter to the King admonishing him for his attempts to divorce his wife and marry Anne, he speaks of the affair lasting 'a long time'. Whatever the truth it was obviously over by early 1526 and thus the lady in the tower could not have been Mary.

By 1524 the King was still without a legitimate son and heir and was becoming increasingly alarmed at the prospect of never having one. Despite the consolation of knowing that he could sire a son, albeit a bastard one, he began to grow increasingly fearful of the activities of his kinsman 'the White Rose' Richard de la Pole. On the execution of his brother Edmund in 1513, Richard had assumed the title of Earl of Suffolk, despite the fact that his elder brother William was next in line to succeed. During his years at the French court Richard had acquired a considerable reputation as a military leader and trusted companion of the French King. In 1521 he had taken part in the invasion of Navarre by the French but then lost his life at the Battle of Pavia in January 1525 when the French Army was soundly beaten by the Imperialists.

Henry was delighted and relieved when he heard the news of Richard's death and as a result took a more benign attitude towards his close kin in England. In the June of 1525 he created his bastard son Henry Fitzroy, Duke of Richmond and Somerset, his cousin Henry Courtenay, Marquess of Exeter, his nephew Henry Brandon, Earl of Lincoln and another cousin Thomas Manners, Earl of Rutland. At the same time he created Thomas Boleyn, Earl of Wiltshire thus seemingly setting the seal on his relationship with Thomas's daughter Mary, who seems to have celebrated by conceiving her second child.

Unfortunately no contemporary portrait of Mary has survived thus we can only speculate about her looks. Clearly she was sufficiently attractive to capture Henry's attention and her personality engaging enough to hold his interest for a number of years. The ability to sing, dance and play a musical instrument were other accomplishments that she must have possessed to a high degree but she did not have that sharp, incisive mind that enabled her sister Anne to hold on to her conquest.

Anne Boleyn first came to Henry's attention in 1521 following the King's plan to marry her to the heir of the Earl of Ormonde in order to settle a dispute over the succession to the title. She made her first appearance at a Court revel in March 1522 and made an immediate impression. Contemporary documents describe her thus 'she was a little, lively, sparkling brunette, with fascinating eyes and long black hair, which she wore coquettishly floating loosely down her back, interlaced with jewels. The beauty of her eyes and hair struck all beholders alike – grave ecclesiastics and spruce young sprigs of nobility'. But Henry's infatuation with Anne Boleyn is thought to have begun in early 1526, perhaps around Shrove Tuesday when he took part in a joust disguised as a tortured lover who was unable to declare his passion for his new love.

When his plans to marry her to Lord Butler fell through, Anne 'formed a deep attachment to the young Lord Percy' unaware that Henry's interest in her was growing every day. Initially he hoped to make her his mistress but her strict upbringing at the French court where 'the society of gentlemen was forbidden to (the French Queen's) maidens' and her general demeanour at the English court was such that it was inconceivable she would even contemplate such a course of action. The French King was very impressed by her and commented that 'She is discreet and modest; and it is hinted amongst the court ladies that she desires above all things to be a nun. This I should regret'.

Lord Percy's interest was brought to an abrupt halt when Henry instructed Cardinal Wolsey to forbid any further communication between the young couple, hence forth she would be the exclusive property of the King. Initially Henry's attentions were very unwelcome forcing Anne to declare 'I beseech your Highness to desist in writing to me... I will rather lose my life than my virtue, which will be the greatest and best part of the dowry I shall bring to my husband...' On another occasion she replied 'Your wife I cannot be because you have a queen already. Your mistress I will not be!' Henry responded thus '... if it pleases you to do the office of a true, loyal mistress, and give yourself body and heart, to me... I promise you not only the name but that I shall make you my sole mistress, remove all others from my affection, and serve you only.'

Henry's attempts to sire a legitimate son by his wife ceased in 1524 and his affair with Mary was over by 1526, thus leaving him a free agent. Whilst his passion for Anne remained unconsummated it would be totally unrealistic to expect him to remain celibate until the winter of 1532, when Anne conceived the future Queen Elizabeth. His offer to Anne in 1527 to forsake all others for her suggests that he might have had other mistresses whilst courting Anne.

Unlike his fellow monarch Francois I, Henry was very discreet in his choice of mistresses, so much so that it very difficult to determine their names. However, two immediately spring to mind, Jane Pollard, wife of Sir Hugh Stukley and Mary Berkeley, wife of Thomas Perrott. Sir Hugh, allegedly a Knight of the Body to the King and Thomas, an Esquire of the Body, certainly had some formal contact with Henry but the claims that Jane and Mary both bore the King bastard sons remains unproven.

At the same time as Henry had fallen under the spell of Anne Boleyn, the King of France was released from his captivity in Spain following his spectacular defeat at the Battle of Pavia. On his return to France, he put aside the cares of state and indulged in a frenzied round of divertissements including hunting, and dancing and imitating Henry took another mistress Madamoiselle d'Heilly, one of the thirty children of the Seigneur de Pisseleu. Anne d'Heilly was Francois's second 'Grande Passion' and remained his principal mistress for the remainder of his life and later became a lady in waiting to his second wife Queen Eleanor and subsequently Governess his daughters the Princesses Madeleine and Marguerite. In return for her love she was given several splendid chateaux at Etampes and Limours and a house in Paris together with a complaisant husband the Sieur de Brosse, who was made Governor of Brittany and later Duc d'Etampes.

Francois's generous treatment of his mistress was in stark contrast to Henry's treatment of Mary. When her husband William Carey died of the sweating sickness in 1528, Henry granted the wardship of her son Henry to her sister Anne and warned her that Mary was in 'extreme necessity'. He then ordered her father Thomas Boleyn to 'take Mary under his roof and maintain her' but assigned her an annuity of £100 'formerly enjoyed by her husband'. There would be no titles, lands and other honours in recognition of her affair with the King.

Although now a widow and her sister the King's new love, Mary's prospects of finding another husband remained high but for five years neither her father or her sister attempted to improve her situation. As the King's ex-mistress no ambitious nobleman sought her hand in marriage therefore she was forced to look elsewhere for a husband. When she made her choice and married without the King's permission Henry and Anne were furious more so when they discovered that she was also with child. Sir William Stafford, was a distant kinsman of the late Duke of Buckingham but the marriage appears to have been a love match. However, Mary was banished from court and her allowance taken away and her remaining days were spent quietly in Essex where she died in 1543.

ELIZABETH BLOUNT, MISTRESS OF HENRY VIII

She was a descendant of kings and princes, including the last Welsh Prince of Wales, Owen Glendower, and a cousin of her Royal Lover Henry VIII and two of his wives. Her kinswoman the Lady Eleanor Butler, was rumoured to have been the first love and possibly the wife of Edward IV, thus she brought a rich and diverse heritage in her wake. It did not matter that some of her descents were on the distaff side because her beauty alone made her eminently fitted to be the wife of a King no less. But fate decreed that she would be a royal mistress and not a royal wife and to live during one of the most turbulent and violent times in English History, the reign of Henry VIII.

Sixteenth century England was dominated by the Tudor Succession Crisis. During a reign of twenty-four years Henry VII was challenged by several rival claimants to his crown but he survived and on his death left the kingdom more powerful, much richer and a major player on the international stage. But he had just one surviving son to perpetuate the Tudor line, Henry VIII, therefore the latter's marriage and the arrival of male heirs was of great importance to the kingdom. Fate, however, denied him a living son until he had reached his forty-fifth year and even then it was feared that this young prince might die young and leave the kingdom in crisis.

Henry VII's choice of the Princess of Aragon as a bride for his eldest son Prince Arthur was designed to increase England's standing amongst the other major monarchies in Europe. It would also, hopefully, ensure the continuation of the Tudor line. As the daughter of the King of Aragon and Queen of Castile, Catherine brought with her an interesting ancestry. The Royal Houses of Aragon, Castile and Portugal were highly interbred and Catherine's ancestry included four descents from Alfonso XI, King of Castile and his mistress Leonor de Guzman and several from Pedro I, King of Portugal via his legitimate and bastard children including an uncle/niece marriage. Bastards featured prominently in her ancestry and she was also a kinswoman of her future husband. But it was for her potential breeding ability that she was chosen and as both of her sisters had borne healthy broods of children, there was no reason to think that Catherine would not follow suit. But the unexpected death of her young husband Prince Arthur jeopardised all of Henry's carefully laid plans and it would be another seven years before the widowed Princess eventually married the Prince's younger brother.

The validity of his marriage to his brother's widow is said to have haunted Henry VIII for the remainder of his life. But he was well aware of holy scripture forbidding such a union and it was only when Catherine had failed to give him a living son that he used it as the reason to divorce her. Although infant mortality was an occupational hazard in any century, Catherine's inability to produce a living male heir had grave political repercussions including the possibility of the young James V King of Scots; Henry's nephew, inheriting the English crown. The young King, the son of Henry's widowed sister Margaret, was born in 1512 and crowned the following year. Like her brother the Queen of Scots also had difficulty in producing a living son, of the six children she bore, four sons and two daughters, only one son survived infancy. The Princess Mary, Henry's younger sister produced just two sons and two daughters of which only the second son and the daughters grew to adulthood, the son dying of consumption at the age of seventeen.

Catherine's sisters on the other hand were very fertile and the eldest Joanna bore six children all of whom survived to adulthood, the youngest sister Maria, Queen of Portugal, bore twelve children of whom two died in infancy. Unlike Catherine, Joanna and Maria were married at seventeen and eighteen respectively and bore their first children in their late teens whilst Catherine was married at twenty-four and bore her first child, a still born daughter, at the age of twenty five. Claude, wife of Francois I of France was married at fifteen and bore her first child at sixteen. Clearly beginning the process of childbearing at a relatively late age was not to be recommended.

The prospect of a foreign prince ruling England after his death was anethema to Henry and indeed to the English nobility in general but neither would he contemplate the succession going to one of his Plantagenet kinsman, such as the Marquess of Exeter or Lord Montague. The only option left was for him to re-marry but initially he would not consider it preferring to conduct several illicit love affairs with some of his wife's maids of honour viz: Elizabeth Blount and Mary Carey and perhaps Lady Elizabeth Carew.

Lady Carew, was the daughter of Sir Thomas Bryan, Vice-Chamberlain to Queen Catherine and was married at the age of fourteen to Nicholas Carew, a Gentleman of the King's Privy Chamber. The King attended the wedding which took place in December 1514 and gave the married couple the manors of Wallington, Carshalton, Beddington, Woodmanstone, Woodcote and Mitcham in Surrey as a wedding present. Immediately after the wedding Carew was made an Esquire of the Body to the King and then in December 1517 appointed Keeper of the Manor of Pleasance in the grounds of Greenwich Palace. In addition to being a cousin of Anne and Mary Boleyn, Elizabeth, was descended from the Countess of Essex, aunt of Edward IV and thus Henry's third cousin. Nicholas, her husband was a firm favourite of Henry's and had been at court from a very early age. He was about five years younger than the King and was also a boon companion of Charles Brandon, subsequently Henry's brother-in-law.

The wedding took place during the Christmas revels at the Palace of Greenwich. A few nights later on Twelfth Night the whole court took part in the first masque ever to be performed in the country with the King and all his courtiers 'disguised after the manner of Italy'. The King's partner was Jane Poppingcourt, a Frenchwoman, who had previously been a maid of honour to Mary Tudor, Henry's sister and was presently the mistress of the Duke de Longueville. The Queen did not take part in the masque as she was once again with child but in the early months of 1515 she gave birth prematurely to another son 'which lived not long after'.

The Manor of Pleasance was a favourite haunt of the King and it is alleged by one contemporary source to have been the residence of one of his mistresses viz: 'the King... in his barge went from Westminster to Greenwich to visit a fair lady whom the King loved, who was lodged in the tower of the park'. Master Carew, who was subsequently knighted was Keeper of the Manor until 1526 when it was granted to William Carey, the husband of Mary Boleyn, another of the King's mistresses. It would seem therefore that the lady he visited was Elizabeth Blount. During her marriage Lady Carew received a large number of precious stones and jewellery from Henry and it is this plus that fact that her residence was used by the King for his amours that suggested she was briefly his mistress.

In the April of 1518, the queen discovered that she was once again with child, the conception having taken place at the beginning of February. Overjoyed, she was asked by Henry to take care of her condition because as he explained to Cardinal Wolsey 'about this time is partly of her dangerous times, and because of that I would remove her as little as I may now'. Sadly, however, when she gave birth in early November it was another girl which died shortly afterwards.

Mistress Blount, the daughter of Sir John Blount, of Kinlet came from a family with a very distinguished ancestry and a record of service to the Tudors that was second to none. Her father was an Esquire of the Body to Henry VIII and her great-grandfather Sir Richard Croft had been Comptroller of the Household to Henry VII and his wife Governess to Princes Arthur and Henry. The blood of the Plantagenets also flowed through her veins.

She came to Court at the tender age of twelve and eventually was appointed a maid of honour to Catherine of Aragon in the hope that the position would increase her chances of finding a suitable husband. But instead she captured a much greater prize, the King! The first time Henry noticed her was during the Christmas celebrations of 1514, when she appeared in a masque in the Queen's chamber dressed in 'blue velvet and cloth of gold, styled after the fashions of Savoy'. Her beauty and other accomplishments captivated Henry and the affair appears to have been consummated in October 1518, after a discreet courtship, in the wake of the celebrations organised by Cardinal Wolsey to mark the betrothal of the Princess Mary to the Dauphin of France. The following year Elizabeth presented him with a bastard son.

Here at last was proof of his virility! No longer would his fellow monarch the French King be able to taunt him for his lack of a son and when the French King asked Henry to be godfather to his second son Henri in 1519, Henry graciously accepted the honour with pride. But unlike her sister in sin, Francoise Dame de Chateaubriant, who became the French King's mistress at that same time as Elizabeth became

Henry's, Elizabeth never achieved the coveted position of *mistress en titre*. Nevertheless the affair was a clear indication that Henry was tired of being the devoted husband but still unwilling to consider a divorce from his Queen as a serious proposition.

Why Elizabeth chose to become his mistress is unclear but it was probably for the usual promises of land, titles and riches for herself and her family. But the surrender of her virginity did not bring the anticipated rich rewards. Any attempt to aim higher and become the King's wife was a much more serious proposal and one that required a woman of strong character, firm principles and nerves of steel like Anne Boleyn. Elizabeth had none of these qualities. Her attraction was purely physical and when Henry grew tired of these a suitable husband was found. But until then she blossomed under the attention that Henry lavished upon her.

Henry's courtship occurred against the backdrop of the intense diplomatic negotiations between Cardinal Wolsey and France which culminated in the Treaty of London in October 1518. By this Treaty Henry agreed to hand back to the French the town of Tournai for the sum of 6000,000 crowns payable in twelve annual instalments. It was also agreed that the English monarch should visit France at the first opportunity the details being left to the Cardinal. The meeting of the Francois and Henry at the Field of the Cloth of Gold in June 1520 just outside Calais was a splendid affair with each monarch attended by a suite of 5000 courtiers, the flower of each nations nobility and gentry plus great officers of state. But Elizabeth was not there. The reason? She had just given birth to her second child, a daughter Elizabeth.

The paternity of this child presents a problem for historians because she declared in June 1542 that she was then twenty-two years old, thus born pre June 1520. As her elder brother appears to have been born in the month of June 1519, it is clear that she was conceived between the beginning of July and September 1519. In order for this child to have been her first legitimate offspring, a hastily arranged marriage would have to take place between the dates already mentioned, whilst she was still recovering from childbirth. But there is no record of Elizabeth as a married woman until 18 June 1522, when she and her then husband Gilbert Tailbois were granted the very rich manor of Rugby in Warwickshire. The day and month is significant being, it is alleged, the birth date of her bastard son.

The first record of Elizabeth as a married woman in 1522 and the subsequent births of two legitimate sons in 1523 and 1524 suggests that she did not marry immediately after the birth of her bastard son but after the birth of her bastard (?) daughter Elizabeth, i.e. post April 1520. If a marriage was being negotiated by Cardinal Wolsey, Elizabeth's mentor, and the Tailbois family, the two year gap between her childrens births is then understandable.

The knowledge that Elizabeth was with child a second time in the autumn of 1519, obviously prevented her from resuming her duties in the Queen's household and the post was filled by Mary Boleyn, who had unfortunately acquired a reputation for gallantry whilst at the Court of France. As daughter of the English Ambassador to that country and niece to the Duke of Norfolk, England's Premier Duke, Mary was a prime catch for any aspiring young nobleman, therefore her marriage to William Carey, a mere Esquire of the Body to the King, was surprising and suggests perhaps that Henry had already declared an interest in her. An affair with a married woman was infinitely preferable because any resulting bastard children were legally the issue of her husband and could inherit his property. This is in marked contrast to the match they tried to arrange for their younger daughter Anne with Sir Piers Butler, a young kinsman, and heir to the Earldom of Ormonde, when she returned from France in early 1522.

Whilst Henry was wooing Mary Boleyn, Cardinal Wolsey was busy arranging Elizabeth's marriage to the King's ward Sir Gilbert Tailbois. At the same time William Carey received a good number of royal grants as a result of Henry's interest in his wife. Elizabeth and her husband also received some of the royal largesse including the very rich manor of Rugby in 1522, probably in celebration of their recent marriage. In addition Sir Gilbert and his father received 'great sums of money, but also many benefits to their right much comfort'.

Eight years later, however, Elizabeth suddenly became a widow with two young sons to support. Now free to chose a husband for herself she was not lost for suitors. At this point in time Henry was engrossed in his love affair with Anne Boleyn but a rumour began to circulate that his desire for a dispensation to absolve him from his marriage to his brother's widow was 'to legitimate by subsequent marriage a bastard son of his' so that he could succeed his father. The source of this rumour, Loys de Heylwigen, was a member of the Holy Roman Emperor's household. But Henry had no intention of marrying Elizabeth and did not forbid any of Elizabeth's suitors paying court to her.

The continuing Tudor Succession problem was now becoming a European 'cause celebre', indeed as early as 1514 a rumour spread that 'the King of England means to repudiate his present wife, the daughter of the King of Spain and his brother's widow, because he is unable to have children by her…'. The source, a Venetian in Rome further speculated that Henry would marry a daughter of the French Duc de Bourbon but the latter did not have a daughter.

Henry's failure to produce a surviving son was reminiscent of Charles VIII and Louis XII of France. Charles never produced a son and the crown was inherited by the next male heir Louis who solved his succession problem by marrying his eldest daughter to the nearest Prince of the Blood, Francois, Count de Angouleme. Henry never seems to have considered marrying his daughter to Henry Courtenay, Marquess of Exeter, his nearest male relative after the King of Scots. As one modern historian would have it 'To a man so prosperous, so splendid, so conscious of nobility, of rectitude, of splendid services to God and the Church, there seemed to be some mysterious paradox in the strange succession of calamities which had overcome the children of this dubious marriage…'.

The French King had no such succession problems. His Queen had borne him three healthy sons who all grew to adulthood but neither of his mistresses the Dame de Chateaubriant or the Duchess d'Etampes bore him any bastard children, unlike Lady Tailbois. Given the French King's reputation this was surprising but the Dame de Chateuabriant was married at the age of fourteen having already borne her husband a daughter who died in her teens. Bearing a child at such a tender age may have prevented her from having any more children as was probably the case with the Lady Margaret Beaufort, mother of Henry VII. In the case of the Duchess d'Etampes, she was one of thirty children born to the Seigneur de Heilly by three wives and for that reason the prospect of having children of her own may not have been her first priority! Either way the Duchess remained Francois's mistress for over twenty years and her predecessor only eight years.

Elizabeth's widowhood was short. One of her suitors Leonard Grey, a son of the Marquis of Dorset, was a cousin of the King. This young man would eventually become Lord Deputy of Ireland and receive an Irish Peerage as his reward but he was suddenly executed for high treason in 1540 for allowing the Earl of Kildare, an Irish rebel, to escape to France. Despite enlisting the aid of Thomas Cromwell, the King's secretary Master Gray's suit was unsuccessful and Elizabeth chose another suitor Edward, Lord Clinton. However, the marriage did not bring Lord Clinton a male heir because Elizabeth only gave him daughters.

Embarking on a second marriage with the possibility of further children was a risky exercise at the age of thirty-two but despite this Elizabeth produced three daughters, Bridget, Katherine and Margaret. Lord Clinton was considerably younger than Elizabeth, twelve years younger in fact and only inherited his father's lands at the age of twenty-three in 1535. Why he chose to marry a much older woman who was also the King's ex-mistress is unclear but it was probably in the hope that he would gain the Royal favour. However, the first fruits of Royal favour only came in the wake of the Pilgrimage of Grace in 1536 when he raised a troop of 500 men from his servants and tenants in Lincolnshire to assist the Royal Army in suppressing the rebels. By this act of loyalty he was rewarded with a grant of the dissolved monastery of Sempringham in Lincolnshire, which became his principle residence, plus the houses and sites of dissolved monasteries in Kent and Norfolk. Elizabeth, however, never fully recovered from the birth of her last child in 1539 and after a brief time as a Lady in Waiting to Anne of Cleves, Henry's fourth wife, died the following year at the age of forty. The Duke of Richmond, her bastard son, had died in 1536, at the age of seventeen, from a rapid consumption.

2

THE JACOBEAN PERIOD

GEORGE VILLIERS, DUKE OF BUCKINGHAM

James I loved 'his favourites better than women, loving them beyond the love of men to women'. Separated from his mother when he was only ten months old and without a father from birth, James was thus doubly disadvantaged. His first male companion John Erskine, was the son of the Earl and Countess of Mar and it was to him that the young prince turned to for the love and affection that was denied him as a child. But a strict upbringing plus a severe grounding in religion left him extremely vulnerable to being manipulated by anyone who managed to capture his affections.

The young prince's love for Master Erskine set the pattern for his relationships with his own sex for the remainder of his lifetime. Lady Mar 'who... kept the King in great awe' during his childhood and youth must therefore take some of the responsibility for this development in his nature.

Sir James Melville, in his memoirs, records that:

> the young King was brought up in Stirling, by Alexander Erskine (brother of the Earl of Mar) and my lady Mar, the latter's widow. He had four principal masters, Mr George Buchanan, Mr Peter Young, the abbots of Cambuskenneth and Dryburgh... plus the Laird of Drumwhasel... Master of the Household.

Master Buchanan, his tutor was a distinguished scholar but he did not hesitate to beat James if he misbehaved and was 'extremely vengeful against any man who offended him'. He also hated women, especially young James's mother the Queen of Scots, whom he blamed for the murder of James's father, Lord Darnley. The violence and uncertainty to which James was subjected during his time as King of Scotland affected him deeply. Indeed Sir John Oglander declared that:

> he could not endure a soldier or to see men drilled, to hear of war was death to him, and how he tormented himself with fear of some sudden mischief may be proved by his great quilted doublets, pistol-proof, also his strange eyeing of strangers with continual fearful observation.

The King's preference for the company of his own sex was the source of much comment in Scotland and amongst the Royal Courts of Europe. His first male favourite, his cousin Esme Stewart, Seigneur d'Aubigny, was old enough to be his father and this perhaps is the key to understanding why James welcomed and embraced him. Esme was the father figure that James never had. He was according to one contemporary 'of comely proportions, civil behaviour, red-headed' and 'honest in conversation' but his appearance at the Scottish court in 1579 caused much speculation and gossip because he came from France as an agent for the Guise family. The Duc de Guise, the uncle of James's mother, wished to promote the cause of his niece and believed that Esme could bring about a new Franco-Scottish Alliance. According to Sir James Melville he 'came in simplicity as if he could meddle with nothing' but events were to prove otherwise. Although not a handsome man by modern standards, he possessed great charm, a sharp brain and a talent for political intrigue which he used to considerable effect in the King's cause.

Within a short time Esme had gained a complete ascendency over James and the French Ambassador wrote in astonishment to his master:

> The success of the Lord of Aubigny is such that it seems certain that he will be made Earl of Lennox and it is thought by many that he will be named successor to the crown of Scotland should the King die without children.

The role of royal favourite was not unfamiliar to Esme for his aunt Helen had been a mistress of James V of Scotland by whom she had a son Adam. Another relative Agnes Stewart, a mistress of James IV of

Scotland, later married Adam Hepburn, Earl of Bothwell and became the grandmother of the celebrated Earl of Bothwell, husband of Mary, Queen of Scots. Agnes's daughter Jean, Lady Fleming rounded off the family tradition by becoming the mistress of Henri II, King of France.

Esme's wife Catherine de Entragues was also connected to the French Royal Family via her sister-in-law, the beautiful Marie de Touchet, one time mistress of Charles IX of France and mother by him of a bastard son, the Duc de Angouleme. Marie's legitimate daughter Catherine-Henriette also chose to follow in the mother's footsteps and went on to become the mistress of Henri IV of France.

Esme's good fortune, however, did not last and within a few years he fell victim to a conspiracy organised by the Earl of Gowrie and was unceremoniously exiled to France, where he died in Paris after a series of strokes. On his deathbed he recommended his children to the care of James and also declared his love and devotion to his sovereign. To his credit James did not forget him or his orphaned children. The eldest Ludovic was immediately given his deceased father's titles and estates and invited to come to Scotland.

After Esme's death James cast his eye elsewhere in his search for another companion. His choice of Patrick, Master of Gray, was singularly unfortunate as he was an 'idle and extravagant' young man, who had accompanied Esme from France but who later was instrumental in persuading the latter's widow to send her eldest son to Scotland in order to inherit his father's titles and estates. Gray had first met Esme whilst a young man during a visit to France and could speak fluent French. He was also a kinsman of James and Esme.

James's affection for those who were close to him in blood was a constant factor in his attempts to establish lasting relationships with members of his own sex. Another to whom he was attracted, Francis Stewart, Earl of Bothwell, the nephew of the infamous Bothwell, was also his first cousin. To this extraordinarily handsome young man, an unscrupulous character, James displayed his customary affection, hanging about his neck and embracing him tenderly. But when the young man attempted to kidnap him, James sought companionship elsewhere from another close kinsman George Gordon, Earl of Huntly, who was also often kissed by James 'to the amazement of many'. His preference for the company of handsome young men clearly had it's origins in his own feelings of inadequacy and lack of good looks but also in his isolation from practically all female contact during his youth.

His obvious affection for Bothwell and Huntly, however, did not prevent James from carrying out his royal duty of seeking a bride and producing children as befitted a sovereign prince. His choice of Anne of Denmark was fortunate as she had a compliant nature, liked eating, drinking and was very fond of jewellery and clothes. What she actually thought of her husband's preference for his male favourites is unknown but she appears to accepted the situation and it is even said that he would 'receive none in favour, but that was first recommended to him by the Queen'.

By contemporary standards the marriage was a success and produced half a dozen children, three of whom survived infancy. But James's attitude to women in general can best be summed up in the advice he gave his son Charles that they 'are no other thing else but irritamenta libidinis'. Having performed his marital duties James now returned once again to his favourites.

The next, James Hay was the younger son of a minor Scottish family of no great distinction and surprisingly unrelated to the King. This gentleman had spent some years serving in the Scots Guards at the court of the King of France and was introduced to James by the French Ambassador in 1603 in London after James had travelled south to claim the crown of England. He was:

'truly a most compleat and well accomplished gentleman, modest and court like and of so fair a demeanour, as made him be generally beloved; and for his wisdom... he was ever great with all the favourites of his time, and although the King did often change, yet he did not' In addition it was noted that he was 'made for a courtier, who wholly studied his master, and understood him better than any other'.

Despite being the new favourite, Master Hay never received the rewards that he thought were his due until many years later when he had been displaced by another young man who had served as one of his pages in Scotland. He was only advanced to the peerage in 1615 just a year before George Villiers was created a Viscount and several years after his successor Robert Carr also received the same honour. All of these young men retained the King's affection and favour but only Hay remained on good terms with everyone.

Robert Carr, a kinsman of the Earl of Lothian, caught the King's attention in 1607 when he fell off his horse and injured himself during a tournament. Struck by the young man's good looks, one contemporary described him as 'straightlimbed, strong shouldered and smooth faced', James offered to teach him Latin and soon they became inseparable, one courtier noting that he 'leaneth on his arm, pinches his cheek, smooths his ruffled garment, and when he looketh on Carr, directeth discourse to divers other…'

As with all of these young men, James lavished money, lands and titles on them and even arranged marriages with wealthy heiresses. The Master of Gray was married to the King's cousin Mary, the daughter of his illegitimate uncle Robert, Earl of Orkney, whilst the Earl of Huntly married Henrietta, daughter of Esme Stewart, Earl of Lennox, James's first favourite. James Hay, married the daughter and heiress of Lord Denny, the niece of Robert Cecil, the King's chief English minister. But Carr's choice of bride was to have dramatic and fatal consequences for himself and his family. He chose Lady Frances Howard, the daughter of the Earl of Suffolk (whose father the Duke of Norfolk had been executed for conspiring to marry Mary, Queen of Scots) but she was already married to the young Earl of Essex.

When the couple fell in love, James set up a special commission to facilitate an annulment to the Essex marriage and in due course Carr and his beautiful bride were wed. James gave her jewels worth £10,000 and also created her husband an Earl. The marriage was not popular with everyone. Sir Thomas Overbury, Carr's advisor and friend, who had written Carr's love letters to Lady Frances, remonstrated with him and declared:

> My lord, I perceive you are proceeding in this match, from which I have often dissuaded you, as your true servant and friend: I now again advise you not to marry that woman, for if you do you shall ruin your honour and yourself.

Unfortunately his warning went unheeded and for his pains he was imprisoned in the Tower of London, and once there, was slowly poisoned by the future Countess.

Not since Catherine Howard's adultery in the reign of Henry VIII, had a daughter of the noble house of Howard caused such a scandal! The Earl and Countess were eventually found guilty of murder and confined to the Tower before being granted a pardon and eventually released. At the same time the Earl and Countess of Suffolk, Robert Carr's in-laws were tried for financial corruption and the family lost all power and influence at court. But Carr had already sown the seeds of his own fall from grace when he refused to acknowledge the rising star of George Villiers. Carr's reaction was one of unconcealed jealousy and rage which prompted James to declare that 'a strange frenzy' had clearly possessed him which:

> so powdered and mixed with strange streams of unquietness, passion, fury, and insolent pride and (which is worst of all) with a settled kind of induced obstinacy, as it chokes and obscures all those excellent and good parts that God hath bestowed upon you.

Unlike Master Hay, Carr could not accept that his brief reign was over and that a new star, promoted by a cabal consisting of the Queen, the Archbishop of Canterbury and the Herbert brothers, one of whom had briefly been a favourite of James, was in the ascent. Bishop Goodman summed up the situation in the following words:

> The true fall of Somerset was this – that love and affection, though they are the strongest passions for the instant, yet they are not of the longest continuance, for they are not grounded in judgment, but are rather fancies that follow the eye; and as beauty itself doth decay, so love and affection abate.

As the younger son of a Leicestershire knight, George Villiers received a pitifully small inheritance; his father had entailed all of his manors and their revenues on the children of his first marriage, leaving George just the tithes of herbage, grain and hay arising from his other manors. Determined that her son should make his mark in the world Lady

Villiers sent him to France at the age of thirteen in order to 'perfect him in all polite accomplishments' and prepare him for a life at court. At that time the French Court was not a place to send a young boy of thirteen. Henri IV of France was a renowned roué who had had many mistresses – he was credited with at least 56 – and numerous illegitimate children. At the time that young Villiers arrived in Paris, Henri was between mistresses, but on his return he came to London and on the advice of Sir John Graham, a gentleman of the privy chamber, sought to 'woo fortune in the court' where he succeeded beyond his wildest expectations.

Despite his relatively modest origins Villiers did have noble connections and was in fact a distant kinsman of King James. But it was his physical beauty that proved to be his saviour. He was according to Sir John Oglander 'one of the handsomest men in the world' and 'from the sole of his feet to the crown of his head there was no blemish in him'. Such a paragon of male beauty was an irresistible attraction for King James and within a very short time he was saw his fortunes rise to dizzy heights.

Villier's success in capturing the affections of the King went hand in hand with a seismic shift in the balance of power, for until now the King's counsels where chiefly dominated by the powerful Howard family in the person of the Earls of Northampton, Suffolk and Nottingham. The characters of these noblemen could not have been more dissimilar. Northampton was described by some of his contemporaries as 'a learned man, but a pedant, dark and mysterious... His rise to favour was almost certainly on account of his family's sufferings for their attachment to James's mother Mary, Queen of Scots. Suffolk's character speaks for itself and he soon fell into disfavour when he was tried along with his wife for financial corruption shortly after his son-in-law Robert Carr was supplanted in the King's affections. Only Nottingham possessed a character worthy of a minister of the crown. The conqueror of Cadiz and architect of the English victory over the Spanish Armada was especially favoured by King James and given as his second wife the King's first cousin the Lady Margaret Stewart; his first Katherine Carey was the grand-daughter of Mary Boleyn, mistress of Henry VIII.

On his succession to the English throne James I inherited:

a country at war, a disaffected church, a revenue system in need of fundamental reform and a parliament determined to seek redress for its perceived grievances.

A more inauspicious beginning to his reign could not be imagined. In time, however, James was able to resolve some of these issues but the question of the royal debt inherited from Elizabeth I remained. With his accession 'royal parsimony was replaced by the most reckless prodigality' to use the words of a noted historian. To be fair to James, however, his expenditure was greater than that of Elizabeth because he had a wife and children to support.

From 1603 until the end of his reign, the sale of titles and offices was the only method by which James was able to raise money to finance his expenditure. The King could not live off the revenues of the 'Crown Estates' as expected by Parliament, because they were simply insufficient for his needs and when he was unable to reach an agreement with the House of Commons on the supply of a fixed income, he was forced to look for other means of raising money. By the end of his reign it is estimated that he had raised at least £600,000 from the sale of titles.

In the first two years James created 1,161 new knights and increased the order threefold. In addition he gave the right of nomination to many of his courtiers thereby further debasing the honour. Thereafter it was bestowed at a more acceptable rate only rising when he was in need of additional cash. In 1611 the Earl of Northampton persuaded James to create a new hereditary dignity of baronet, with the number fixed at 200 at a price of £1,095. By 1619 the price had fallen to £700 and by 1622 to just £220. The increase in creations occurred when James allowed his courtiers to acquire the right to nominate a baronet which was then sold on. In 1615 James adopted a similar policy on the creation of peerages.

It will come as no surprise, therefore, to discover that for the remainder of his reign George Villiers and his family were the main beneficiaries of the sale of honours. In 1624 a courtier paid him £8,000 for a barony and £8,000 for an earldom but the main area of his interest was the sale of Irish titles, over which he had a virtual monopoly. His stranglehold over the sale of honours would be the main charge against him when Parliament attempted to impeach him in 1626.

During his years as the king's favourite Buckingham accumulated great wealth and built up a vast clientele of office-holders and monopolists headed by his family and friends. But his greatest success was in gaining control of royal policy making in the later years of the King's life. Unfortunately, however, Buckingham did not possess the necessary skills to become an effective statesman and this factor plus his tight control of Royal Patronage gained him many enemies amongst the old English nobility. But according to one contemporary he sought to overcome these deficiencies by:

> the drawing or flowing into him of the best instruments of experience and knowledge, from whom he a sweet and attractive manner to suck that might be for the public or his own purpose.

When Villiers decided to take a wife he chose an heiress Catherine Manners, daughter of the Earl of Rutland. His choice did not please the bride's father but despite his opposition they were eventually wed. The lady brought with her some illustrious connections for not only was she directly descended from Anne, sister of Edward IV but also from the noble Duke of Buckingham, who was executed by Henry VIII for treason. She was also first cousin of the infamous Lady Somerset, who had poisoned the unfortunate Sir Thomas Overbury. It was the first of several splendid marriages that Villiers arranged for himself and his family. The strength of this family bond was particularly evident with his brothers of the whole blood but the marriages that he arranged for them were to have unfortunate repercussions.

John Villiers, his elder brother, aspired to marry Frances, daughter of Sir Edward Coke, 'a lady of transcending beauty'. However, Sir Edward and his daughter found his suit most distasteful because they believed she 'might expect a more advantageous alliance than any member of the Villiers family could offer.' Buckingham's reaction was swift. After expelling Sir Edward from the Privy Council and threatening him with 'the terrors of the Star Chamber for some portion of the legal reports he had published' he was eventually persuaded to change his position and now looked with favour on a marriage that he had once viewed with such distaste.

Unfortunately, however, his daughter would not change her mind and he had to resort to tying her to the bedpost and giving her a good whipping until she agreed to it. But Lady Frances had her revenge when she took as her lover Sir Robert Howard, brother of the infamous Lady Somerset, and bore him two bastard sons. The affair did nothing to enhance the reputation of the Howard family and the effects of it were to reverberate over succeeding generations when the eldest bastard son of Lady Frances and Sir Robert Howard went on to make a claim to her deceased husband's titles. Similarly the bastard son of Sir Robert's sister Lady Knollys also claimed the titles of her deceased husband. Neither was successful but nevertheless still assumed the dignity, thus displaying a flagrant disregard for the laws of succession.

The nature of James I's relationships with all of his male favourites is still a matter of much debate. A good many of his contemporaries believed that the relationships were physical and indeed the extravagant language that they used in letters between them could be used to support such a belief. In one letter to his King, George wrote:

> I naturally love your person, and adore all your other parts, which are more than any ever one man had' and I desire only to live in the world for your sake'. In turn James wrote 'I had rather live banished in any part of the Earth with you than live a sorrowful widow's life without you... God bless you, my sweet child & wife, and grant that ye may ever be a comfort to your dear dad and husband.

Whatever the truth, Villiers went on to captivate the next generation of the Stuarts in the person of James's eldest surviving son Charles, Prince of Wales, but three years after Charles had succeeded his father in 1625, the favourite died at the hands of a madman, leaving a young widow and three small children.

3

THE STUART PERIOD

Lucy Walter

She was the daughter of William Walter, a Pembrokeshire gentleman, of Roche Castle and his wife Elizabeth Protheroe, a descendant of the Vaughans of Golden Grove and niece of John (Vaughan), Earl of Carbery, Comptroller of the Household to Charles I. Her ancestor John Walter, an Englishman from Essex had migrated to Pembrokeshire in the wake of Henry VII's victory against Richard III at Bosworth Field but the many intermarriages with the local welsh gentry removed almost all trace of the family's English genetic inheritance. However, alliances with some of the county's more prominent families brought connections with the noble families of Howard, St John and Berkeley and several descents from the Royal House of Plantagenet. Amongst her more distant kinfolk were such figures as Anne and Mary Boleyn, wife and mistress of Henry VIII; Catherine Howard, wife of Henry VIII and Sir John Perrott, Lord Deputy of Ireland, alleged bastard son of Henry VIII, whose mother Mary Berkeley was Lucy's direct ancestor. Lucy was also a distant kinswoman of her Royal Lover Charles II. In addition three successive generations of the Walter family, including Lucy's father William, married descendants of that great Celtic warrior Sir Rhys ap Thomas, who was as famous for his mistresses as he was for his military exploits at the battle of Bosworth.

William Walter was a proud and passionate man whose wife and cousin Elizabeth Protheroe came with a dowry of £600, a very welcome addition to his own rather meagre income. Unfortunately, however, John Protheroe, Elizabeth's father died suddenly shortly after the marriage and his daughter's portion was never paid but the marriage produced three surviving children, Richard, Justus and Lucy, the latter born about 1630. In 1638 the whole family had moved from Pembrokeshire to 'the backside of Kinge Street, Covent Garden', where the children were able to visit their grandmother Mrs Gwinne (the widow of John Protheroe), who lived close by in St Giles-in-the-Fields, a fashionable district much favoured by Court Society.

But the marriage was not a happy one and in 1641 William deserted his wife and returned to Pembrokeshire leaving her without any maintenance because he declared 'he had more than a suspicion of her incontinency'. When Elizabeth petitioned the House of Lords they ordered him to pay her £60 per annum from his meagre income of £100 per annum. But when he refused the Lords ordered the sequestration of his estates. In support of his niece the Earl of Carbery appealed to the Lords and he followed this up in 1643 by taking possession of Roche Castle in the King's name after Charles had raised his standard at Nottingham. It remained in Lord Carbery's possession until it was surrendered in the spring of 1644 to Roland Laugharne, on the orders of Parliament. Elizabeth once again petitioned Parliament lamenting how her husband had committed 'that grosse and abominable sin of adulterie with divers other woemen with and by whom he hath had many other illegitimate children'. But this time Parliament found in favour of her husband and ordered that he 'shall have his children sent home to him for their keeping and education because the Mother was too much beggared by the Father that she could not afford to keep them'.

Whether Lucy remained in London or returned to Pembrokeshire is unclear but between February 1647 and March 1648 she made the acquaintance of the Edward Somerset, Marquess of Worcester and allegedly accompanied him to the continent chaperoned by her 'kinsman' John Barlow, of Slebech, Pembrokeshire where they joined the exiled Royal Court in Paris. The Marquess and Mr Barlow were forced to flee to the continent following their unsuccessful attempt to raise the siege of Raglan Castle, the Marquess's home. As a result Mr Barlow's estates were confiscated by Parliament and given to the same Rowland Laugharne who had sequested the estates of Lucy's father, William Walter.

Henceforth Lucy assumed the name of her protector Mr Barlow but he was quickly followed by Colonel Algernon Sidney and then his brother Colonel Robert Sidney until she finally caught the attention of the Prince of Wales. A woman of great determination Lucy was quite prepared to defy contemporary conventions and make her own way in life regardless of the consequences. Her father's lecherous and lewd manner of living had also made a deep impression upon her and laid bare the obvious double standards that were employed in relation to women's rights. Like her kinswoman Barbara Villiers, she believed that if a man could have mistresses, a woman could have lovers. A maxim that she followed for the rest of her short life but like Barbara she gained the unenviable reputation of being thought of as a loose woman, a whore even. Coincidentally their paths never crossed but they had much in common. 'Her beauty was' according to a contemporary 'so perfect that when the King saw her... he was so charmed and ravished and enamoured that in the misfortunes which ran through the first years of his reign he knew no other sweetness or joy than to love her, and be loved by her'.

Colonel Algernon Sidney was an officer in Cromwell's New Model Army and was serving in Ireland until April 1647. Upon his return he is alleged to have been captivated by Lucy's beauty and made her the dishonourable offer of fifty broad pieces if she would become his mistress. He allegedly made her acquaintance at the home of her uncle Mr Gosfright in London but was then called away to be with his regiment and the lady promptly left for Holland, presumably in the company of the Marquess of Worcester and Mr Barlow. Many years later, probably during the Exclusion Crisis, Colonel Sidney allegedly recounted his experience to the Duke of York (later James II) adding for good measure that on arriving in Holland she promptly became the mistress of his brother Robert Sidney, then Groom of the Bedchamber to the young Prince of Wales.

Lucy did not proceed to Holland but went directly to Paris where the Prince of Wales was residing in the Louvre. They arrived in March 1648 and if indeed as is alleged she became the mistress of Robert Sidney, it was a brief affair. The subsequent doubts caste upon the royal paternity of the future Duke of Monmouth by James II were clearly politically motivated in an effort to discredit him, therefore the alleged statement by Robert Sidney that Lucy was already with child when she became Charles's mistress must be viewed caution. The Duke of Monmouth was born 9 April 1649, therefore provided that Lucy carried him to full term he could not have been conceived earlier than 25 June 1648. On that date the Prince of Wales left Paris for Calais on his journey to Holland where he arrived at Helvoetsluys on 9 July. Exactly when Lucy became Charles's mistress is uncertain but Monmouth was clearly conceived between 25 June and 22 July 1648; on the latter date the Prince of Wales set sail from Holland for the English Downs abroad the ships that had mutinied from Cromwell's Navy and he did not return until 1 September.

The young Prince's affair with Lucy was not his first sexual experience; that honour is usually accredited to his former nurse Mrs Christabella Wyndham, whose daughter-in-law Winifred Wells would also become Charles's mistress. But Lucy would not enjoy her success unopposed. Within a year of her conquest Charles had taken another mistress Mrs Boyle, the wife of Francis Boyle, son of the Earl of Cork and daughter of Sir Robert Killigrew. After the birth of her son in Rotterdam in April 1649, the infant Monmouth was left in the care of a prosperous Dutch merchant and his wife and Lucy immediately retired to France in order to be with Charles. The execution of his father in January 1649 had been a bitter blow to the young Prince but the birth of his son four months later was some small consolation. But Charles sought to ease the pain of his bereavement by indulging in several love affairs, firstly with Mrs Boyle and then with the beautiful and bewitching Duchess de Châtillon.

When Anne of Austria and her son Louis XIV entered Paris in state on 18 August 1649, Lucy and Charles went to the palace of St Germain-en-Laye to pay their respects to Henrietta Maria and advise her that he planned to go to Jersey in an effort regain his father's crowns. The Prince left for Jersey on 27 September 1649 and did not return until 21 February 1650. The affair with Mrs Boyle, whose husband was subsequently created Viscount Shannon, produced a daughter Charlotte who was born in 1650 at Paris. The Prince's itinerary in 1649/50 suggests quite strongly that it was a very brief affair which probably took place pre September 1649 when he left for Jersey.

Mrs Boyle, previously a maid of honour to Henrietta Maria was married at the age of seventeen and considerably older than Charles. Her father, Sir Robert Killigrew, Vice-Chamberlain to Henrietta Maria had married Mary, the daughter of Sir Henry Wodehouse which match provided connections with Anne and Mary Boleyn plus Jane Seymour, the notorious Frances, Lady Somerset, and Barbara Villiers etc. Lady Killigrew married as her second husband Sir Thomas Stafford, Usher to Henrietta Maria and it was her wish that her daughter should marry the son of the Earl of Cork.

As a maid of honour the young bride was married in the presence of the King and Queen and the proud father-in-law, the Earl of Cork, recorded the event in his diary:

24 October 1639

This day my fourth son, Francis Boyle, was married in the Kings chapple at Whitehall to Mrs Elizabeth Killoghgreev... The Kinge with his own Royall hand gaue my son his wife in marriadge, and made a great Feast in court for them, wherat the Kinge and queen were both presente, and I, with 3 of my daughters satt at the King and queens table, amongst all the great Lords and Ladies. The King took the bryde owt to dawnce; and after the dawncing was ended, the King led the Bryde by the hand to the bedchamber, where the queen herself, with her own hands, did help to vndress her. And his Maty and the queen both staid in the bedchamber till they saw my son & his wife in bed together; and they both kissed the bride and blessed them, as I did; and I beseech god to bless them.

Thereafter the young bridegroom by the King's licence departed for the continent and did not return for another three years. In 1646 Mr Boyle and his wife and servants obtained a pass to go into Holland where they appeared to have remained until April 1648, when they were escorted back from the Hague by their brother-in-law Dr Robert Boyle. From March 1646 until July 1648 Charles was based in France until he left for Holland when the news reached him that part of the English Fleet had mutinied and declared for him. When Mr Boyle and his agreeable and beautiful wife returned to the continent is unclear but when they did Charles made an instant conquest of her with the inevitable result.

Mrs Boyle's daughter was never publicly recognised by Charles or granted the Royal Arms with suitable marks to denote bastardy. Fate, however, decreed that her first husband would be Mr James Howard, son of Colonel Tom Howard, Lucy's ex-lover. She was married at the tender age of thirteen but did not bear her first child until she was twenty. The child was baptised Stuarta, in honour of her royal ancestry and she became a maid of honour to Mary II but never married, dying in 1706 at the age of thirty-six. For a brief time she was engaged to marry Hans William Bentinck, William III's favourite but when he broke off the engagement, Stuarta's half brother, Lord Paston, challenged him to a duel and shot him. Bentinck survived but the affair caused a tremendous stir.

Whilst engaged with Lucy and Mrs Boyle Charles also found himself falling for the charms of the beautiful Duchess de Chatillon whom he had first met in the spring of 1648 at a Court Ball given in his honour by his cousin La Grand Mademoiselle, just before the arrival of Lucy and her protector Mr Barlow. Isabelle Angelique de Montmorency-Bouteville, the daughter of Francois (de Montmorency), Comte de Luxe was descended from one of France's most ancient and noble families and had been the mistress of the Prince de Conde, a Prince of the Blood, and the Duke de Nemours, a member of the Royal House of Savoy. On his return from his disastrous expedition to Scotland, Charles weary of his affair with Lucy laid siege to the beautiful Isabelle. During his absence in Scotland the Duchess, then a widow, had given birth to a son of uncertain parentage. It could have been her husband's or perhaps her lover's, the Duke de Nemours. It would be her only child which suggests that the birth was probably difficult and traumatic resulting in her inability to have further children. What ever the reason her appeal to Charles was obvious, beautiful, cultured, witty and an excellent hostess she was admired by all. She remained Charles's principal mistress until his departure from France in 1654 and fully deserved to be recognised as the Prince's first official *mistress en titre*.

Charles's deplorable treatment of Lucy during these additional affairs, however, caused her considerable anguish and as she was in a foreign land with no family of her own, the fragility of her position was all too apparent. The path she had chosen was paved with major uncertainties and difficulties but the prospect of marriage to an ordinary country gentleman clearly held no appeal for her, especially as she had no dowry to offer. Either way her family were not resigned to the path she had chosen indeed Mr Gosfright, the husband of her aunt blamed Lucy's mother 'for leaving her daughter abroad in an ill way of living' to which Mrs Walter replied 'he was mistaken, for her said daughter was married to the King'. Mrs Walters died in 1655 but did not mention Lucy or her children in her will. The belief that Lucy and Charles were married was widespread in post Restoration England but accounts vary about the time and place.

The marriage of a reigning monarch to a lady of lesser rank was not unusual in England. Edward IV had married Elizabeth Woodville and Henry VIII had wed in succession, Anne Boleyn, Jane Seymour, Catherine Howard and Catherine Parr but the Stuarts had a much more exalted view of monarchy and only a Royal Bride was suitable for Charles. Indeed before he left for France in 1646 his father had already begun negotiations for the hand of the Princess of Portugal, the eight year old Catherine of Braganza, which at the time came to naught and which was immediately followed by a plan to marry him to 'La Grande Mademoiselle', his extremely wealthy cousin.

When Charles was requested to leave France by Cardinal Mazarin in July 1654, the rumour spread that before leaving he married the Duchess de Châtillon. It was of course untrue but he did spend his last days on French soil at her country chateau. During his progress to Germany he also spent a few hours at Liege where he appears to have met Lucy before moving on. It is here that one account alleges that Charles and Lucy were married at an inn, with the just the innkeeper and his wife as witnesses. Another much later account alleges that Lucy and Charles were married in the presence of three members of the clergy, Henry Glemham, later Bishop of St Asaph (uncle of Barbara Villiers), William Fuller, subsequently Bishop of Lincoln and Dr John Cosin, later Bishop of Durham.

It was Thomas Ross, tutor to the young Monmouth, who first put the idea into Monmouth's head that he was the King's legitimate son. According to James II he 'would have Bishop Cosin to certify that he had married the King and Mrs Walters, who refused it with indignity, and gave immediate notice of it to the King, who removed Ross from about him'. The discovery of a marriage certificate in the archives of the Duke of Buccleuch in the reign of Queen Victoria infers that Ross had drafted a document for signature and this was then destroyed by the Duke. The full story of this event is given in a letter from Sir Frederick Barnewell, Bt to the Baronne d'Aulnoy dated 26 May 1905 viz:

> A good many years ago the late Sir Bernard Burke, whom I knew very well, told me that the Duke of Abercorn had told him that he had heard from the late Duke of Buccleuch that one day, looking through papers in the muniment room at Dalkeith, he came across the marriage certificate of Charles II and Lucy Walter, that after considering the matter for some time he decided to destroy it, and thereon threw it into the fire, and it was burned.

Shortly after the Second World War, Sir Hew Dalrymple, KCVO when searching the Buccleuch papers came across the following document which claimed that:

> The certificate of marriage was found by Henry, Duke of Buccleuch and President Hope amongst some old papers at Dalkeith and the Duke thought best to burn it. It does not seem clear whether it was an original or a copy of one at Liege where they were married by the then Archbishop of Canterbury...

As there was no Archbishop of Canterbury between 1645 and 1660, Sir Hew was clearly mistaken about the title of the alleged officiating minister.

When Charles left Liege for Germany Lucy returned to Brussels and within a short time had acquired a prospective husband, Sir Henry de Vic, the King's resident there. According to the Memoirs of James II;

'she imposed on Sir Henry de Vic... to go with her to Cologne to marry him, but all in vain'. Lucy had indeed gone to Cologne with De Vic and young James to ask for Charles's permission to marry but her request was refused and de Vic was reprimanded for leaving his post. Mother and child returned to Brussels and all hope of Lucy making a respectable marriage finally disappeared. However, her visit to Cologne did result in the King's promise that he would not take her son from her and a pension of £400 per annum (5,000 livres) payable in quarterly instalments. The visit to Cologne took place in December 1654 but Lucy's pension was not granted until January 1655/6. News of De Vic's visit was common knowledge in royalist circles. The King's aunt, the Queen of Bohemia wrote to Sir Edward Nicholas 'I have the reason of Sir Henry de Vic's journey to Cologne: since it is doting time for the King's ould Ministers of State. I thank God your wife is yet alive, for feare you should fall in love again.' This was followed by another letter in January 1654/5 viz: 'I am sorry for poore Sir Henry de Vic for the match break or goe on: it is every way ill for him'.

After the de Vic episode Lucy took up with Colonel Tom Howard, younger brother of the Earl of Suffolk and a distant kinsman, who was Master of the Horse to Mary, Princess of Orange. The affair lasted several years but exactly when it began is unclear. However, Howard was seen to 'much frequent her company' in August 1655 at the Hague where Lucy was then living, therefore it would be safe to assume that it began between January and August 1655. Lucy's sojourn at the Hague lasted until April 1656 when she left to take ship from Flushing to London in the company of her brother Justus, two children James and Mary and Colonel Howard. On the journey she met Charles at Antwerp or Brussels in order for him to have sight of his son.

Evidence has now come to light which suggests that Lucy's daughter Mary was born in 1655 and not 1651 as claimed by the Dictionary of National Biography. From November 1654 until January 1655/6 Charles was living in Cologne and Lucy at the Hague. The only recorded visits by Lucy to Charles were in August 1654, December 1654/January 1655 and again in June/July 1656. However, the meeting at Liege in August 1654 was only for a few hours, whereas the later meetings were clearly of much longer duration. It was during this period November 1654 to June 1655 that a series of letters has survived in which it is alleged there is proof of Lucy's marriage to Charles. The first dated 9 November 1654 and written by the Princess of Orange to Charles from the Hague, is worth quoting in full viz:

> Your Mothere says that the greatest thankfulness she can show for the honnour of your kind remembrance is to have a special care of you(r) wife for feare her husband here may make her forget them that are absant. Your wife thanks you in her own hand and still though she begs me very hard to help her!

The veiled reference to your wife and her husband here would seem to refer to Lucy and Sir Henry de Vic but it is odd that Henrietta Maria should take such an interest in her son's mistress. Two further letters from the Princess dated 20 May 1655 and 21 June 1655 from the Hague and Hounslerdike again refer to 'your wife' viz:

> Your wife is resolving whither shee will writ or no: therefore I am to say nothing to you from her; but will keepe open my letter as long as the post will permitte, to expect what good nature will worke, which I find now does not al all; for 'tis now elven of the clock, and noe letter comes.

> Your wife desires me to present her humble duty to you which is all she can say. I tell her 'tis because shee thinks of another husband and does not follow your example of being as constant a wife as you are a husband: tis a frailty they say is given to the sex, therefore you will pardon her I hope.

These references to 'your wife' were clearly made with tongue in cheek and are not first hand evidence that Lucy and Charles were married, had that been the case she would not have asked for permission to marry Sir Henry de Vic.

The paternity of Lucy's daughter Mary has always been ascribed to Lord Taaffe, subsequently Earl of Carlingford. The authority for this was the 'Memoirs of James II'.

she lived so loosely when he [Charles] was in Scotland that when after Worcester fight he came to France and she came thither, he would have no further commerce with her. She used in vain all her little arts. She tried to persuade Doctor Cozins that she was a convert and would quit her scandalous way of life, and had at the same time a child by the Earl of Carlington, who grew up to be a woman, and was owned by the mother as hers, as like the Earl as possible.

The double standard used here is typical of the seventeenth century. A man was free to have as many mistresses as he chose provided he was discreet about it but the mistress was expected to remain faithful to her lover. The evidence therefore such as it is now suggests that Mary was the daughter of either Sir Henry de Vic or more likely Tom Howard. Lord Taaffe who was in Holland during the first six months of 1655, including the Hague in April and again in July, was based in Ireland, in 1650/1 the date the DNB claims Mary was born.

Tom Howard's relationship with Lucy was a stormy one and during the first year of the affair she is alleged to have 'miscarried of two children by phissick'. Daniel O'Neile, the author of this quote, further claimed that 'Hir last miscarriage was since Mrs Howard went, ass the midwyf says to one, that I imploy to hir. Doctor Rufus has given hir phissick, but it was allwayes after her miscarrying' 14 February 1656/7. During this time from June 1656 to the spring of 1657 Charles held his court in Bruges, in what was then termed Flanders, from where he could travel easily to Ghent, Antwerp and Brussels. In April 1657, with the permission of Don Juan, Governor of the Spanish Netherlands, the bastard son of the King of Spain, he established a small court at Brussels consisting of just seventy persons.

At the little court that he had established at Bruges Charles took another mistress Catherine Pegge, an English Catholic exile of good family, who bore him two children in quick succession. Don Carlos, the son, was educated as a catholic and subsequently created Earl of Plymouth but his sister did not survive infancy. Lady Green, as she later became, was the daughter of Thomas Pegge, of Yeldersley, Derbyshire and grand daughter of Sir Gilbert Kniveton, Bart. Unlike Lady Shannon and Lucy, however,

Lady Green did not have any royal connections despite being descended from some very respectable catholic gentry families.

After returning from visiting England in the wake of her mother's death Lucy arrived in Bruges with her children and Tom Howard and within a short time of their arrival in August 1657, an incident occurred that finally ended their relationship when 'a kinsman or servant of Mrs Barlow stabed Tom Howard through the arm with a dangerous wound and escaped.' The following year Howard took out a lawsuit against Lucy for the recovery of his papers and the incident was relayed by Sir George Downing, the Parliamentary Ambassador to the States General to Mr Secretary Thurloe, in London viz:

> Tom Howard, brother of the Earl of Suffolk had a whore in this country, with which he trusted all his secrets & papers; these two afterwards fell out, a person of this town [the Hague] got all the papers from her; whereupon Tom Howard began a suit in law against the said party to the value of £10,000, & did plead in open court, that the reason why he began the said suite, & upon pretence of so high damages, was because he did not know, but that he might fall to be heir to the Earl his brother, and that there were among the said papers some which if discovered would be his ruin.

Sir George, whom Pepys called 'a perfidious rogue' was a 'vain, ruthless but extremely able man' who was knighted at the Restoration and allowed to keep his post at the Hague having given valuable information to the King. Henceforth Tom Howard took no further part in Lucy's life and the remainder of her short life was taken with fighting for the custody of her son and daughter.

Charles's attempts to get his son from his mother are well known. Initially the task was given to Sir Arthur Slingsby but his methods aroused the indignation of the people of Brussels, especially when he tried to have her arrested for debt and carried to one of the public prisons in the city. The King's orders were to carry out the assignment 'in a quiet and silent way' but not with the 'noise and scandal that hath happened'. Lucy for her part retaliated by declaring that 'if Your Makesty did not send her pension she would post up all your Majesty's letters to her'. When young

James was finally separated from his mother Lord Crofts was appointed his Governor and Thomas Ross, his tutor. He was then sent to school at Port Royal in Paris where remained until the Restoration.

Despite being separated from her son Lucy followed him to Paris where she died the following year. From Bishop Kennet we have the following account of the event: 'The late Master of the Charterhouse William Erskine, Esq, who was long in the service of King Charles II abroad, had care of Mrs Barloe and buried her in Paris'. Prior to her death she sort comfort from Bishop Cosin, the same ecclesiastic who refused to sign the certificate alleging that she had married Charles. What happened to her daughter Mary in unclear but many years later she referred to a pension that Charles had given her when she was but a child, therefore he did make provision for her. When she married for the first time in 1670, she was living in the household of her appointed guardian the Earl of Carlingford in Ireland.

CATHERINE SEDLEY

The only one of James II's mistresses who ever came close to being acknowledged as an official *mistress en titre* was Mrs Sedley, whom he created a Countess with a pension and a house in St James's Square. Catherine Sedley was the daughter of Sir Charles Sedley, Bart, the famous Restoration wit and writer who when taxed with his ingratitude to King James at the time of the Glorious Revolution wittily replied: 'the King having made my daughter a Countess; it is fit I should make his daughter a Queen'.

The Sedley's were from relatively undistinguished protestant stock but not so the Savages who were Catholics. Catherine Savage, Catherine's mother, was the daughter of John Savage, 1st Earl Rivers and his first wife Catherine Parker, the daughter of William, Lord Morley. The marriage was a step up on the social ladder for Sir Charles but his wild debauched behaviour often in the company of Lord Buckhurst, Nell Gwynn's first lover, destroyed the delicate balance of Lady Sedley's mental health and drove her insane. In her distress she believed that she was a Queen and asked to be addressed as 'Your Majesty'; later she was shipped off to a Benedictine convent in Ghent, in the company of a catholic priest where she remained until her death in 1705.

Unlike the Sedley's, the Savage family could boast of being of Royal Descent most notably from the Plantagenets via Edward IV's sister, the Lady Anne St Leger and also from John of Gaunt via his bastard issue. Lady Sedley was also the cousin of Lady Shrewsbury, mistress of the 2nd Duke of Buckingham and another luminary and major player of the post Restoration era, Barbara Villiers, the mistress of Charles II, was also a kinswoman. The characters of these individuals left much to be desired and indeed the family were well known for their eccentricities. Lady Sedley's cousin, the 1st Duke of Bolton was a good example. This gentleman was according to a contemporary:

> a man of strange mixture [who] had a spleen to a high degree, and affected to an extravagant behaviour, for many weeks he would not open his mouth until such an hour of the day when he thought the air was pure. He [also] changed the day into night, and often hunted by torch light, and took all sorts of liberties to himself, many of which were disagreeable to those about him. He was a man of profuse expense, and of almost ravenous avarice to support that and though much hated, yet he carried matters before him with such authority and success, that he was in all respects the great riddle of the age.

As for the character of Lady Shrewsbury we need only quote Anthony Hamilton viz: 'she is prodigious; I would take my oath that a man might be killed for her every day, and she would only hold up her head the higher on account of it. You would think she received plenary indulgence for everything that she did'. Earl Rivers, Lady Sedley's nephew also enjoyed a reputation as 'one of the greatest rakes in England in his younger days' and according to Jonathan Swift on his death:

> ...left legacies to about 20 paultry old whores by name, and not a farthing to any Friend, Dependant, or Relation; he has left from his only child, lady Barrimore, her mother's estate, and given the whole to his heir-male, a Popish priest, a second cousin, who is now earl Rivers, and whom he used in his life like a footman. After him it goes to his chief wench and bastard.

The Sedley baronetcy was conferred in 1611 on Sir William Sedley, the grandfather of Sir Charles when Robert (Carr), Earl of Somerset was the reigning favourite of King James I. The idea of a new hereditary dignity was first mooted by Francis Bacon, in 1606 but it was not until 1609 that the government began to take the idea seriously as a means of future revenue for the crown. King James guaranteed that the number of creations would not exceed 200 and only families who could prove that they had been armigerous for three generations with land worth £1,000 per year were eligible. The cost was £1,095 payable to the Exchequer. Unfortunately, however, the King was unable to keep his promise and the creation of baronetcies spirelled out of control.

Sir Charles was distinguished for his wit and his gallantries and 'as a critic too he was so much admired, that he became a kind of oracle among the poets, and no performance was approved or condemned until [he] had given judgement. King Charles used to say, that nature had given him a patent to be Apollo's viceroy'. Bishop Burnet's assessment of him was equally flattering viz: 'he had a sudden and copious wit, but it was not so correct as Lord Dorset's, nor so sparkling as Lord Rochesters'. His behaviour, however, left much to be desired. On one occasion when in the company of Lord Buckhurst and Sir Thomas Ogle he caused a riot by appearing naked on the balcony of the Cock Tavern in Bow Street, for which he was heavily fined and briefly imprisoned.

Whilst Sir Charles's antics kept the court highly amused the actions of his wife's cousin Lady Shrewsbury caused horror, dismay and shame in equal measure. Although not prone to taking her clothes off in public Lady Shrewsbury did nevertheless take them off in private for her numerous lovers:

> This beauty, less celebrated for her conquests than for the woes which she occasioned, piqued herself on being more capricious than the rest; and though nobody could brag that he alone had been more kindly entertained by her, equally there was no one who could contend that his suit had been ill received.

After presenting her husband with a son and heir a year after their marriage and another five years later whose paternity raises a question mark, Lady Shrewsbury grew bored and took up with the first of her lovers, the Earl of Arran, husband of the Duke of Buckingham's niece and brother of Lady Chesterfield who was briefly mistress of the Duke of York. He was then followed by Tom Howard, husband of the Duke of Buckingham's sister; who won universal plaudits for his character and of whom, according to the 'Memoirs of the Comte de Gramont', 'there was not a braver nor handsomer man in all England. Though his air was cool and his manners seemed mild and pacific, there was nobody, in point of fact, prouder nor so easily disposed to wrath'. He was then replaced by Harry Killigrew, brother of Lady Shannon, a one time mistress of Charles II, and brother-in-law of Lady Sedley, who 'though he possessed a merry wit and considerable charm, was one of the most abominable and debauched scoundrels who ever disgraced a Court'. Killigrew was quickly replaced by the Duke of Buckingham, cousin of the King's mistress Barbara Villiers and son of George Villiers, the favourite of James I. The last sudden change in lovers was a notorious affair and caused a public scandal.

Lady Shrewsbury's affair with Tom Howard was in full swing by August 1662 but almost immediately he had a rival for the lady's affections, Harry Jermyn. Honour would only be satisfied by a duel and the event duly took place:

On Monday Tom Howard, brother to the Earl of Carlisle and Mr Dillon, brother to Lord Dillon accosted H. Germaine and Giles Rawlins, drew upon them before... door, coming from the Tennis Court, and Tom slew Giles dead in the place, and after that fell on Harry, and wounded him in three or four places, which prove but slight hurts, which done, Tom said 'Now we have done justice, let's be gone' and having their horses hard by, with pistols at the saddle bow, they presently fled, and 'tis thought that Howard had some hurt, or he was seen to bear himself up on his pummell...

How long Tom Howard remained Lady Shrewsbury's lover is unknown but Harry Killigrew's reign as her ladyship's lover began in 1663 and ended in 1665/6 when he was replaced by the Duke of Buckingham; Lady Shrewsbury's second son John was baptised in February 1665/6. The Duke of Buckingham's courtship is believed to have begun in the summer of 1666 whilst he was 'living in great state in Lord Irwin's House at York' but at that point Lord Shrewsbury was seemingly completely indifferent to his wife's latest amour.

Suddenly, however, the situation changed and Lord Shrewsbury issued a challenge to the Duke. On hearing of the news the King issued instructions forbidding it but it still took place. Shrewsbury was seriously wounded and several months later died of his wounds at Arundel House. On hearing of her husband's death Lady Shrewsbury went openly to live with the Duke, who immediately installed her in his London residence. She later bore him a son who despite being a bastard was buried in Westminster Abbey with the title of Lord Coventry!

With such a catalogue of misdeeds continually keeping her in the public eye the exploits of Sir Charles were viewed almost as childish pranks and nothing more. However, he was saved by his undoubted literary talents and as a result earned himself a reputation as a man of culture. Indeed according to a recent historian:

'he had taste and ability without being too serious, and he was learned without being a pedant or a systematic scholar' and 'among the books from his library, sold at auction at Tom's Coffee-house, [after his death in 1703] the classical authors were well represented. He had works of Livy, Virgil, Juvenal, Terence, Plutarch, Seneca, Suetonius, Sophocles, Martial, Pulartus, Cicero and Lucan...' also 'The contents of Sedley's library, rich in the classics, almost as rich in French literature, also containing several Italian volumes and a couple in Spanish, are testimony to the interest Englishmen took in the state of art outside England...

But what of the education of his daughter Catherine? Nothing is known and in view of this it leads one to surmise that Sir Charles did not take any special measures to ensure that she was educated above the standard that was expected for a woman in the seventeenth century. But what Catherine might have lacked in education she made up with a natural shrewdness and a great deal of coarse wit, laced with large helpings of common sense. In 1670 when Lady Shrewsbury bore the Duke of Buckingham's bastard, Catherine was just twelve years old but as her father's heiress already a very desirable marriage prospect for an aspiring nobleman or well bred gentleman. Suddenly, however, two years later her father fell in love and went through a bigamous marriage with Ann Ayscough and went on to produce two sons William, who died an infant and Charles on whom he doted.

The births of these children, however, did not alter the fact that Catherine was her father's legitimate heir. Her first suitor, Sir Edward Hungerford, KB, was twenty-six years older than Catherine and desperate to restore his fortunes by marriage to a wealthy heiress having dissipated his own fortune with riotous living. Another possible candidate was Catherine's cousin Richard Savage, who was described by John Mackay as:

> A gentleman of very good sense and very cunning; brave in his person, a lover of play, and understands it perfectly well; hath a very good estate and improves it every day; something covetous; is a tall handsome man of very fair complexion.

Sir Edward's suit being unsuccessful he was immediately replaced by the penniless but handsome John Churchill, a Groom of the Bedchamber to the Duke of York (later King James II), whose father Sir Winston was eager for the match. Predictably Catherine was smitten with this irresistibly handsome soldier who had the added appeal of being only eight years her senior and an ex-lover of the notorious Barbara Villiers, the mistress of Charles II! Sir Winston and Sir Charles duly entered into negotiations to bring the match to a suitable conclusion in the autumn and winter of 1676 but fate intervened when Sir Charles discovered that the young soldier was in love with one of the Queen's maids of honour, Sarah Jennings. By the spring of the following year the marriage was off:

> Mrs Sedley's marriage with Jack Churchill neither is nor ever will be any more talked of, both the Knight [Sir Charles] and the Colonel [Sir

Winston] being willing to break off fairly... which important matter is referred to me by both parties, and for both their goods I think it is best it should cease.

To compensate her for her loss Catherine was appointed a maid of honour to the Duchess of York and unwittingly fell into the arms of the Duke of York.

Catherine's failure to find a husband was unfortunate but given contemporary views on the institution of marriage understandable. Indeed Catherine's own father wrote a very witty poem of the subject entitled *The Happy Pair* viz:

The man values not the woman, but her store: Extends his treacherous pledge to golden charms, And joins his hands to none but spangled arms. He weds her jewels and her amber chains, But her rich self [that merits all] disdains; Her face he praises, but he courts her ears, Catching the glittering pendants that she wear; Each eye no longer he esteems a star Than flaming rubies hung upon her hair: And judging love, without her gold, a curse, He scorns her virtue, and adores her purse.

The woman too, no less debased than he Gives not herself, but her gratuity; Soothes like a merchant with inveigling art, Demands her jointure and keeps back her heart. On terms and articles with pride proceeds, And seals her cold affections to her deeds: Stands off and treats like an imperious state, And baulks her happiness to be made great; Proclaims her fortune of a goodly size, And he that offers most obtains the prize'.

This witty and irreverent poem encapsulates perfectly the legalistic and business like approach that most contemporary families adopted when seeking to supplement their own fortunes by making a suitable marriage.

If the institution of marriage held no charms or obvious financial benefits for Catherine then the prospect of gaining the like from her position as *mistress en titre* to the Duke of York was a very risky option. As an heiress in her own right with a dowry of £4,000 she had no reason to take that route but the fact that she did so points to another reason.

There was no prospect of becoming his wife because he was already married but the status she would acquire as his official *mistress en titre* was the next best thing. James was captivated by Catherine's personality and wit but she could not understand his infatuation 'It cannot be my beauty, because I haven't any; and it cannot be my wit, because he hasn't enough to know that I have any'. When the lovely Sarah Jennings retired from her position as Maid of Honour to the duchess in April 1678 in order to marry John Churchill, James arranged for Catherine to fill her place. A sweet revenge for her failure to capture John Churchill as a husband. By the end of July the consequences of her actions were all too apparent when she was discovered she was with child by the Duke. Four years earlier the Duke had pledged to give himself body and soul to his wife but on the death of a short lived son for whom 'the duke was never known to grieve so much at the death of any of his other children' he went back on his word and sort consolation in his mistress's bed and did not return to the marital bed for another four years.

After the birth of Catherine's child's in March 1679, the Duke and his Duchess travelled to Brussels for a self imposed exile until the political situation in England had stabilised only returning in September and then leaving almost immediately for Scotland where he remained until early 1680. However, the Duke's return to England was deemed premature and he was sent back to Scotland as the King's Viceroy and remained until May 1682. In August the Duchess gave birth of his fourth child, a daughter Charlotte, who died two months later from convulsions. Meanwhile during the Duke's absence Catherine remained in London with her child at the residence James had given her in St James's Square.

After two further miscarriages in October 1683 and May 1684, the Duke's attention to his wife wandered again and he resumed his visits to Catherine and in the September of 1684 she bore him a son who was named James after his father. However, rumours circulated that she had also been intimate with James Grahme, another member of the Duke's household, who believed that he was the father of her children. The truth of the matter was that James and Catherine would meet for secret trysts at Colonel Grahme's house near Bagshot thus giving rise to the rumour.

On his accession in 1685 James promised his wife that he would no longer see his mistress and for a short time kept his word but his brothers-in-law the Earl of Clarendon and Earl of Rochester intrigued to bring her back because they believed that if the King had an official protestant mistress it would increase his popularity. However, the only outcome was that James created his mistress Countess of Dorchester and Baroness Darlington. Many years later when setting down some moral instruction for his son James lamented the fact that he had been 'bewitched by women who were not chaste. One and all, they wanted from a prince money and power, if not for themselves for their relations and friends. They never truly loved a prince. They were never faithful, they were vipers, and their lovers were galley slaves'. Unable to face the thought of dismissing his mistress in person James sent a letter by one of his courtiers Lord Middleton asking her to retire to Holland. When she refused he suggested Dublin and she duly left England for Ireland but did not stay long returning in September 1686. On her arrival she swept into the Queen's drawing room looking radiant and caused a sensation. She then bought a country house close to London, Ham House, but her days as James's *mistress en titre* were now effectively over.

There is no evidence to suggest that during her years as James's mistress, Catherine used her influence to enrich her immediate family at his expense. Admittedly James did grant her an annual pension of £3,000 in 1686 with a proviso that this would be increased to £5,000 in 1691. But Catherine was already of independent means and could manage quite well without his help. Despite James's rather brutal dismissal of her she remained loyal to him for a number of years after he retired to France in 1688. Not so her cousin Richard Savage, who towards the end of James's reign became a leading member of the Treason Club 'an informal gathering of like-minded whig army officers, aspiring politicians, and former army officers with ties to the Duke of Monmouth'. Under his leadership the group laid plains to defect from James to the Prince of Orange and when William invaded England he, together with Harry Wharton, William Jephson and Charles Godfrey, Arabella Churchill's husband, was the first to join the prince. Amongst William's retinue was Lieutenant-Colonel Sir David Colyear, who would later become Catherine's husband.

The post Revolution years were full of turmoil and danger for Lord Savage and Sir David. Both served in the prince's army in Ireland, Richard distinguishing himself at the siege of Cork where the Duke of Grafton, Charles II's bastard son was mortally wounded whilst Sir David was appointed Governor of Limerick when it was surrendered by the Jacobites. Sir David then went on to serve in Flanders and then on the death of his first wife, a Dutch lady, immediately paid suit to Catherine a thirty nine year old spinster and ex-royal mistress with a bastard child in tow. It cannot have been for her looks because she had none. Against all the odds, however, she accepted his suit bore him two fine sons and watched as he rose through the ranks of the army before being created a peer of the realm. After exemplary service in Flanders he was created Lord Portmore and Blackness in the peerage of Scotland and following another stint in the War of the Spanish Succession was created Earl of Portmore.

In 1710 Portmore was made Commander-in-Chief of the British Armed Forces in Portugal and in 1712 served in Flanders under the Duke of Ormonde. However, on the accession of George I, he became disenchanted with the new regime and in 1716 provided the Jacobites with military advice on a possible landing in England. Because of his discontent, he did not receive any further posts until the accession of George II in 1727, when he was sent to raise the siege of Gibraltar and become its next Governor. John Mackay described him as 'one of the best foot officers in the world; is very brave and bold; hath a great deal of wit; very much a man of honour and nice that way, yet married the Countess of Dorchester, and hath by her a good estate; pretty well shaped; dresses clean; but one eye'.

Shortly before Catherine's marriage in August 1696, her cousin now Lord Colchester began an affair with the Countess of Macclesfield, who at the time was separated from her husband but she was unable to conceal the births of her two bastard children and was promptly divorced. Colchester's infatuation with Lady Macclesfield did not survive the birth of her second child in 1697 and she then proceeded to marry a second time to Lieutenant-Colonel Henry Brett, a great friend of Coley Cibber. According to the latter Brett had 'an uncommon Share of Social Wit, and a handsome Person, with a sanguine Bloom in his Complexion'. Indeed he made such an uncommon impression on Lady

Macclesfield that 'in about ten Days [of meeting her] he marry'd the Lady'. The lady also made a deep impression on Coley Cibber who according to James Boswell 'had so high an opinion of her taste and judgment as to genteel life and manners, that he submitted every scene of his 'Careless Husband' to Mrs Brett's revisal and correction'.

Catherine, of course, had given up all thoughts of extra marital gallantries. Her marriage to Sir David was blissfully happy and he was all that she could want in a husband. But as the years passed so did her memories of the time she held the position of *mistress en titre* to the exiled King James. But when he died at St Germain-en-Laye in 1701 it did not sever her links with the Jacobite Court, because her daughter Lady Anglesey, later to become Duchess of Buckinghamshire, who was inordinately proud of her royal blood, was a fervent Jacobite supporter and kept in close touch with her half brother the 'Old Pretender'.

With the relatively peaceful accession of the Elector of Hanover in 1715 and the failure of the Rising of 1715, there appeared to be no hope now of a Restoration of the Royal House of Stuart. But despite this Catherine's husband sought to maintain his Jacobite connexions and relinquished his colonelcy in the Scots Guards in preparation for participating more actively in their intrigues. His contempt for the Elector and his son was well known but his support of the Stuarts was probably just one of self interest, like so many of the nobility and gentry, but for the remainder of George I's reign he was not appointed to any public posts and in the October of 1717 his wife suddenly died. With her death any thoughts he might have had of joining the exiled Court at St Germain disappeared and he settled down to wait for a change in monarch. This occurred ten years later in 1727 but he did not survive for much longer dying whilst Governor of Gibraltar in 1730.

BARBARA VILLIERS, DUCHESS OF CLEVELAND

Charles II first met and fell in love with Barbara Villiers just before he returned from exile in 1660. She had arrived at the exiled court in Breda with her husband Roger Palmer, conveying secret messages from

Lord Mordaunt, the King's agent in England and a gift of £1,000. The timing of their arrival was exceedingly fortuitous because the King's household was in 'incredible and fearful want' and with enormous debts the Palmers gift was warmly welcomed. Her sinister and exotic beauty captivated Charles and she quickly acquired a hold on his affections. An exceptionally beautiful woman with magnificent raven black hair, a dazzling white complexion and an exquisitely formed figure, she was the finest woman of her age. But it was her vivacity and witty conversation that captured and held the King. Never before had anyone seen such grace and beauty united with such spirit.

She came from one of England's most recently ennobled families, who owed their rise to power and fame to George Villiers, 'one of the handsomest man in the world,' the favourite of King James I. Barbara's father Viscount Grandison, an honourable man, had died fighting for his King during the Civil War. 'A young man of extraordinary hope' according the Lord Clarendon, he was much admired by all who knew him, but he left Barbara a penniless orphan at the age of three and she never forgot the poverty of her early years. He had unwisely lent considerable sums of money to his near kin the Earl of Southampton and the Buckinghams, but due to the ravages of the Civil War they were never repaid. This reduced her mother to extremes of want and effectively prevented the family from providing her with a dowry suitable to her station and in the process killed all chances of her making a grand marriage. So when she met the king on the eve of his Restoration and saw how the wind of change was blowing, she determined to become his mistress.

Charles liked witty and amusing people and nobody was more witty and amusing than Barbara. Courtiers found her lazy, languishing way of talking and unexpectedly exaggerated descriptions of people in comic situations irresistibly funny. But her wit, like that of her cousin the Duke of Buckingham, was of a biting and cruel nature. She was quite unlike any of Charles's previous mistresses. She had exceptional strength of character and fervently believed that 'the virtue of women is only an invention of men'. It was a view point that outraged many of her female contemporaries. To prove her point she took almost as many lovers as the King and thus gained a dubious reputation. To some she was the finest woman of her age, to others the fairest and lewdest of the King's concubines! Ambition and greed were the main stays of her character and she grew proud and haughty as her power and influence over the King increased over the years. She truly believed that 'the first thing a woman ought to consult is her interest and establishment in the world; (and) that love should be a handle towards it' and used her sexuality as an instrument to accumulate riches, titles and lands.

Like many of her female contemporaries she received very little education – her spelling and writing were atrocious – and idled away her time playing whist, ombre or basset. Not for her the domestic virtues. It was a state of affairs that Bishop Burnet roundly condemned declaring:

'Gaming is a waste of time, that rises out of idleness and is kept up by covetousness. Those who can think, read or write to any purpose and those who understand what conversation and friendship are will not want such a help to wear out the day'. He further declared that 'the breeding [of] young women to vanity, dressing and a false appearance of wit and behaviour without proper work or a due measure of knowledge and a serious sense of religion is the source of the corruption of that sex'.

As she spent her most impressionable and informative years without the guidance of a father figure she was spared to a large degree, the pressure to conform to the 'overwhelming ideology of female subordination and inferiority, drilled into every member of society by clerical sermons, state regulations, marital handbooks and elite and popular culture, which induced a certain docility in most wives...' This gave her the freedom to determine her own destiny in life and she seized the opportunity with both hands.

In her pursuit for power and wealth she made many enemies including the Earl of Southampton and Lord Clarendon both kinsmen; the Lord Treasurer because he owed her mother a great deal of money which he never repaid and the Lord Chancellor because in his opinion she epitomised all that was bad in the post civil war era. She was almost certainly: the inspiration of (his) famous, furious indictment of the society that had grown up in the years of the Civil War. A time when 'young people thereof of either sex [were] educated in all the liberty of vice, without reprehension or restraint...' When '... young women conversed without any circumspection or modesty, and frequently met at taverns and common eatinghouses...'. Where 'The daughters of noble & illustrious families bestowed themselves upon the divines of the times, or other low & unequal matches...' and where 'In the place of generosity, a vile and sordid love of money was entertained as the truest wisdom, and anything lawful that would contribute to being rich.

The King was not her first lover; that honour went to Lord Chesterfield and despite her marriage to Roger Palmer, a good, honest Catholic country squire, the affair continued right up to her meeting with Charles. From the moment he first saw her, this unfortunate man fell under her spell and against the advice of his father and the wishes of his family married her, the rest is history. Sir James Palmer, Roger's father, having a strong premonition that the marriage would not be a success, declared:

> if he was resolved to marry her he foresaw he should be one of the most miserable of men in the world'. How right he was! 'A gay wife, great expenses and a slender fortune' would be his lot. Unlike some of his contemporaries who believed that '... it is no offence either to husband, father or God to succeed in being loved by one's prince.

Mr Palmer did not consider it an honour to be cuckolded by the King! What Barbara's mother thought is not on record.

In return for his loan and to compensate him on the loss of his wife, Charles created the poor man an Irish Earl, his ministers having refused to pass the patent for an English title, and sent him abroad as one of his ambassadors. On his return he quarrelled violently with his wife, now the mother of two bastards by the King, hastily arranged a legal separation and publicly declared that he was not responsible for any of her debts. In return, Charles gave her a magnificent apartment over the Holbein Gate in the Palace of Whitehall overlooking the privy garden close to his own apartments and visited her every day.

Barbara's very large extended family all benefited from her royal conquest. But she never managed to completely control royal patronage on the scale achieved by her uncle the Duke of Buckingham. Nevertheless she was able to promote her relatives to some very prestigious posts within the Royal Household and thus ensured that her cousins provided the Stuarts with the next generation of royal favourites. Her uncles Sir Edward Villiers and George, Viscount Grandison, helped her secure grants and places for the family and her nominees despite the opposition of the Lord Treasurer and Lord Chancellor. Money was channelled to her from various sources over which neither had control.

'Her principal business wrote Lord Clarendon, was to get an estate for herself and her children'. 'All the suits she made of that kind [grants of land] were with reference to Ireland, he added, where they had not title to obstruct nor natural opportunity to know, what was granted; and in that Kingdom she procured the grant of several great quantities of land, like to prove of great benefit and value to her or her children'.

She was wildly extravagant and in one night alone lost £25,000 at cards but Charles always paid her debts.

Lady Suffolk, her aunt, was appointed Mistress of the Robes to Queen Catherine, whilst the Duchess of Buckingham became a Lady of the Bedchamber. Another aunt, Lady Frances Villiers – a gentle warm hearted woman – became governess to the Princesses Mary & Anne, the daughters of the Duke of York, later King James II and her daughters became companions to the young princesses. Sir Edward Villiers, husband of Lady Frances, became Master of the Robes and Groom of the Bedchamber to the Duke. She also ensured that her Churchill cousins John and Arabella were appointed to the Duke's household, John as a page and Arabella as a maid of honour. When Lady Frances became the princess's governess they lived at Richmond Palace just four miles from Whitehall and when Barbara quarrelled with the King she invariably retired there because of its close proximity to Whitehall.

When the Duchess of Richmond, another of Barbara's kin took great exception to the latter's attempts to retrieve the money owed to her father, she headed a court faction that sought to replace her with 'La Belle' Stuart. They quarrelled violently, the Duchess calling her 'Jane

Shore' and hoping that she would come to the same end. The Duchess and her brother Buckingham had been childhood companions of the king and were much loved by Charles I, who treated them as if they were his own children. But they resented being displaced in the royal favour by their younger cousin. In her younger days the Duchess was an 'extremely beautiful' woman but she was also virtuous and one of the very few women who managed to capture the heart of Prince Rupert, the King's cousin; there was even talk of marriage. Testimony once again of the enduring fascination that the Villiers family exercised over the Stuarts.

Sir Edward's daughters Elizabeth, Anne and Barbara were all spirited and amusing children who made the most of their opportunities and very soon won the trust and affection of the young princesses Mary and Anne. Elizabeth despite her lack of beauty was exceedingly witty and intelligent and followed in her cousin's footsteps by becoming the mistress of William of Orange, whilst Anne, married the Earl of Portland, the Dutch prince's favourite; their younger sister Barbara became governess to the Duke of Gloucester, the son of Queen Anne and was 'as witty and pleasant a lady as any in England'.

Other members of the family included Lady Purbeck, who scandalised the court by committing adultery with her lover Sir Robert Howard and running away from her husband. The affair produced two illegitimate sons. This was followed some years later by another scandal when Barbara's aunt, Lady Eleanor Villiers gave birth to an illegitimate daughter after she was seduced by Henry Jermyn, Chamberlain to Henrietta Maria, the Queen Mother. Many years later the Chamberlain's nephew Harry Jermyn became one of Barbara's lovers.

During her reign as the King's mistress Barbara had numerous rivals but she scorned them all. The most serious was Frances Stuart, a distant cousin of the King and 'the prettiest girl imaginable and the most fitted to adorn a Court'. Barbara foolishly befriended the girl thinking that perhaps by doing this she could retain the king's interest. Mistress Stuart was just fifteen years old when she arrived at court and Charles was instantly intrigued by her beauty. For four long years he pursued her but despite his best efforts she never surrendered her virtue and only saved her good name by eloping with the Duke of Richmond much to the anger and frustration of the King. Nevertheless as the model for Britannia, as she became, her beauty was there for all to see. In the mean time Barbara continued to reign supreme as the King's official mistress secure in the knowledge that her position was virtually unassailable.

Another of the King's amours was Winifred Wells, a big, beautiful, blonde creature and maid of honour to the Queen who was very accommodating and surrendered at the first assault but received little reward in return. Mistress Wells came from an ultra royalist family and was one of the Queen's original maids of honour. She is alleged to have been the king's mistress on and off for over ten years but no children were born of the liaison. She was followed by the comic actress Nell Gwyn, a protégé of Barbara's, whose greatest talent was that she could always make the King laugh and the aristocratic, high born and baby faced beauty Louise de Keroualle, formerly a maid of honour to the Duchess of Orleans, the King's sister.

Charles loved children but the Queen proved to be barren. Barbara on the other hand was a very prolific woman. During their relationship she presented him with a child each year. She had a total of seven, but the King would not acknowledge the paternity of the penultimate daughter and only grudgingly recognised the youngest. The eldest, a daughter, was a wayward child who craved for affection and was married at a very young age to the Earl of Sussex. After her marriage she conceived an overwhelming passion for the company of the Duchess of Mazarin, one of her father's mistresses, who had befriended her. The Duchess, a niece of Cardinal Mazarin, Louis XIV's first minister, had come to England to enlist the aid of the king in recovering her inheritance after she had run away from her husband. She firstly fled to the Duke of Savoy, a former admirer but on his sudden death, she headed for England.

Hortense Mancini was an incredibly beautiful woman whose bohemian ways appealed to both sexes. An accomplished and skilful rider she could also shoot and fence and enjoyed long country walks either cloaked or in men's clothing. But she had a chequered past and was quite amoral. After running away from her husband because of his cruelty, she gave birth to a child whose paternity was attributed to the

Chevalier de Rohan's page, to whom she had taken a violent fancy. She was not therefore suitable company for such a young and impressionable girl as Lady Sussex. Nevertheless she made an instant conquest of her and they soon became boon companions.

Her arrival in England in the winter of 1675 caused a sensation in court circles. She was accompanied by the Comte de Gramont, who performed a similar service for Barbara when she left for France to avoid her creditors, and was met outside the capital by Ralph Montagu, the former English Ambassador to Paris, who planned to use her to supplant the reigning mistress, Louise de Keroualle. Initially she resided at the home of Lady Hervey, Montagu's sister, and when she began to visit the apartments of her cousin the Duchess of York several times a week, Charles got to here of it and made sure he was in attendance.

Hortense also visited the apartments of Lady Sussex and on occasion would stay the night to nurse the poor woman who was very young and pregnant with her first child. Again when the King visited his daughter to check on her health in the mornings he was delighted to find Hortense there and before long they fell in great familiarity. Eventually, however, Lord Sussex grew exceedingly jealous and removed his wife from court and their friendship ended abruptly.

Despite the King's protection Barbara was very conscious that their relationship was deeply frowned upon by the Church. They were committing double adultery and to protect what was left of her good name, it was essential that they should try and observe all contemporary conventions and keep the births of their children secret. In an attempt to do this Barbara's children were spirited away at birth by her coachman, a service he performed on several other occasions before being handed over to a wet nurse, but it was not long before she threw caution to the winds and placed them in a nursery in her lodgings at the palace which Charles began to visit to a regular basis to play with them.

As there was no Madame Scarron to take on the role of surrogate mother, Barbara would raise them herself. It was a truly scandalous situation. No other English monarch had dared to allow his bastards to be brought up in the royal palace at such a young age. It was a complete break with tradition. But the lady did not care! Polite society however was enraged and shortly after the birth of her fourth child they expressed their displeasure in no uncertain terms. As she crossed St James's Park one evening with just a maid and footman after a visit to the Duchess of York, she was accosted by three masked men, almost certainly courtiers, and verbally abused. They called her a plain whore and every variation on the word and forced her to run towards to the Palace of Whitehall where she fainted in her room. When the King heard he rushed to her side and ordered the park gates to be locked and everyone inside to be arrested. Being the King's mistress clearly had it's price!

Unlike her contemporary Mme de Montespan who was given the Chateau de Clagny as her principal residence, Barbara fared badly by comparison. Clagny was situated just a few miles from Versailles and completely rebuilt for Mme de Montespan who refused to move in because she said it was the sort of thing one gave to opera singers! The King ordered the architect Mansart to design a new chateau and commissioned La Notre to design the gardens. The result was a beautiful and enchanting chateau.

Only when Charles tired of her did Barbara receive a residence of her own. The King gave her Nonsuch Palace and Berkshire House, formerly occupied by Lord Clarendon whom she detested, both of which she promptly demolished in order to lease out the land and with the proceeds built a smaller house in the gardens of Berkshire House which she renamed Cleveland House. Lord Clarendon had occupied the house shortly after the Great Fire of London and only moved out when his new mansion in Piccadilly was finished.

Barbara's eventual fall from favour swiftly followed that of her bitterest enemy the Lord Chancellor and the marriage of Mistress Stuart to the Duke of Richmond. In encompassing the downfall of her rival and her bitterest enemy she had engineered her own downfall. The fallen Chancellor was under no illusions that 'the lady and her party' had encompassed his downfall. During the whole his term of office he had blocked, impeded and refused to pass any patents or orders in her name. When he stopped a grant of £2,000 a year to her uncle Viscount Grandison she retorted that 'I have disposed of that place and do not doubt in a little time to dispose of yours'. The King for his part was mortally offended in the highest degree when he was told 'that the Chancellor had a principal hand in the marriage of the Duke of Richmond'. He simply had to go. Weary also of his mistress and her tantrums, Charles stopped sleeping with her and decided to return to the marital bed for a few years in order to fulfil his duty and sire legitimate children.

To purchase Berkshire House, Charles was forced to borrow £11,500 from Alderman Backwell, a city banker, on the security of two Customs tallies. Once Clarendon had left, Barbara moved in immediately and had the property valued and the house re-furnished. Charles visited her every day. It was an extraordinary situation given that only the previous year Barbara had given birth to a child that was clearly not the King's but Harry Jermyn's! The King's forbearance was truly astonishing! But it did not last long. Shortly after moving in, Barbara discovered that the King had seduced her maid and she was with child. His visits ceased immediately when he discovered that the poor woman had been thrown out on the street at midnight by his enraged ex-mistress.

In the early days following his Restoration the King planned to build a new palace at Greenwich in the grand style of Andrea Palladio, including apartments for Barbara, but when he ran out of money he was forced to abandon the project and spend what little money he had on renovating the Royal Palaces of Whitehall and Hampton Court. Barbara had apartments in both. The King spent his honeymoon at Hampton Court and after many tantrums and tears forced the Queen to accept his mistress as a Lady of the Bedchamber. Barbara also ensured that her aunt Lady Suffolk was appointed to be the Queen's Mistress of the Robes and Keeper of the Privy Purse.

When the King's interest in her eventually began to wane, he took other mistresses. Barbara retaliated by taking up lovers of her own. In quick succession she took up with Charles Hart, the actor, Harry Jermyn, Jacob Hall the tight rope artist, William Wycherley, the poet and playwright, John Churchill, the future Duke of Marlborough and John Sheffield, Earl of Mulgrave. In keeping with her ground breaking views on equality between men and women, when it came to the subject of sex, she paid handsomely for her pleasures and in the case of John Churchill provided him with the money that formed the base of his subsequent fortune. Unlike the King, however, who managed to carry off these new amours with an easy charm, some panache and a degree of style, Barbara was portrayed as ruthless, extravagant, avaricious and sexually promiscuous. Whilst Charles managed to maintain some of the 'mystery and romance that men had invented to ennoble their passions', Barbara recognised that they were but 'the thirst and necessity of pleasure; a taste founded on the senses; a blind sentiment which does not presume any merit in the person who inspires it'. Noble sentiments indeed but as an early advocate for women's emancipation she was clearly proving to be her own worst enemy.

At the same time the King finally succeeded in breaching the defences of 'La Belle Stuart' and also pursued and won the actress Nell Gwyn and her colleague Moll Davies. He also continued to enjoy the charms of Mistress Wells but Barbara's star was eventually eclipsed with the appearance of the baby faced French beauty Louise-Renee de Penancoet de Keroualle, who arrived on the scene in 1670.

The result of all these later liaisons was the birth of Barbara's two youngest daughters, both destined to become nuns. The elder was the result of her affair with Harry Jermyn, whilst the latter named after her mother, the fruit perhaps of her relationship with John Churchill, but also possibly by Charles. The affair with Churchill lasted longer than most but he plundered her finances to such an extent that she was forced to retire to France in order to recover. 'She has given him the value of more than £100,000' commented the French Ambassador 'In one way or another he has got so much money out of her that in desperation she is obliged to go to France to live quietly for some time'.

Her infatuation with Churchill was easy to understand as he was one of the handsomest men in England who possessed an extraordinary charm and graciousness of manner that made him irresistible to men and women alike. Nevertheless his behaviour cost him a colonelcy in the Regiment Royal-Anglais in the French Army and serving the King of France. When the French Ambassador heard of his plans he immediately wrote to Louis 'Monsieur Churchill is too keenly devoted to his own pleasure to be likely to acquit himself well with such a responsibility.

What is wanted is a man who will make the Regiment... both his vocation and his mistress'.

When Barbara arrived in Paris, all of the great French ladies stayed away. But eventually she succeeded in establishing herself and soon had a number of beaus in tow, including the Archbishop of Paris and the Marquis de Châtillon. News of her success reached England where it was noted that 'She driveth a cunning trade, and followeth her old employment very hard there, especially with the Archbishop of Paris, who is her principal gallant'.

The Archbishop was quickly followed by a much younger man, indeed twenty years his junior. Alexis, Marquis de Châtillon was First Gentleman of the Bedchamber to the Duke of Orleans, brother of the King of France. Barbara became besotted with him, and at first, the affair was carried on with a great deal of discretion. However, when letters written by the lovers came into the hands of the English Ambassador 'some of which abounded with gross and unseemly things in the trade of love, some with disrespect to His Majesty' he immediately sent them to Charles causing a diplomatic crisis. According to Barbara the Ambassador aspired to become her lover but she had spurned his advances. In revenge he sought to compromise the good name of her daughter Lady Sussex, who had temporarily separated from her husband and retired to a convent. Montagu vehemently denied any wrong doing with Lady Sussex and claimed that the cause of the uproar came about as a direct result of Barbara's clandestine couplings with her lover the Marquis de Châtillon. Apparently when Lady Northumberland had called on her uninvited, and was in consequence refused admission, she had returned home in high dudgeon to report the incident to her husband the Ambassador. He then took it upon himself to remonstrate with Barbara about her behaviour at which she turned on him in a rage. Fortunately for all, Charles refused to rise to the bait and the matter was eventually resolved to the satisfaction of all concerned.

Before her departure for France, Barbara ensured that her children by the King received the titles, lands and money that was their due. In character the children duly resembled one or other of their parents. Anne, the eldest and Henry inherited their mother's fractious and disagreeable nature whilst the remainder resembled their father. Anne was married to her cousin, who was created an Earl for the occasion, and given a dowry of £20,000. Charlotte received a dowry of £18,000 and her husband was also made an Earl. The boys fared better, the eldest Charles was created Duke of Southampton and married to an heiress. Henry the second son was also created a Duke and married to an heiress whilst George, the youngest son, had to wait for his dukedom until the penultimate year of his father's reign. When George did eventually marry after his father's death, it was to a beautiful penniless widow. Barbara's youngest daughters fared less well. The eldest went on to have an affair with the Duke of Hamilton and bear an illegitimate child before entering a nunnery, whilst the youngest Barbara took her vows at the age of eighteen and went on to became the Prioress of an Abbey in France.

After returning from France in the autumn of 1679, Barbara settled down to live for her a very quiet life. With a gift of £25,000 from the royal coffers she spent the years up to the King's death in 1685, delighting to the regular appearance of her royal grandchildren. By 1685 Lady Sussex had two daughters and her sister Lady Lichfield, five children, whilst the Duke of Grafton only one. The Duke of Southampton did not have any children from his first marriage and the Duke of Northumberland remained childless. However, this rather idyllic phase of her life did not last. Even before the King's death, she cast her eyes in the direction of the theatre for her next love and took up with the handsome and popular actor Cardonell 'Scum' Goodman, who was then all the rage on the boards of Drury Lane.

'Scum' as he was known to his enemies, was a handsome, amusing rogue who was formerly a page of the backstairs to Charles II but was dismissed on a charge of negligence. He had turned to the theatre to make his living because all other careers were barred to him. His gentlemanly manner and fine appearance were used to great effect when playing the leading roles in Julius Caesar, Othello and Alexander the Great, but his fortunes rose when he caught the Duchess's eye and he became her lover. The affair did not last because in addition to acting, he was not averse to a spot of highway robbery in order to supplement his income. However, his downfall, came when he was accused of attempting to poison the Duchess's two sons the Dukes of Grafton and Northumberland.

After the death of King Charles, Cleveland House, Barbara's residence, continued to be the centre of a raffish social circle. Among the visitors was a young kinsman, Lord Arran, eldest son of the Duke of Hamilton who came to pay court to Barbara's daughter by Harry Jermyn. If Barbara was expecting that he came with honourable intentions she was rudely deceived. The object of his attentions was convent bred and was almost as beautiful as her mother. Her marriage prospects however were very poor given that she was illegitimate, but that did not stop her from entertaining the idea that the young Lord Arran might ask for her hand in marriage given that he was recently made a widower. Unchaperoned, however, the young lady quickly displayed all of her mother's amoral characteristics and succumbed to Arran's dishonourable advances. Within a short time, she showed unmistakable proofs of her error. The result was a son, Charles Hamilton, who grew up to be much loved by his grandmother. Having ruined her marriage prospects, the young lady eventually ended her days in a nunnery. A few years later Lord Arran caused the lady further pain and distress by contemplating marriage with her cousin Lady Henrietta Villiers, daughter of Sir Edward, but his mother was horrified at the suggestion reminding him that 'You have by my mother the honourablest part of that alliance and I admire you ever took that into consideration, knowing how mad the father was! The Duchess's mother was a niece of George Villiers, 1st Duke of Buckingham.

When Barbara's husband died in 1705, she found herself not only a widow but also the target of one of histories most rapacious fortune hunters i.e. 'Beau or Handsome Feilding'. Feilding came from a respectable Warwickshire family and was closely allied to the Earls of Denbigh. He had already married two heiresses and disposed of their fortunes. In addition he was a bully, prone to acts of violence, a lecher and a spendthrift. But all of this did not seem to matter because his physical beauty blinded almost all to the defects in his character. He was according to one contemporary 'the universal flame of all the fair sex; innocent virgins sighed for him as Adonis, experienced widows as Hercules...' 'Woman was his mistress and the whole world his seraglio'. For once Barbara had met her match and here was the mirror image of herself in the opposite sex.

Not content to woo Barbara, Feilding also attempted to seduce another rich widow, Mrs Anne Deleau, with a fortune of £60,000. In order to do this he approached the lady's hairdresser a Mrs Villars, reputedly an illegitimate daughter of the Duke of Buckingham. Realising that Mrs Deleau would have nothing to do with such a fellow as Feilding, she decided to dupe him and asked for £500 to arrange a meeting. When he agreed she passed off a common prostitute as the widow and deceived him into marrying her. When Feilding found out, he assaulted Mrs Villars and beat her about the head and face shouting 'God eternally damn you, you bitch, how could you think that woman a wife fit for I, Major General Feilding?'

In the mean time, the rogue had also persuaded the Duchess to marry him and had moved into her Bond Street house. When Mrs Villars and her companion informed Barbara that he had committed bigamy, he proceeded to beat the Duchess as well until she screamed 'Murder' from the window. When the watch arrived he was arrested. To avenge himself on the Duchess, he then seduced her grand daughter Charlotte, who was living with her temporarily. The child she bore was a daughter but Feilding showed no interest in it and after a few years it disappeared from the pages of history.

The effect on Barbara of this final humiliation was to permanently damage her health and she fell into a decline from which she never recovered. The end came in 1709 after she had swelled to a monstrous size, the result of dropsy. In retrospect this remarkable woman led a quite extraordinary life. Born in the Civil War years which saw the emergence of radical ideas about social, economic, sexual and political equality, she proceeded to turn the accepted status quo on the role of women in society on its head. She made a conscious decision to forgo the security to be found in marriage and like a man sought her fortune by other means. Like Ninon de L'Enclos her famous French counterpart she rebelled against the injustice of the unequal conventions surrounding the conduct of the opposite sexes and resolved the right to follow nature's course and act like a man! And so she did much to the horror and dismay of many of her contemporaries. She now lies buried in Chiswick.

Elizabeth Villiers, Countess of Orkney

When William of Orange invaded England in 1688 and seized the crown from his father-in-law James II, he brought with him the next generation of royal favourites, male and female. A very discreet and secretive man he is often portrayed as a closet homosexual, but despite the obvious affection and high regard he had for his childhood companion Hans Bentinck and later Arnold van Keppel, there is no evidence to support this allegation. The secret to his character lies in his birth and upbringing. He was an orphan and a child of state. His father died before his birth and his mother when he was ten. At a very young age all of his companions who had been with him since the age of four were taken away, save one Hans Bentinck, thus leaving him isolated and lonely. To use the prince's own words 'I was born in misfortune and reared in misfortune'. As a result, over the years his attachment to Bentinck grew stronger and this goes a long way to explaining his affection and enormous regard for him. His Calvinist upbringing also ensured that he was careful in his relationships with both sexes and in this respect he resembled his grandfather Charles I. But that did not stop him from having a mistress Betty Villiers, one of his wife's maids of honour.

Elizabeth Villiers, a cousin of Barbara Villiers Charles II's mistress, was to be his confidante and mistress for at least fifteen years. Although not a great beauty she possessed a lively intelligence and ready wit which made her very agreeable and entertaining company. Unlike her cousin Barbara she made no attempt to flout or break the contemporary standards of behaviour that were demanded of women. The relationship did not produce children, which suggests that the affair may have been more platonic than sexual. But the whole affair was conducted with much dignity, discretion and a great deal of self control on William's part, who was ever mindful of his marriage vows and strict religious upbringing.

Elizabeth was one of the six daughters of Sir Edward Villiers, half brother of the famous Duke of Buckingham, the notorious male favourite of James I and later his son Charles I. She was also the niece of the infamous Lady Somerset, wife of Robert Carr, Buckingham's predecessor as favourite of James I, both of whom were imprisoned in the Tower of London for the murder of Sir Thomas Overbury. It is surprising therefore that this double connection with two such notorious people should have produced such a well balanced individual as Elizabeth.

Elizabeth and her sisters received the standard education for women of their time viz: lessons in music, dancing, French and deportment etc, but there is no evidence that they were caught up in the prevailing fashion in some aristocratic circles of providing higher education for the female members of their families. However the Howards, her mother's kin, were renowned for insisting that their daughters were given a sound education. Elizabeth's great-aunt Katherine, Lady Berkeley was taught amongst other things Latin, French, Italian, natural philosophy and astronomy. Although not as clever as her aunt, Elizabeth was a gifted conversationalist, with a keen and enquiring mind – she was able to converse with many of the countries leading politicians on important political issues – and possessed many other sterling qualities, including the ability to fascinate all those with whom she came into contact.

The Villiers children, including Elizabeth, were brought up in the palace of Richmond as companions of the Princesses Mary and Anne and shared in all of their activities. Sir Edward had been appointed keeper of the palace, park, lodges and game shortly after the Restoration. It was here that his niece Barbara, Charles II's mistress, would sometimes retreat whenever she and the king had quarrelled. The princesses joined the Villiers household after the death of their mother in 1671 when Lady Frances was appointed their governess. They were joined by a small group of carefully selected well born young ladies such as Frances Apsley, Sarah Jennings and Anne Trelawny; Frances, a close relative of Elizabeth's, became an instant favourite with Princess Mary who began a passionate correspondence with her that lasted many years.

The fame and fortune of the Villiers family rested solely on the activities of the notorious George Villiers, 1st Duke of Buckingham, the male favourite of James I and Charles I. Three generations of the family – men and women alike – exerted an irresistible fascination upon three generations of the Stuarts, they included the 1st Duke, his son the 2nd Duke, Barbara Villiers and Elizabeth Villiers.

Sensing perhaps that their day was over, the Howards attempted to cling onto some of the power they had once possessed by forming a number of matrimonial alliances with the Villiers family. The most notable of which were between Frances Howard, daughter of the Earl of Suffolk and Sir Edward Villers; Mary Boteler, niece of the 1st Duke of Buckingham and Edward Howard, Baron Howard of Escrick; Colonel Thomas Howard and Mary Villiers, Dowager-Duchess of Richmond. and James Howard, 3rd Earl of Suffolk and Barbara Villiers, aunt and namesake of Lady Castlemaine later Duchess of Cleveland.

But it did not take this influx of Villiers blood to produce a family that was prone to scandal. Elizabeth's first cousin Lady Betty Felton, a famous beauty, was the mistress of James, Duke of Monmouth, the bastard son of Charles II and Lucy Walters. Tom Howard, Master of the Horse to Mary, Princess of Orange, and Elizabeth's uncle, succeeded Charles II as the lover of the beautiful Lucy Walter. In addition there was Elizabeth's aunt and namesake who scandalised the court of Charles I when she bore her lover two bastard children and the beautiful Lady Frances Howard, who with her husband's help poisoned Sir Thomas Overbury and was committed to the Tower of London. Finally there was the infamous bawd Moll Howard, grand daughter of the above mentioned Baron Howard of Escrick.

When Princess Mary married her cousin the Prince of Orange in November 1677, Elizabeth was appointed one of her Maids of Honour and together with her sisters, prepared to leave for Holland. Shortly before the wedding, however, Lady Frances, Elizabeth's mother caught the smallpox from her charge Princess Anne and died. The same week in which the princess was married saw the new Duchess of York give birth to a son, the Duke of Cambridge, the death of the Archbishop of Canterbury and the death of Lady Frances. Although Princess Anne recovered she passed the infection on to her infant half brother. At his birth he was described as 'little but sprightly and lightly to live' but within a month was dead, the event being attributed to neglect. 'In the opinion of the physicians' remarked Dr Lake 'he might have lived many years had not Mrs Chambers and Mrs Manning, his dry nurse, struck in the humour which broke forth under his arm ... instead of putting on a coal leaf to draw it out'. The Duke was distraught and 'never known to grieve so much at the death of any of his other children'.

Shortly after their arrival in Holland Elizabeth's sister Anne married Hans Bentinck, the favourite companion of the Prince of Orange. Bentinck, who was appointed page to the Prince in 1664 would be a loyal friend for the remainder of his life. On entering the Prince's service he was described as 'a pleasant looking, upstanding youth... with reddish blond hair' who liked the outdoor life and country pursuits. He showed exemplary loyalty and devotion to the prince and once in 1675 when the Prince was seriously ill with small pox volunteered to sleep by his side because it was the belief that 'the violent progress of the disease could only be stopped if a young man of the same age... exposed himself to the dangerous contagion'. The Prince duly recovered only for young Bentinck to succumb to the infection and although seriously ill for some time he eventually recovered.

Although much taken with his young wife on account of her beauty, gaiety and gentle charm, it was clear to William that she could not provide the intellectual companionship that he desired. Even Bentinck fell short in that department, therefore he was delighted and pleasantly surprised when he discovered that he could converse on political matters with his wife's maid of honour. His interest in Elizabeth despite her youth was such that by 1679 reports of their intimacy had even reached the French Court. In all of his relationships William was very discreet and for his wife to remain unaware of his interest in her maid of honour for so long is abundant evidence of how successful he was in keeping the relationship a secret.

The marriage of her sister to the Prince's favourite companion put Elizabeth into a very strong position and allowed her to have access to him without raising undue suspicion. Although there were no suitors for her hand in marriage her sisters Katherine and Barbara made good marriages, the first to the Marquis de Puissars and the second to John Berkeley, later Viscount FitzHardinge; John's elder brother Charles had been a great favourite of Charles II but he was killed at sea fighting the Dutch in 1665. Katherine and her husband – an exiled Huguenot – had a suite of rooms assigned to them in the Binnenhof Palace whilst Anne,

Lady Bentinck, also a firm favourite of the Princess was lodged in an apartment with her husband that immediately joined that of the Prince.

Among the many men that Elizabeth seduced with her mind, none was more taken with her than Jonathan Swift, who records that her only fault was that she squinted like a dragon, 'I always forget myself and talk of squinting people before her' he exclaimed. The reports of her lack of beauty are much exaggerated and surviving portraits show that she was a very attractive woman. Lady Fitzhardinge, her sister, who was 'as witty and pleasant a lady as any in England' became a very good friend of Sarah, Lady Marlborough and another great favourite of the Princess of Orange. But despite being appointed Governess to the young Duke of Gloucester, Princess Anne's son, she was not liked by that princess. 'Remember none of that family (the Villiers) were ever good for anything' the Princess declared adding for good measure that the Duchess of Somerset and Lady Fitzhardinge were also 'two of the most observing, prying ladies in England'. Her warning appears to have been based on the contents of an anonymous letter that was sent to her:

... have a care of what you say before Lady Fitzhardinge, remember she's Lord Portland's & Betty Villiers sister. You may depend upon't that these two are not ignorant of what is said & done in your lodgings... Upon the whole matter he's the luckiest gentleman in England [reference to Edward Villiers, Earl of Jersey, brother of Lady Portland, Elizabeth Villiers & Lady Fitzhardinge] whose sister [Betty Villiers] governs the King [the Prince of Orange now William III] & his wife [Mary] the Queen & is the entire confident of poor deluded Lady Marlborough.

The occasion for these outbursts was a falling out between Mary and her sister Anne. 'In all this' declared Mary 'I see the hand of God and look on our disagreeing as a punishment upon us for the irregularity by us committed upon the Revolution'.

It was eight years into the marriage before the Princess of Orange discovered that her husband was visiting the apartment of her maid of honour Betty Villiers. At first Betty had resisted his advances but the

Prince persisted and eventually won her over. When the liaison was discovered the prince attempted to appease his wife by remarking 'What has given you so much pain is merely an amusement, there is no crime in it'. Lady Bentinck was appalled at her sister's behaviour and the Princess resolved to be rid of her by sending her on a mission to England, with the instruction that she was not to return. When Betty did return, the Princess refused to see her and she was forced to take up lodgings with her sister Katherine.

Now that the affair was out in the open the Prince hastened to assure his wife that 'I swear to you by all that is most sacred that what has caused you pain was simply a distraction, that there has been no crime...' Bentinck meanwhile gave his sister-in-law and the Prince a piece of his mind and wrote to a friend of the '... pain and resentment that I have in seeing that by her [Betty's] own choice and the wish of her father [Sir Edward Villiers] she pursues a course of conduct so opposed to her interests, to her honour and to what she promised me in speaking'. Eventually, however, the Princess accepted her husband's explanation and the Orange household returned to it's normal routine.

The timing of the revelation could not have come at a worse time because the princess was still grieving over the death of her uncle Charles II from apoplexy earlier in the year. This event transformed her status from that of a Stadholder's wife to heiress presumptive to the crowns of England, Scotland and Ireland and thus increased the status of her husband on the European political stage. Elizabeth meanwhile kept quietly in the background and left the stage clear for her cousin Lady Betty Felton to make a big noise in the world.

Lady Betty's mother Lady Suffolk (*nee* Barbara Villers) had been Mistress of the Robes and 1st Lady of the Bedchamber to Catherine of Braganza and on occasions was called upon by Charles II to use her influence to assist him in patching up his many quarrels with his mistress who also happened to be her niece. Of the daughter it was said that:

> Madam Betty had a beauty and youth that were almost dazzling, and won her the love of all who saw her, and being of a very gay disposition, she seldom frightened her loves away by her looks.

Unfortunately, however, the defects in her character damaged her reputation causing Lady Sunderland to comment on 'the fine airs of the great beauty my Lady Betty Felton who turns the heads of all the men, and quarrels with all the women, and lies in bed & cries when things are not altogether to her taste.'

When Lady Betty decided to marry it was to Thomas Felton, then just a Groom of the Bedchamber to Charles II. Naturally her parents disapproved of the match because they felt their daughter could find a much richer husband. After the birth of their only child, a daughter, the couple separated. The cause of the separation was due to the following incident 'Lady Betty Felton' declared Lady Russell 'threatens to mortify [Lady Arundell] above all sufferance; for she will not suffer Lord Shrewsbury to adore there any longer... And for my Lord Thanet, she says the world shall see how much more powerful her charms are than those of a great monarch'. When the King heard of her behaviour he was enraged 'Lord Newport came yesterday morning' declared Lady Russell '& says he never saw the King more enraged; he sent for Lord Suffolk to chain up his daughter & forbid her the Court, so at present neither Lord or Lady Suffolk sees her & little Felton is leaving her' A short while later Lady Betty died from mortification and apoplexy. When the Duchess of Portsmouth, Charles II's last mistress, left England for France after the latter's death, the title of *mistress en titre* was briefly filled by Catherine Sedley, whom James II created Countess of Dorchester and upon the accession of William of Orange by Elizabeth Villiers. However, the contrast between the first two and Elizabeth could not have been more striking. Unlike her predecessors Elizabeth did not wish to be publicly acknowledged and never sought to gain from her royal connections. That she was able to achieve this degree of anonymity was remarkable but greatly facilitated by the fact that the major part of William's munificence and generosity was directed towards his male favourites, Hans Bentinck and Arnold van Keppel, both of whom he raised to the peerage with the titles Earl of Portland and Earl of Albemarle.

Unfortunately, William's public displays of affection for these two gentlemen aroused much speculation about the exact nature of their relationship. So much so that it was commonly assumed in Holland

and later England that it was homosexual in nature. When William was made aware of this he was genuinely shocked and disgusted. As a great-grandson of King James I, who was notorious for the number of his male favourites, it is easy to caste doubt on his sexuality but given that there were many similarities in their upbringing including the lack of a father figure and the pronounced lack of feminine company during their most impressionable years it is easy to see how they came to depend upon the affection and companionship of members of their own sex. As William declared 'It seems to me very extraodinary that it should be impossible to have esteem and regard for a young man without it being criminal'.

Meanwhile in the post Glorious Revolution years Elizabeth finally began to turn her attention to the task of finding a husband and in her endeavours she was assisted by William. Unfortunately, however, some years were to pass before she achieved her objective and in the mean time several of her closest kin had passed away. Her sister Lady Bentinck was the first. After bearing her husband five children this unfortunate lady was taken seriously ill and passed away on the eve of William's invasion of England. Elizabeth and her sister became estranged after her relationship with William had been made public and had not spoken in awhile but on her deathbed she forgave her. The ladies death was reported to her husband by his secretary '... It has pleased providence – and on me falls the task of telling your Lordship – to call hence out of this world into eternal happiness... your lordship's highly-born wife, my highly-born mistress, to the great affliction not only of her Royal Highness who stayed with her till her last sigh and with bitter tears left the body, but also of all the bystanders and servants...' The following year Sir Edward Villers, Elizabeth's father died. The character of this gentleman is a mystery but a clue can be found in the correspondence of the Duchess of Hamilton. The Duchess on being told that her eldest son and heir wished to marry Elizabeth's sister Henrietta exclaimed 'I beseech you not to think of the Knight Marshals daughter. You have by my mother the honorablest part of that aliah [alliance] and I admire you ever took that into consideration knowing how mad the father was'. The Duchess's mother Lady Mary Feilding, was a niece of the 1st Duke of Buckingham.

Although Elizabeth still retained some influence with the King it is possible that the prospect of an alliance with a former royal mistress and kinswoman was not appealing enough for the Duchess despite the promise of a dowry of £20,000; Henrietta eventually married the Earl of Breadalbane. The tables were turned, however, the following year when Elizabeth married one the Duchess's younger sons George bringing with her a dowry of only £8,000 plus an income of £5,000 per annum from the Irish estates that William had granted her in 1691 after the defeat of King James. George for his part brought £60,000 in ready money, an income of £7,000 per annum plus three great houses. Elizabeth was under no illusions and accepted that this was an arranged marriage and to her husband declared with refreshing frankness that 'she had been on very good terms with a certain person [William III], but she did not wish to hear any reproaches or insinuations on that score'. In the event the marriage turned out to be a very happy one and it produced three daughters.

Despite being renowned for the discretion she exercised in all of her affairs, in the year before her marriage Elizabeth suddenly found herself thrust into the public eye when Edward 'Beau' Wilson, was killed in a duel with John Law, the famous financier. The resulting court case and her connection with these two gentlemen has been ignored by the majority of historians. But the most interesting aspect of it was the part played in it by one of England's most prominent statesmen Charles Talbot, Duke of Shrewsbury. The latter, son of the beautiful but notorious Anna Maria Brudenell, Countess of Shrewsbury, mistress of George Villiers, 2nd Duke of Buckingham, Elizabeth's cousin was renowned for his aversion to the married state and for twenty-nine years fought off all attempts by his family to provide him with a wife. When he did finally marry it was to a penniless, eccentric and very peculiar Italian widow who was later described by St Simon as:

> a large person, tall, fat, and mannish – both before and behind – she had been beautiful, and still claimed to be so. She wore very low cut dresses, and tucked her hair behind her ears in bunches, tying them up with ribbons, she rouged heavily, with many patches, and was very mannered,

talking loudly in bad French, and speaking familiarly with everyone. Her behaviour was that of a lunatic; but her gambling, her magnificence and her informality made her the fashion.

Like Han Bentinck and Arnold van Keppel, Shrewsbury became a great favourite of William III. The secret of his success in befriending William was due to 'a sweetness of temper that charmed all who knew him'.

According to some modern historians Shrewsbury was bi-sexual and it was this aspect of his character that threatened to be exposed as a result of the Wilson/Law affair. Edward 'Beau' Wilson was a young, well connected but poor gentleman, of pleasing looks who caught Shrewsbury's fancy whilst he was a leading member of the government. Within a short time Wilson had an income of £6,000 per annum, a fine house, a coach and six horses and was able to redeem his father's estate and give marriage portions to his sisters.

The cause of the duel was a woman. One story alleges that Wilson was the lover of Elizabeth but the trial records only refer to a Mrs Lawrence, who appears to have been Law's mistress. Many years later, in 1723, an anonymous pamphlet appeared in London claiming that Wilson was having a homosexual relationship with an unnamed nobleman and Law was used to remove him. When the duel was fought in 1694, Shrewsbury also had a mistress Mrs Lundee, daughter of the Governor of Londonderry and William III was trying, unsuccessfully, to persuade him to take up office in his government. In an attempt to persuade him otherwise William employed the services of his mistress Mrs Villiers but even her efforts proved fruitless. 'You are an ill natured devil', Mrs Lundee declared.

Eventually, however, Shrewsbury accepted the post of Secretary of State and for his pains was created in April 1694, Duke of Shrewsbury and Knight of the Garter. The duel between Wilson and Law was fought on 9 April and Shrewsbury was made a Duke on 30 April. It is plain to see therefore that Elizabeth was asked by William to protect Shrewsbury's reputation by joining forces with Law to remove Wilson from the equation. The King's and Shrewsbury's subsequent help in arranging Law's escape from prison would seem to add substance to the charge. But the story does not end there for by a curious twist of fate Law subsequently took as his mistress Elizabeth's cousin, Katherine Knollys and by her had two bastard children.

As the year drew to a close William sustained an irreparable loss when his wife Mary died suddenly of smallpox. The effect on his relationship with Elizabeth was immediate. She was dismissed and then granted the Irish estates once owned by James II worth £30,000 but on William's death they were re-possessed and broken up for sale to more worthy individuals. Elizabeth's marriage to her cousin George Hamilton and his subsequent ennoblement by William, however, finally gave her the respectability and status that was her due. George, although only the fifth son of the Duchess of Hamilton, brought a considerable fortune to the marriage and it was to all intents and purposes a very happy one. A soldier by profession he had served in William's armies at the battles of the Boyne and Aughrim and later fought at the battles of Namur, Steenkirk and Landen; shortly before his death in 1737 he was created Britain's first Field Marshal.

The marriage was not accepted by all of her husband's family, indeed his sister-in-law the Duchess of Hamilton refused to speak to her because of her previous royal association. Despite this, however, Elizabeth had many admirers one of whom was Dean Swift who described her 'the wisest woman I ever saw'. The effect she had on people was simply amazing but to some she was a figure of fun. In 1727 at the coronation George II, Lady Mary Wortley-Montagu described her thus: 'she exposed behind a mixture of fat and wrinkles, and before, a very considerable protuberance which preceded her. Add to this the inimitable roll of her eyes and her gray hair and 'tis impossible to imagine a more delightful spectacle'.

Upon the death of Queen Anne and the succession of George I, the position of *mistress en titre*'was occupied by ladies of continental extraction but fate decreed that the Howard family would yet again provide another royal favourite in the person of Henrietta Howard, wife of Charles (Howard), subsequently 9th Earl of Suffolk, Elizabeth's first cousin. Henrietta is believed to have become the mistress of George II in 1715, when he was Prince of Wales and continued so until 1734 when she was succeeded by Mary, Countess of Deloraine, another Howard cousin!

The story of Elizabeth and her kin and their success in fascinating several generations of the Stuarts and the Guelphs in turn is quite remarkable. No other family in England's history managed to reach such dizzy heights of royal favour. Lady FitzHardinge, Elizabeth's sister and her brother Lord Jersey all shared the confidence and favour of Queen Mary and William III. Lord Jersey especially was much liked by William, a pleasant and amusing man he had 'a good figure in his person, being tall, well shaped, handsome'. William often dined with him at his lodge in the Park.

William's enjoyment of Lord Jersey's company was remarkable in view of the latter's latent Jacobite sympathies. Indeed the Countess of Jersey was an avid Jacobite and after her husband's sudden death in 1711, she retired to Paris and was granted the title of Countess by the titular James III. Mathew Prior, a great friend of Lord Jersey was much afflicted by his sudden death, and sought sympathy from Sir Thomas Hanmer, the Duchess of Grafton's second husband, who wrote 'I know you loved my Lord Jersey – the Queen, the nation, mankind, has lost a pattern of honour, integrity and good manners'. But on Elizabeth's death in 1733, another chapter in the story of this remarkable family was about to begin.

Arabella Churchill, Mrs Godfrey

'I do not believe there are two men who love women more than you and I do' declared Charles II to the French Ambassador 'but my brother, devout as he is, loves them still more'. The Duke of York who subsequently succeeded his brother as James II had two principal mistresses, Arabella Churchill and Catherine Sedley but during the years immediately following the Restoration he also bedded in rapid succession a bevy of beauties including Anne, Lady Carnegie, Elizabeth, Lady Chesterfield, Mistress Goditha Price and Margaret, Lady Denham.

Lady Carnegie – the bosom friend of Lady Castlemaine, subsequently Duchess of Cleveland and mistress to Charles II – was a member of the powerful Hamilton family and a direct descendant of James IV of

Scotland and his mistress Katherine Boyd. When the Duke first took an interest in her is unclear but it is alleged in the 'Memoirs of the Comte de Gramont' that the affair began prior to the King's marriage to the Portuguese Infanta in May 1662. By her husband Lady Carnegie is said to have had two sons and if the date mentioned is correct it raises a question mark over the paternity of the second child.

The affair caused Lord Carnegie considerable embarrassment and in revenge it was alleged that 'he went into the most infamous places, to try to pick up the most infamous disease which they could furnish him; he was successful, but his vengeance was only half complete for, after he had resorted to the most extreme methods to cure himself of it, my Lady, his wife, gave it back his present, having no further commerce with the person for whom it had been so industriously prepared'. The rumour was repeated by Pepys, the diarist and Andrew Marvell, the poet much to Lord Carnegie's amusement but it was untrue. Many years later Bishop Burnet recorded that 'It looked like a peculiar strain of revenge, with which he (Lord Carnegie) seemed much delighted. But I know he has, to some of his friends, denied the whole story very solemnly'.

Lady Carnegie was quickly followed by Lady Chesterfield, the wife of Lady Castlemaine's first lover. Lady Chesterfield, a member of the famous Butler clan in Ireland, was related to Mary Carey, mistress of Henry VIII and also Mary Berkeley, the mother of Sir John Perrott, an alleged illegitimate son of Henry VIII. This affair began in the autumn of 1662 and it was not long before Lord Chesterfield was provided with ample proofs of the Duke's interest in his wife. Whilst Lady Carnegie had been tolerably handsome, Lady Chesterfield was one of the Court's leading beauties who 'knew how to arm her attractions with all that is seductive in a woman's nature when she desires to please'. At first she had played the role of dutiful wife but on perceiving that her husband was indifferent to her obvious charms she caste her eyes elsewhere.

The Duke of York the happy recipient of her amorous glances needed no encouragement but was so indiscrete in the conduct of the affair that it became the talk of the Court. Indeed on one occasion whilst playing cards in the Queen's presence the lady's husband observed later to another courtier that 'The Duke was close by. I do not know what had become of his hand, but I know very well that his arm had disappeared right up to the elbow. He returned around and saw me, and was so disconcerted by my presence that, in drawing away his hand he came near to completely undressing Lady Chesterfield'. Chesterfield enraged by the Duke's behaviour took his wife off to his country estate and there nine months later she gave birth to her second child, a daughter Elizabeth, who married the Earl of Strathmore and became ancestor of Elizabeth Bowes-Lyon, the Queen-Mother.

With Lady Chesterfield's departure the Duke returned to the arms of his wife with the result that she produced in quick succession two children one of whom, Anne, eventually succeeded her elder sister as Queen. But the Duke's amourous instinct's eventually re-surfaced and before long he had taken a fancy to Mrs Price another of his wife's maids of honour.

Goditha Price, was the daughter of Sir Herbert Price and a cousin of the famous Restoration beauties Jane and Eleanor Needham and also Lady Byron, Charles II's seventeenth mistress abroad. Unable to make the Duke acknowledge her publicly, Mrs Price was reduced to making her way to his apartments by way of the backstairs. The affair produced no material rewards whatsoever for the lady or her family and was over almost as soon as it had begun. However, this was not to be the case with his next mistress the fair Lady Denham.

Margaret Brooke and her sister Frances, the daughters of Sir William Brooke, came to court at the behest of the Earl of Bristol, a relative of their step-father the Earl of Bedford. The plan was to excite the interest of the King and in this design they were very successful. When he saw them Charles was immediately struck by the beauty of Margaret, the younger sister. Unfortunately, however, Lady Castlemaine got wind of the plot and together with Harry Brouncker, a member of the Duke of York's household, conspired to engage the Duke's interest in the lady. At the same time Sir William arranged for his daughter to marry Sir John Denham, Surveyor General of the King's Works and thirty years her senior. Sir John 'an old, snarling, troublesome, peevish fellow, in love with her to distraction and, to complete her misery, a perpetual attendant on her person', was tall with rather bent shoulders and a pronounced limp and in the words of the diarist Evelyn, 'A better poet than architect'. His wife's affair with the Duke affected his reason to such an extent that he became temporarily deranged.

By the June of 1666 Pepys observed that the Duke was 'wholly given up to his new mistresse, my Lady Denham, going at noon-day with all his gentlemen with him to visit her in Scotland Yard; she declaring she will not be his mistresse as Mrs Price, to go up and down the privy stairs, but will be owned publicly; and so she is'. Why she chose to become his mistress is unknown but like so many of the ladies in this book she probably hoped that she could make the family's fortune by surrendering her virtue. But like her ancestor Elizabeth Blount, the mistress of Henry VIII, the affair brought her no benefit whatsoever. Indeed within a year of becoming the Duke's mistress she died quite suddenly, rumour attributing her sudden demise to poison administered by the Duchess. The rumour was of course false but it did untold damage to the Duke's reputation.

With Lady Denham's passing the Duke quite naturally sort consolation elsewhere and within a short time found comfort in the arms of one of his wife's new maids of honour, Arabella Churchill, sister of John Churchill, the future Duke of Marlborough. Arabella's appointment was almost certainly due to the influence of her cousin Lady Castlemaine, Charles II's mistress, who at the time was carrying the King's fifth child, the future Duke of Northumberland. Indeed it is alleged by Mrs de la Rivere Manley that subsequently 'The Duchess [of Cleveland] gave 6,000 crowns for a place in the prince's bedchamber for him [John Churchill]' and 'called about her person his fair and fortunate sister who became the mistress of the prince'. The following year John, became the Duke's page of honour. Arabella's arrival coincided with the beginning of the Duke's affair with Lady Denham and she did not make an immediate impact on James. The Memoirs of the Comte de Gramont which are very disparaging of Arabella, paint her in a very unattractive light but the portrait of her at Althorp shows that she was in fact very beautiful as one would expect from a sister of the handsome John Churchill.

Arabella's decision to sacrifice her reputation and prospects of making a good marriage by becoming the Duke's mistress cannot have been motivated purely by the example of her cousin Lady Castlemaine. Had that been the case she would have fought a great deal harder for the same status and riches. The key to understanding her decision must lie in her character. The memoirs of the Comte de Gramont describe her as lazy, therefore content with the little that she was given. Unlike Barbara she had no wish to challenge the establishment and fight for women's rights.

Sir Winston Churchill was not a wealthy man and like any father took a keen interest in seeking marriage partners for his offspring. For his eldest son John, he sought the hand of Catherine Sedley, only child of Sir Charles Sedley. Catherine, who made up in wit what she lacked in beauty, was a very desirable catch who stood to inherit a fortune but unfortunately it was not to be. John had lost his heart to Sarah Jennings, a beauty without a fortune but still with some aristocratic connections; she was a cousin of the Duke of Norfolk and kinswoman of Elizabeth Villiers, mistress of William of Orange

Arabella's affair with the Duke began in earnest after the death of Lady Denham in January 1667 and continued until he abandoned her for Catherine Sedley in 1678. During that time she bore him four children, retiring to France each time for the birth.

According to contemporary accounts 'the Duchess was outraged by a choice which seemed to infringe her own especial province, in a degree far greater than had any of her previous rivals' but before the year was out Arabella had given the Duke a daughter who was named Henrietta after his mother. Shortly thereafter Arabella moved into a house in St James Square, bought for her by the Duke, with a pension of £1,000 per annum.

The Duchess who always 'conducted herself with… prudence and circumspection… (and) found the secret of pleasing everyone' was a kind and intelligent woman who spent all of her married life in a state of perpetual pregnancy. In ten years of marriage she produced eight children, four sons and four daughters before dying of cancer in her early thirties. Two sons survived infancy only to die before reaching their fourth year.

Unlike the Duchesses children, Arabella's offspring thrived and her eldest daughter Henrietta was followed by a son James, who was born at Moulins in the Bourbonnais whither she had retired for the occasion. However, her sons – the second Henry was born in 1673 – spent the first seven years of their lives in England before being sent to France under the care of Father Gough/Goff, a Jesuit priest who had been selected for the purpose by their father; Father Goff had performed a similar service for the Duke of Monmouth, the eldest bastard son of Charles II before the King decided that he should be raised as a protestant. James and Henry were placed in the Jesuit Seminary of Juilly but on Father Goff's death shortly thereafter they were sent to the college of Plessis to continue their education. At the age of fourteen and after a brief visit to England the boys returned to France and completed their education at the College of La Fleche. The youngest daughter, however, died at the age of thirty having been plagued by illness all of her life.

The decision to abandon all prospects of making a good marriage by becoming the Duke's mistress obviously carried many risks for Arabella because the Duke could caste her aside when ever he wished but to his credit he protected her, gave her some financial security and carefully supervised their childrens education. Her parents reaction to her decision is not on record but she was not mentioned in her father's will or her mother's. Within a few years her brother John followed suit by becoming the lover of the King's ex-mistress the Duchess of Cleveland. Charles who was still visiting the lady became very jealous and on one occasion almost caught the pair in bed together declaring 'I forgive you because you do it for your bread'. The child that the Duchess subsequently bore was attributed to John but as Charles was also still visiting her, the paternity is in doubt, although Charles is alleged to have said 'You may tell my lady that I know the child is not mine, yet I will acknowledge it for old times sake'. As he resolutely refused to acknowledge the child that the Duchess bore in 1667, he must have believed that there was a very good chance that he was the father and was simply attempting to save face.

The affair is alleged to have lasted a number of years and during that time young Churchill systematically pillaged the Duchess's finances. 'She has given him the value of more than £100,000' declared the French Ambassador 'In one way or another he has got so much money out of her that in desperation she is obliged to go to France to live quietly for some time'. The Ambassador also predicted that 'If Churchill goes abroad she will set up house with him again'. True to form whilst her lover was away Barbara took up with John Sheffield, the Earl of Mulgrave, a notorious rake, and after the affair was rumoured to be carrying his child but nothing further was heard of it.

John certainly did benefit from his association with Barbara but not to the extend that has been suggested. In fact he only received £4,500 which he wisely invested for an annuity of £500 per annum. Barbara was forced to leave England because of the vast debts that she had accumulated and whilst in Paris became in rapid succession the mistress of the Archbishop of Paris and then the Marquis de Chatillon. The Archbishop was a well known womaniser and grandson of Jacques de Harlay, Seigneur de Champvallon, the lover of Marguerite de Valois, Queen of Navarre, first wife of Henri IV of France. His cousin Charlotte de Essarts was also a mistress of Henry IV and for good measure the beautiful Diana de Poitiers, mistress of Henri II of France could be numbered amongst his ancestors.

Upon the death of his first wife the Duke of York immediately began to look for a replacement but it would be another two years before he found a suitable bride. Maria de Este was only fourteen years old when she was married by proxy to the Duke on 30 September 1673. The month before the wedding Arabella had given birth to her youngest child Henry and was now the proud mother of four surviving children but henceforth the Duke devoted himself to the role of devoted husband and his mistress was obliged to remain in the background. The only condition that the Duke laid down was that his wife should be beautiful. As the niece of the celebrated Hortense Mancini, who would later captured the heart of Charles II and was described by the Duke of York as 'the most beautiful girl in the world', the young princess had much to live up to but the Duke was not disappointed.

Despite his good intentions, however, the Duke immediately resumed his visits to his mistress but eventually settled down to his duty of providing England with an heir. Unfortunately, however, he had no more success than with his first wife and during the first twelve years of marriage she only managed to produce one son who died within a month of his birth. The child's death from smallpox was a tragedy and sensing the grave political implications the Duke was 'never known to grieve so much at the death of any of his other children.

Amongst the young ladies appointed to the Duchesses household at the time of her marriage was the lovely and bewitching Sarah Jennings, a young maid with a fiercely independent mind and a resolute will. Her elder sister Frances had been Maid of Honour to the Duke's first wife and at one time had even been pursued by the Duke in an attempt to make her his mistress. La Belle Jennings 'had a complexion of dazzling fairness, with perfect blond tresses' according to a contemporary and 'Nature had endowed her with all those charms which it is impossible to express'. But she was also 'prudent and high minded'and turned a deaf ear to all the Duke's attempts to engage her interest. The King seeing his brother's predicament was sufficiently interested in the lady himself to believe that he could succeed where his brother had failed but in doing so he severely jeopardised his relations with Miss Stuart whose resistance to his advances were beginning to tire him 'but Miss Stuart, as it happened, was not inclined to countenance the King's design' and intervened where upon his interest quickly faded.

Although not as beautiful as her elder sister Sarah was sufficiently attractive to capture the attention of John Churchill, who was also attached to the duke's household. It was a mutual attraction but she was a very difficult, wayward and peevish woman with very strong will who was determined to have her own way at all times. The courtship was anything but smooth and John was frequently driven to distraction by her behaviour. Since coming to Court Sarah had become a favourite of the Princess Anne, which no doubt was an added reason why John showed such an interest. This friendship would have immense and grave consequences for John and Sarah and it's beginning's are recounted thus in Sarah's own words:

> the beginning of the Princess's kindness for me had a much earlier date than my entrance into her service... We had used to play together when she was a child, and she even then expressed a particular fondness for me. This inclination increased with our years. I was often at Court, and the princess always distinguished me by the pleasure she took to honour

me, preferably to others, with her conversation and confidence. In all her
parties famusement, I was sure, by her choice, to be one.

As a great favourite of the Duke because of his military abilities,
John appeared to be set for a great future. Unlike Arabella, he was an
opportunist and determined to make his way in the world but marriage
to Sarah was not in his original plan. She was after all not a great heiress
and had only a modest dowry. True she was allied albeit distantly with
the Howard family and was a relative of Elizabeth Villiers, the mistress
and confidante of William of Orange but John's parents much preferred
a marriage of Catherine, the daughter of Sir Charles Sedley.

Upon her marriage to John, Sarah was obliged to resign from her post
as Maid of Honour to the Duchess of York and Miss Sedley was chosen as
her replacement. The appointment of Miss Sedley was to have momentous
consequences for Arabella and the Duchess because within a short time she
became the Duke's mistress and remained so for a good number of years.
As she was not a beauty Miss Sedley was surprised by the Duke's interest
in her and declared 'It cannot be my beauty, because I haven't any; and it
cannot be my wit, because he hasn't enough to know that I have any'. But
clearly she fascinated the Duke as only an intelligent and clever woman
can and for many years held him spell bound with her personality. Unlike
Arabella she was also made a Countess much to his wife's annoyance.

Within a short time of becoming a maid of honour, Catherine gave
birth to a daughter, the Duke's child and the event was recorded in
contemporary letters. Unlike Arabella, Catherine was not a member of
the extended Villiers or Howard clans but she was cousin to the infamous
Anna Maria, Lady Shrewsbury, mistress of the 2nd Duke of Buckingham
and more distantly related to Elizabeth Jones, Lady Kildare, who for a
brief period in the sixteen eighties became a mistress of Charles II.

Neither Arabella or Catherine achieved the status or riches enjoyed by
Charles II's mistresses Barbara Villiers, Duchess of Cleveland and Louise
de Queroualle, Duchess of Portsmouth but they both provided James
with illegitimate offspring. Whereas Arabella did not wish to be publicly
acknowledged as the Duke's mistress Catherine Sedley had no such
qualms. Indeed by 1686 Catherine was enjoying an income of £5,000 per

annum and had purchased Ham House, near London, as her principal residence. Arabella by contrast had only £1,000 per annum and a town house in St James Square, which she eventually sold for £8,000.

Mrs Sedley's appearance on the scene and the Duke's abandonment of Arabella now presented her with the opportunity of looking to the future and perhaps making a good marriage. As the ex-mistress of the Duke of York her prospects were not good but eventually she married Colonel Charles Godfrey, a very well connected Catholic gentleman and a fellow officer of her brother John. The marriage, by all accounts was a happy one and she duly presented her husband with four children, a son and three daughters.

Colonel Godfrey was a companion in arms of the Duke of Monmouth, Charles II's eldest bastard son and served in the French Army distinguishing himself at the siege of Maastricht in 1673. Godfrey came from a catholic family but seems to have converted to Anglicanism. Prior to James II's flight to France in 1688, he was a member of the Treason Club together with Richard Savage, Lord Colchester (cousin of Catherine Sedley), Henry Wharton and William Jephson, which met at the Tavern Club in Covent Garden and was one of the first to join the prince of Orange when he invaded England.

Despite Arabella's fall from favour her brother John continued to enjoy the Duke's favour. John's eagerness to follow a military career clearly impressed him and at the age of seventeen he became an ensign in Colonel Russell's Regiment of Foot Guards. Over the years he saw service in Tangiers and on the continent and took part in the siege of Maastricht when he saved the life of the Duke of Monmouth, Charles II's eldest bastard son. But his finest hour came at the battle of Enzheim in 1674, when his coolness under fire and his general conduct captured the admiration of the great Marshal Turenne. Eventually James simply could not do without his company 'So long as I am from him [i.e. the King] I would not willingly have Churchill from me'. Indeed James asked of his brother a peerage for his favourite and this he duly received in 1682.

A title for John but not for Arabella, which illustrates the great differences in their characters. The latter was clearly content to forgo the public status and possible riches that came with the role of *mistress en titre* and she fell into the traditional role expected of a kept woman unlike her cousin Barbara and Catherine Sedley. It was clearly her preference and in return she saw one of her sons raised to the peerage and achieve considerable fame as one of Europe's greatest generals.

Although John and Arabella, once married, remained faithful to their spouses the errant Villiers blood still flowed strongly in the veins of their children with the most unfortunate results. Indeed, to use the words of Winston Churchill 'Something in that errant, vivacious, brilliant blood, with its wonderful looks, passed an electric current into the stocks with which it mingled'.

As a widow, Henrietta FitzJames, Arabella's eldest daughter, discovered that she was in a condition that no widow should find herself in and to save face retired to a convent to await the birth. Her niece Arabella Dunch allegedly had two illegitimate children by Sir George Oxenden, whilst Henrietta, John & Sarah's eldest daughter, became the lover of William Congreve, the writer and poet and then gave birth to a daughter at the age of forty two. Not to be outdone her younger sister Mary, Duchess of Montagu was credited with affairs with Charles FitzRoy, 2nd Duke of Grafton & subsequently William Villiers, 2nd Earl of Jersey. The source for this rumour was the Duchess's own sister-in-law, Lady Anne Harvey, who on being told that she was a fool by her sister-in-law in May 1711 declared that 'at least she was an honest fool and had not wronged her husband's bed, whereas Her Grace had had affairs with the Duke of Grafton and the Marshal [the Earl of Jersey]'.

The affair with Lord Jersey was common knowledge by the December of 1711 and recorded in a letter written by Lady Strafford viz: 'The Duke of Montagu and Lord Jersey are the dearest friends that ever was, which is a great jest to the town, because the Duchess and Lord Jersey had been so a great while'. During the early years of her marriage the Duchess bore three children, a son John in 1706, and two daughters Isabella in 1708 and Mary in 1711. The son was almost certainly by her husband but shortly after his birth her affections were soon directed elsewhere.

Charles FitzRoy, 2nd Duke of Grafton was unmarried at the time of his association with the Duchess and already had a reputation for gallantry, as one would expect of a grandson of Charles II and Barbara

Villiers. Indeed he was already the father of a bastard son who bore his name and it would appear that he may have been conducting an affair with the Duchess and the mother of his bastard son at the same time. It was a feat he would repeat again with the Princess Amelia and the Lady Burlington! To use the words of Bernard Falk 'If true, that were a subtle form of revenge, Charles II's grandson serving Marlborough's daughter in the same fashion as Marlborough, when a penniless ensign, had served the King's mistress, Lady Castlemaine'. The affair, however, did not last long and soon after the birth of her daughter Isabella (the choice of name was significant as Grafton's mother was Isabella Bennet, daughter of Henry, Earl of Arlington) in 1708, the Duchess had transferred her affections to Lord Jersey; the latter, a kinsman of the Duke of Grafton, was probably the father of the Duchess's daughter Mary, born in 1711.

During the momentous years leading up to the invasion of England in 1688 by William of Orange, Arabella remained firmly in the background and devoted herself to raising her four children by Charles Godfrey. The daughters were given the standard education suitable to young ladies of their class and the elder married Hugh Boscawen, 1st Earl of Falmouth. All of Arabella's children by King James were brought up in the Catholic faith and the youngest daughter became a nun at Pontoise in France. Disappointed with her prospects in France Henrietta, the eldest, left her husband, returned to England and settled at Navestock in Essex, the country seat of her son James, Earl Waldegrave.

Although the role of royal favourite had always sat rather uncomfortably on Arabella's shoulders, this was not the case with her brother John and his wife Sarah. As the favourite of James II before he ascended the throne, John, rose rapidly through the ranks of the royal army and by 1685 had acquired considerable influence over his royal master. In turn Sarah had become the complete mistress of Princess Anne's affections thus ensuring her husband's pathway to future glory. The errant Villiers blood had once again triumphed! And if this was not enough their cousin Elizabeth Villiers was the favourite and confidante of William of Orange and her sisters of his wife Mary.

John's part in the defeat and capture of the Duke of Monmouth at the battle of Sedgemoor in 1685, only served to enhance his military reputation as did his direction of the siege and capture of Cork and Kinsale during the Jacobite invasion of Ireland in 1690. During the siege of Cork, his cousin the Duke of Grafton was killed; his nephew Berwick also arrived during the siege with 4,000 Jacobite troops but on seeing that the situation was hopeless retreated. But on his return to England John was arrested and imprisoned in the Tower of London for corresponding with his old master James II at St Germain-en-Laye, not until 1698 was he restored to royal favour.

But John's years of greatness as the 'Saviour of Europe' against Louis XIV would not have been possible without the support of Sidney Godolphin in his role as Lord Treasurer and Robert Harley as Speaker of the House of Commons and later Secretary of State. This triumvirate was severely tested during Godolphin's term of office but despite this he continued to support the war effort and ensured that his colleague received all of the financial backing that was necessary to achieve victory. Without this support Marlborough – John had been made a Duke by Queen Anne – would not have been able to defeat the French at the battles of Blenheim (1704), Ramillies (1706), Oudenarde (1708) and Malplaquet (1709). Harley for his part managed the Commons with great skill and provided Marlborough with the political support to continue the war.

Sadly, however, all their efforts were to be undermined by Marlborough's wife Sarah whose relationship with Queen Anne was continually under strain from her uncompromising and bullying attitude. At the beginning of their relationship Sarah '… began to employ all her wit and all her vivacity, and almost all her time, to divert and entertain and serve the Princess; and to fix that favour which now one might easily observe to be increasing towards her every day'. But as time went on Sarah grew tired of her role of Royal Favourite and began to stay away from court and neglect the Queen. In addition she took up and befriended a poor relation, Abigail Hill with whom she spent most of her time thereby making the Queen jealous. Eventually the relationship ended in bitter recriminations which was exacerbated by the behaviour of Sarah's daughter Lady Montagu who shortly after her marriage embarked on affairs with the Duke of Grafton and then the Earl of Jersey. The end came at the beginning of 1712 when Marlborough and Sarah were dismissed from their posts and retreated to the comforts of private life. Thus ended one of the most extraordinary tales of Royal Favouritism in English History.

But what became of Arabella? Her marriage to Mr Godfrey was a very happy one but at heart he remained a soldier, despite serving time as an MP in the House of Commons. They did not benefit from Marlborough's good fortune but despite this were loyal and supported him in all his endeavours. Arabella eventually died in 1730 at the age of eighty-two; her rival Mrs Sedley had died in 1717.

NELL GWYN

Like Moll Davis and Peg Hughes, Nell Gwyn's origins are shrouded in mystery but attempts have been made to prove that she came from relatively distinguished stock. Even in her own lifetime it was suggested that she was the granddaughter of a clergyman named Edward Gwyn, who was a Canon of Christchurch Cathedral in Oxford. Her father, the canon's bastard son Thomas, allegedly died in a debtors prison in Oxford having served under Sir Thomas Dallison in Prince Rupert's Horse during the 1st English Civil War.

Nell was born, according to her horoscope, on Saturday 6 February 1650/1 at 6 o'clock in the morning, place unknown but tradition asserts it was one of the following, Cole-Yard, an alley off Drury Lane, the Hop Garden off St Martin's Way, both in the Covent Garden District, Oxford or possibly Pipe Well Lane in Hereford. The truth will probably never be known because the registers of St Paul, Covent Garden and St Thomas, Oxford do not begin until after Nell's birth. Nevertheless it is possible to piece together a plausible scenario around the main events in her mother's life and thus come to some reasonable conclusions.

Old Madam Gwyn was renowned in her youth for being 'skilled in the arts of gallantry' and on her death lampoons celebrated with tales that she had been 'Maid, punk and bawd, full sixty years and more' and that 'Bawd was her life, and common-shore her death'. One in particular stated that she had been a chief matron (bawd) who went to great expense:

to find out an ingenious method to restore lost maidenheads, that so she might to her abundant profit make a double mortgage to such buffoon beauty hunters who daily accosted her for the procuration of some rosebuds though June be passed, as likewise to find out a private tincture for to sprucify her daughter's decayed physiognomy.

The most famous of the seventeenth century London bawds were Madam Cresswell and Damaris Page, the former operating from Clerkenwell and the latter from the Ratcliffe Highway and Rosemary Lane in the east end of London. Both were contemporaries of Madam Gwyn and they remained at the top of their profession for over thirty years.

According to the antiquarian Anthony á Wood, Old Madam Gwyn died on 20 July 1679:

Elen Gwynn, commonly called old Madam Gwynne, being drunk with brandy, fell in a ditch neare the Neathouses, London and was stifled. 'Mother' to Nell Quin. Lived sometimes in Oxford.

Ten days later she was buried in great state at St Martin-in-the-Fields the event being celebrated by Lord Rochester in his amusing lampoon entitled *A Panegyrick on Nelly* viz:

Nor was the mother's funeral less her care, No cost, no velvet, did the daughter spare: Fine gilded Scutcheon's did the Herse inrich, To celebrate this Martyr of the Ditch; Burnt brandy did in flaming Brimmers flow, Drank at her funeral, while her well-pleas'd shade Rejoyc'd, even in the sober Fields below, At all the drunkenness her Death had made.

The escutcheons relate to the coat of arms that Nelly was granted by the Garter King of Arms at the Royal College of Heralds in London. Ever desirous of pleasing her, the King ordered the heralds to find her suitable armorial bearings and she was granted 'per pale indented or and argent, a lion rampant', very similar to the arms borne by Cadwgan, Prince of Powys. The arms borne by Nell's alleged grandfather were 'Sable three horses' heads argent' but she was not entitled to used them because her alleged father Thomas Gwyn, was the canon's bastard son and bastards could not use the same arms as their father unless of course you were a Royal Bastard. Captain John Gwyn, 'who taught Charles II military exercises when he was Prince of Wales, and served throughout the civil war' also bore the same arms as Nell and thus may have been a relative.

Madam Gwyn's origins are also shrouded in mystery and the reference to her being born in St Martin-in-the-Fields and sometimes living in Oxford are the only clues we have to her possible early life. The likeliest scenario is that she was baptised in Oxford in St Thomas's parish, where the registers no longer survive pre 1655, brought to St Martin's London as a small child, married in Westminster/London and then returned to Oxford during the first Civil War, only returning to London when Oxford was captured by the Parliamentary forces in 1647.

Charles I arrived in Oxford in December 1642 and 'kept the Christmas season with ceremony and splendour at Christ Church College'; he remained there until forced to leave in 1647, following the surrender of the city to Parliament. When he arrived he left behind him a city where 'trade was sluggish, the theatres closed, the Court gone, the traffic in and out of the city strictly controlled and a monthly fast day imposed'. London was also 'chill, drab, and uneasy with suspicion. Food was dear because of disturbances on the roads and waterways'. Small wonder therefore that Madam Gwyn should chose to decamp and follow the King and the Royal Court to her home city of Oxford.

Prince Rupert's Horse in which Nell's father is reputed to have served was stationed in Oxford for more than half the year in 1643 and 1645 but less than two months in 1644, the remainder of the time it was away on campaign. Old Mrs Gwyn's presence in Oxford, therefore, would seem to support the belief that she had relatives in the city. When she began her activities as a bawdy house keeper is unknown but it was probably on her return to London. When Nell was born in 1650/1 London was just beginning to come to terms with the abolition of the monarchy and the execution of Charles I but there was still much unrest in the city and the remainder of the country.

A month before Nell's birth, her future lover Charles II was crowned King of Scotland at Scone and shortly after prepared to resist Cromwell's continuing attempts to conquer that ancient kingdom. After the initial English victory at Dunbar, Cromwell suffered a severe illness which almost paralysed any military activity on his part for several months. In the mean time Charles was able to invade England and head south along the west coast. When he arrived at Worcester the city was immediately surrounded by Cromwell's Army which had closely traced his movements since leaving Scotland. The battle which followed on 3 September 1651 was another resounding victory for Cromwell and Charles was forced to flee the country

The deterioration of public morals in the Covent Garden area of London that followed the King's departure for Oxford in 1642 was common knowledge and celebrated in the following amusing tract entitled *Saint Hilaries Teares* viz:

> If you step aside into Covent Garden, Long Acre and Drury Lane, where those Doves of Venus, thos Birds of Youth and Beauty – the Wanton Ladies – doe builde their Nestes, you shall finde them in suche a Dump of Amazement to see the Hopes of their Tradeinge frustrate ... [Before 1642] Ten or Twentie Pound Suppers were but Trifles to them... they are nowe forc'd to make doe on a diet of cheese and onions.

The situation was further compounded by the lack of any suitable health and sanitary precautions or as one modern historian has put it:

> The disposal of waste water and human waste was an awkward problem. At a convenient time chamberpots and night commodes would be carried down to the basement and emptied into the cesspit or thrown onto a compost heap in the garden. More often than not the servants would save themselves the drudgery of this unpleasant job by emptying the contents out of a window into the 'kennel' [gutter].

This picture of loose morals and squalor was all too familiar to Nell but despite the dreadful disadvantage of having a bawd for a mother she ultimately triumphed over such terrible conditions and rose from the gutter to a royal bed! But the lure and magic of the theatre was with her from birth and although the theatres had been officially closed to Londoners since the King's departure:

> again and again, defying the ordinances, those actors left in London gave clandestine performances. Needless to say, the plays were frequently interrupted by the arrival of soldiers who would remove the costumes and arrest the players. By 1649 most of the playhouses had been dismantled or had had their interiors stripped completely' but 'Attempts were still made to train actors or give secret performances, but the theatre had effectively been suppressed.

But 'by the mid-1650s references to irregular performances began to reappear' and 'actors at the Red Bull Theatre in Clerkenwell were raided whenever they tried to act in 1654 and 1655 but they still attempted to perform'. Only with the Restoration of Charles II in 1660 did their fortunes revive.

When Charles II was restored in 1660 old Mrs Gwyn was in her early forties with two fatherless daughters, the youngest of whom, Nell, was only ten years old. Her active life as a bawd was rapidly coming to an end and her looks were fading. More and more she turned her talents, such as they were, to making a living as the small time proprietor of a bawdy house, which quite naturally she preferred to call a drinking establishment. In support of her point of view it should be said that 'the true brothels were large establishments in Moorfields, Whetstones Park, and Dog-and-Bitch Yard, kept by such famous procurors as 'Lady' Bennet, Madam Cresswell, 'Mother' Temple and Damaris Page' but clearly old Mrs Gwyn could not compete with such luminaries.

Many years later a Satire written by a Mr Lacy summarised Nell's first steps from bawdy house to the stage:

> Witness the royal line sprung from the belly
> Of the anointed princess, Madam Nelly,
> Whose first employment was, with open throat,
> To cry fresh herrings, even at ten a groat;
> Then was by Madam Rose exposed to the town,

I mean to those that would give half a crown,
Next, in the playhouse she took her degree,
As men commence in the university
No doctors till they've masters been beforehand

So no player till first she has been a whore.
Look back and see the bitch in so high equipage;
And every day they do the monster see,
They let ten thousand curses fly at thee.

A few years later the satire was further embellished in 'A Panegyric' of 1681:

Even while she cinders raked, her swelling breast
With thoughts of glorious whoredom was possessed.
But first the basket her fair arm did suit,
Laden with pippins and Hesperian fruit.
This first step raised, to the wondering pit she sold
The lovely fruit, smiling with streaks of gold.

Nell's formative years serving strong waters to the gentlemen had clearly made her 'wise beyond her years and cynical about such mere abstractions as truth, honour and virtue' according to one historian and thus prepared her fully for the uncertainties and vagaries of her future profession as an actress. Indeed her reputation as a whore fitted in well with the current fashion then in vogue where 'Love and gaming were the two principal pastimes' particularly at the Royal Court in Whitehall and 'both diversions were also indulged in by the gentlemen of the town'. In fact if you did not keep a whore you were 'ill looked upon at Court'. The actors in the theatres were not much better. Tom Killigrew reported to Pepys, the diarist, that he had to 'keep a woman on purpose at 20s a week to satisfy eight or ten of the young men of his house, whom till he did so he could never keep to their business, and now he do'!

Nell's first appearance on the stage as one of 'His Majesty's Servants' was scheduled for the production *Thomaso or The Wanderer* a comedy by Tom Killigrew in which she was selected to play the part of 'Paulina, a courtesan of the first rank'. The play was heavily influenced by Mateo Aleman's picaresque novel 'Guzman de Alfarache' and would have an all female caste including Anne Marshall as Angellica and Mary Knep as Lucette. However it never reached the stage and Nell was forced to wait until the following year before making her debut.

It came in the production of *The Indian Emperor*, an heroic drama by John Dryden and Sir Robert Howard (his brother-in-law) in March 1665 where she played the part of Cydaria, the daughter of Montezuma and her fellow actor Charles Hart, Hernanado Cortez, the conquistador. This pairing of Nell with Charles Hart was to prove a very successful partnership both financially and artistically. Hart, of course, went on to become one of the many lovers of Barbara Villiers who is reputed to have been Nell's patroness for a short time.

The Indian Emperor was rapidly followed by *All Mistaken or the Mad Couple* a comedy by James Howard, another brother-in-law of John Dryden, in which Nell and Charles Hart once again played the principal roles. However, with the onset of the plague in that year the King ordered the theatres to be closed and Nell's budding career as an actress was put on hold. The theatres did not re-open until December 1666 after the Great Fire of London but during the hiatus fortune worked it's magic and so influenced events that Nell's life would be changed forever.

In December 1665, Barbara Villiers, gave birth to her fifth child by the King in the chamber of one of the fellows of Merton College at Oxford and thereafter slowly began to lose the King's favour. The cause was her passion for one of his courtiers Harry Jermyn whom she took as her lover before the years end. Unlike previous years Lady Castlemaine did not present the King with another bastard child in 1666. It would prove to be a fallow year and one that she used to pursue and capture the unfortunate Jermyn. What attracted her to him was at first a mystery for he was by repute 'small; had a big head and spindle shanks; his features were not exactly disagreeable, but there was much affectation in his bearing and in his mannerisms'. However, rumour suggested that he made up for these short comings in his private stature! But when she became with child and it became public knowledge in July 1667, the King firmly denied any responsibility for her condition because he had not lain with her at the time it was conceived! Miss Stewart's marriage in the March of that year to the Duke of Richmond followed by Lady Castlemaine's betrayal in July, left the King without a love interest for the first time in his life therefore without further ado sought looked elsewhere for comfort and distraction. Enter Nell!

Following Nell's absence from the stage during the Plague and the Great Fire she conducted an affair with her leading man Charles Hart but it was of short duration and quickly followed by another with Lord Buckhurst, cousin of Lady Castlemaine and close friend of Lord Rochester, perhaps the most notorious of the post Restoration Rakes. Buckhurst was a witty fellow and also a cousin of the Howard brothers, all of whom were either poets or playrights and thus indirectly related to the famous John Dryden who wrote the play *Secret Love* in which Nell played Florimel, her most successful role. In 1661 Buckhurst with five other men had been 'apprehended for killing and robbing a tanner' and two years later was involved in an 'indecent escapade' at the Cock Tavern in the company of Sir Charles Sedley. But again the affair did not last and Nell was back on the stage again this time for a Royal Command Performance in 'Secret Love'. Her star was rapidly rising and her performance delighted the King.

Nell followed this up in May 1667 with another success as the sprightly Mirida in the tragi-comedy *All Mistaken or The Mad Couple* by James Howard, Lord Buckhurst's cousin, with Charles Hart playing the part of Philidor. A great part of the play's success was due to the song that Nell sang in the epilogue, which was a parody of Moll Davis's 'My Lodging it is on the cold ground'. In addition her performance in rolling from side to side on the stage in tumbled petticoats fired the passions of Lord Buckhurst to such an extent that he offered her an annuity of £100 to become his mistress. Hart with whom she was then involved grudgingly consented as he did not have the wherewithal to compete with such a rival:

> Take her, my lord, quoth Hart, since you're so mean
> To take a player's leavings for your quean,
> For though I love her well, yet as she's poor
> I'm well content to prefer the whore.

Nell's rise to the position of 'royal whore' was engineered by the Duke of Buckingham who on falling out with his cousin Lady Castlemaine 'studied to take the King from her by new amours'. To this end he enlisted the aid of Colonel Tom Howard and his brother Sir Robert Howard who were also eager to promote the charms of Nell's rival Moll Davis from the King's Players. When Nell 'was first brought to the King, she asked only five hundred pounds a year' but Charles refused and instead took up with Moll who being managed more cleverly by the Howard brothers was happy to accept just his gifts. However, it was only a temporary setback for Nell because Buckingham knew that in time *gaiety of humour would take much with the King* and Mrs Davis was no match for her rival in the humour stakes. At the same time the King was also amusing himself with one his wife's Maids of Honour Winifred Wells described rather waspishly by Gramont as:

> a big, splendidly handsome creature, who dressed finely, had the carriage of a goddess and whose face, though made in every detail like those which pleased most, was, as it happened, among those which were least attractive. Heaven had granted her a certain air of indecision, which gave her the physiognomy of a dreamy sheep. And this, in it's turn, gave a bad impression of her intelligence; and, as bad luck would have it, her intelligence lived up in every point to the reputation it had acquired.

After Lady Castlemaine and Mrs Stewart, Mrs Wells was one of the leading beauties at Court but 'it was reported that she had put up a rather feebler resistance than would have been proper; that she surrendered at discretion, without ever having been vigorously attacked'. Intelligence was not a quality that the King demanded of his mistresses all he required was to be entertained and as Nell was 'the wildest and indiscreetest creature that ever was in a court' there was no competition. When Charles's interested in Mrs Wells waned he took to sleeping in turn with his wife and then Moll Davis. However, the desire to begat a son an heir faded after several miscarriages and the Queen's place in his bed was taken up by Nell. But whilst Charles was careful not to sire any children by Moll he threw caution to the winds with Nell and by

November 1669, she discovered that she was with child! Immediately Charles arranged for her take up residence in Lincolns Inn Fields in preparation for the child's birth.

Contraception was not widely practised in England in the seventeenth century but condums were commonplace having been invented by the famous Italian physician Gabriele Fallopio in the mid-sixteenth century. The condum was manufactured from a sheep's intestine and worn originally as 'a protection against the ravages of syphilis then sweeping over Europe'. During the post Restoration period Dutch condums were imported into England from France by Dr Fernando Mendes, Court Physician to Catherine of Braganza who supplied not only Sir John Birkenhead but also the Duke of York. The virtues of using such a devise were wittily summed up by the Earl of Rochester in his poem *Signior Dildo* and *Panegyric upon Condums* in 1674 viz:

> You ladies all of merry England
> Who have been in to kiss the Duchess's hand
> Pray did you lately observe in the show
> A noble Italian called Signior Dildo?

> The Signior was one of her Highness's train,
> And helped to conduct her over the main
> But now she cried out 'To the Duke I will go;
> I have no more need for Signior Dildo...'

> You'll take him at first for no person of note,
> Because he appears in a plain leather coat,
> But when you his virtuous abilities know,
> You'll fall down and worship Signior Dildo.

> That pattern of virtue, her Grace of Cleveland,
> Has swallowed more pricks than the nation has land;
> But by rubbing and scrubbing so large it does grow
> It is fit for just nothing but Signior Dildo

Our dainty fine Duchesses have got a trick
To dote on a fool for the sake of his prick;
The fops were undone did their graces but know
The discretion and vigour of Signior Dildo

Doll Howard no more with his Highness must range
And therefore is proffered this civil exchange:
Her teeth being rotten, she smells best below,
And needs must be fitted for Signior Dildo...

Although not entirely happy at having to use them, Charles was eventually forced to realise that he could not continue to sire bastard children forever and after the birth of his last child, by Moll Davis, in 1673, he stopped sowing any more wild oats.

With the birth of her son on 8 May 1670, which was duly noted by the popular broadsheets of the time viz:, 'Elianor Quin, one that belongs to the King's play house, was brought to bed of a boy in her house in Lyncoln's Inns feilds, – the King's bastard', Nell appeared to be looking to a much brighter future but although Charles acknowledged the child, her situation did not alter significantly. But once again fate intervened and gave her cause for concern for within a week of the child's birth Charles caught sight of the beautiful Louise de Penancoet de Querouelle, maid of honour to his sister the Duchess of Orleans during the latter's brief visit to England and was instantly smitten. When the Duchess died suddenly several months later Charles immediately arranged for Louise to become one of his wife's maids of honour and she was duly shipped over to England and given an apartment in Whitehall.

After a brief return to the stage Charles arranged for Nell to have the leasehold of a fine house in Pall Mall close to the Palace of Whitehall, which had previously been occupied by the Earl of Scarsdale but was originally built for Harry Jermyn's uncle the Earl of St Albans. Her immediate neighbours were Edward Griffin, a Groom of the Bedchamber to the Duke of York to the west and the Countess of Portland to the east. The freehold of the property was eventually conveyed to her on 6 April 1677 but only after she had reminded Charles that she 'had always conveyed herself free under the crown, and always would, but that she would not accept the house until its freehold was conveyed free to her by the Crown.'

Although vastly popular with the majority of Londoners, Nell's success in raising herself from a bawdy house to the stage and then the Royal Bed, was not acceptable to all. Indeed the appearance of Louise de Querouelle on the scene was positively welcomed by the Earl of Arlington as a refreshing change and one who was more fitted to be the King's mistress. Indeed he said as much to the French Ambassador:

> it was well for the King's good servants that his Majesty should have a fancy for Mademoiselle Keroualle, who was not of an evil disposition and a lady. It was better to have dealings with her than with lewd and bouncing orange-girls and actresses, of whom no man could take the measure.

But despite the threat of being supplanted by the King's new love interest, Nell's position proved to be unassailable because 'she acted all persons in so lively a manner and was such a diversion to the King that even a new mistress could not drive her away'. Further proof of her success came in December 1671 when she gave birth to her second son by the King and named him James.

Nell's new status as a royal mistress also brought other members of her family into prominence. Her elder sister Rose had recently acquired a husband one John Cassells by name who claimed that he had served under the King's ensigns whilst he was in exile and his father had 'lost a plentiful estate in Ireland for his loyalty'. As one historian has already pointed out John Cassells 'bears a suspicious resemblance to the highwayman and burglar of those names' who in September 1671 only just escaped hanging after attempting to rob Sir Henry Littleton's house. For his impudence Charles gave him a captain's commission in the Royal English Regiment commanded by his bastard son, the Duke of Monmouth. Also serving in the regiment was Lieutenant Francis Hawley, the future husband of Judith Hughes, sister of Peg Hughes, mistress of Prince Rupert and Richard Savage, later Earl Rivers, cousin of Lady Dorchester, mistress of James II.

The regiment which formed part of the English Brigade in the French Service, was shipped over to France in April 1672 'only to find that the

French had not provided adequate provisions or quarters'. It comprised sixteen companies totally 2,000 men but by October 'eight of its companies were broken up and replaced by a battalion commanded by Bevil Skelton'. Although the Duke of Monmouth was commander of the brigade whilst it remained in the service of the King of France the regiments were divided between the various theatres of war and never fought together as a corps.

During his service in the regiment Captain Cassels was present at the siege of Maastricht in 1674 and fought in the battles of Sintzheim and Entzheim in 1674. At the latter battle 'the brunt of the fighting fell upon the English and Irish Regiments, especially's John Churchill's [known as Skelton's or the 2nd Battalion of the Royal English] which had half its officers killed or wounded in the bitter struggle for a wood that lay between the two armies'. Although Marshal Turenne was delighted with the performance of the English troops this was of little comfort to Rose Cassell whose husband was killed.

However, shortly after his departure for the continent Captain Cassell's meagre army pay was supplemented by the welcome addition of a pension of £100 on the Irish Establishment and after his death this was increased to £200. But after the departure of James II for France in 1688 the pension fell into arrears and Rose had re-married to a gentleman called Guy Forster but he also predeceased her. Nell's only other known relative William Chomley was originally a member of the 'Black-Guard' which consisted of 'tattered waifs (and) ink-boys, whose smoking torches lighted wayfarers through the pitch black streets at night' but in 1678 Nell secured a commission for him to be an ensign in Colonel John Russell's Regiment of Foot, which had been formed in 1660; in 1681 he was appointed a captain in the Coldstream Guards.

The year following Captain Cassells death, the King granted Dukedoms to his sons by Lady Castlemaine (now the Duchess of Cleveland) and Louise de Querouelle (now Duchess of Portsmouth) but Nell had to wait until the end of 1676 before her eldest son was created Earl of Burford and the younger, Lord Beauclerk; the elder was eventually created a Duke in 1684. It was a bitter sweet moment for Nell because although she had to all intents and purposes reached the pinnacle of success in having her children publicly acknowledge by the King, her position as a royal mistress was threatened by the sudden appearance of the famous Italian beauty the Duchess de Mazarin, who had once been canvassed as a possible bride for the King shortly before the Restoration.

The Duchess of Cleveland, sensing that her days as a royal mistress were now well and truly over departed for France with her children in order to avoid her creditors and left the field clear for Nell and the two Duchesses. The situation was wittily it rather coarsely summed up by an anonymous satirist in the following words:

> Since Cleveland is fled till she's brought to bed,
> And Nelly is quite forgotten,
> And Mazarine is as old as the Queen,
> And Portsmouth, the young whore is rotten,
> Since women at helm have ruined the realm,
> And statesmen have lost their anchors,
> The Lords and the Commons know what will come on us,
> But the kingdom must break like the bankers.

However, Nell need not have feared for the Duchess de Mazarin's star blazed brightly for just eighteen months and then slowly faded away, whereupon the King returned to the arms of Nell and the Duchess of Portsmouth. But before doing so Lady Harvey attempted to introduce Mrs Myddleton's beautiful sixteen year old daughter into the King's seraglio but her plans were defeated despite using Nell as a means of gaining access to the King.

By this time Nell had an income of £5,000 per annum from the treasury and other sources but it was paid very irregularly often in sums of £250 or £500 and in arrears. However, this was a very good income for someone of her background but of course nothing like the pensions acquired the Duchesses of Cleveland and Portsmouth. But to the people of London Nell was a very wealthy woman and her situation was even celebrated in rhyme by the mysterious poetess 'Ephelia' – now thought to be Mary Villiers, Duchess of Richmond:

So bright your beauty, so sublime your wit,
None but a prince to wear your chains is fit
I could wish something, but all Heaven's store
Cannot afford one single blessing more;
Honour nor wealth you want, not any thing
Unless I wish you a perpetual spring
Of youth and blossoming beauties, such as may
Make all your envious rivals pine away.

Several years later the duchess of Richmond was engaged in an attempt with her brother and divers others, including Nell it would seem, to supplant the Duchess of Portsmouth with the lovely Jane Lawson her husband's niece. A contemporary satire on the situation warned the lovely Mrs Lawson of the perils in becoming a 'whore':

O yet consider e're it be too late
How near you stand upon the brink of fate.
Think who they are who would for you procure
The great preferment to be made a whore:
Two reverend aunts, renowned in British story
For lust and drunkenness with Nell and Lory.
These, these are they your fame will sacrifice,
Your honour sell, and you shall hear the price:
My Lady Mary nothing can design,
But to feed her lust with what she gets for thine;
Old Richmond making thee a glorious punk,
Shall twice a day with brandy now be drunk;
Her brother Buckingham shall be restored
Nelly a Countess, Lord a lord.

Other contenders were the beautiful Carey Frazier, daughter of the King's physician Sir Alexander Frazier, and a descendant of Mary Carey, mistress of Henry VIII plus Elizabeth Jones, subsequently Countess of Kildare, kinswoman of the notorious Lady Shrewsbury and Lady Dorchester, mistress of James II. Only the Lady Elizabeth appears to have captured the King's interest but the affair was over almost as soon as it had begun.

MARY OR MOLL DAVIES, LATER MRS PAISIBLE

In the seventeenth century, actresses, although few in number, were considered by many to be little more than common prostitutes, and therefore it is not surprising that attempts were made to provide Nell Gwyn and Moll Davies with more exalted origins. In Nell's case it was suggested that her father was a royalist officer who had fallen on hard times and died in a debtors prison in Oxford. Moll, on the other hand, was given noble ancestry no less; it was claimed that she was the illegitimate daughter of the Earl of Berkshire, although other sources suggest she was the daughter of a blacksmith, from Charlton in Wiltshire.

Whatever Moll's origins she came under the protection of Colonel Howard at a very early stage in her acting career and he acted as her pimp in his efforts to capture the King's interest. If Moll really was an illegitimate daughter of one of the Howards, then she was cousin to several other royal mistresses, some of whom were her contemporaries viz: Elizabeth Villiers, Lady Orkney (William III), Mary Howard, Lady Deloraine (George II), Henrietta Howard, Countess of Suffolk (George II) and for good measure Lady Elizabeth Felton, (James, Duke of Monmouth). A more distant connection was Mary Carey, the mistress of Henry VIII.

The Howard family already had links with the Restoration theatre. Sir Robert Howard, Edward Howard, Colonel Henry Howard and James Howard, sons of Thomas Howard, 1st Earl of Berkshire all wrote plays for the King's and Duke's theatres. Sir Robert Howard's drama *The Indian Queen* co-written with John Dryden, his brother-in-law, was later set to music by Henry Purcell. Edward Howard's play *The Change of Crowns*, also a drama, was much admired by Pepys and proved to be a great success but it's leading player John Lacy was imprisoned because he offended the King with his improvisations. Nell Gwynn made her first appearance on the stage in James Howard's play *The English Monsieur*.

Moll's first recorded appearance on stage appears to have been as a member of the Duke's Company when Samuel Pepys saw her play the part of Viola on 18 February 1662 in *The Law against Lovers* at the Lincolns Inn Playhouse. Several days later he saw her perform in *The Slighted Maid* when he noted that 'the play hath little good in it, being most pleased to see the little girl dance in boy's apparel, she having very fine legs, only bends in the hams, as I perceive all women do'. Her next appearances were in October 1663 as Violanda in *The Step-Mother*, and March 1664 as Aurelia in *The Comical Revenge* etc.

The Duke's Company was established by Sir William Davenant, shortly after the Restoration in Lincoln's Inn Fields. Amongst the original caste were Thomas Betterton, James Nokes, Cave Underhill and Mary Saunderson, who subsequently married Betterton. The latter a major talent and Nokes, a brilliant comedian were the companies leading players but in order to preserve the good name of his actresses Davenant had them live in his own house adjacent to the theatre and paid their wages out of his own pocket. It was therefore under Davenant's careful eye that Moll learnt her craft.

The actors and actresses 'were expected to play a new part every two or three nights on average and to learn ten or more new roles in a season'. However, the two forms of acting 'comedy' and 'tragedy' required radically different techniques. Comedy was performed with a 'formal naturalness' that matched the ideals of contemporary Restoration society, a naturalness that would be completely alien to modern society. Tragedy meanwhile was performed with an 'operatic style of gesture' accompanied by a chanting style that 'was partly derived from the delivery of chanting preachers'. This rather stilted style however was performed with great skill by such actors as Betterton and Charles Hart and helped to establish their reputation as the leading actors of the post Restoration period.

Moll's next performances clearly illustrate her skill in alternating between Comedy and Tragedy. In March 1664 she appeared in the comedy *The Comical Revenge* followed by the tragedy *Heraclius*, and then as Princess Anne in the Earl of Orrery's play *Henry V* on 13 August. However, the King's first sight of her appears to have been in the play *Mustapha* which was performed on 3 April 1665 at the Duke's Theatre, where she played the part of the Queen of Hungary. The play, a tragedy, was written by Roger Boyle, Earl of Orrery and Thomas Betterton, the leading Restoration Actor, played the part of Sulyeman the Magnificent. Amongst the audience was Pepys, his wife, the King, Lady Castlemaine, his mistress and Nell Gwyn; the play was performed again the following year in the King's private theatre in the Cockpit at Whitehall. The Earl a member of the Irish Boyle family was also husband of Lady Margaret Howard, daughter of the 2nd Earl of Suffolk and thus a possible kinsman of Moll.

Shortly after her performance in *Mustafa* the King ordered the playhouses to be closed because of the plague and the whole Court retired to Syon House then Hampton Court and Salisbury until it finally reached Oxford in September 1665. It remained at Oxford until the epidemic had run its course and then moved back to Hampton Court and then Whitehall in February 1666; the theatres did not re-open until November 1666. The epidemic began in Westminster and St Giles-in-the-Fields and slowly made its way towards Holborn and then the city. At the end of August 1665 Pepys recorded that:

> In the city died this week 7496; and of them, 6102 of the plague. But it is feared that the true number of the dead this week is near 10,000 – partly from the poor that cannot be taken notice of through the greatness of the number, and partly from the Quakers and others that will not have any bell ring for them.

The plague was followed in September 1666 by the Great Fire of London but there is no record of Moll during this period. Like the majority of London's more wealthy citizens and the court she probably retired to the country.

Although not a great beauty, Moll was an incomparably better singer and dancer than Nell Gwyn and her talents made a great impression on

114

the King. Samuel Pepys was a great admirer and noted in his diary her performance in *The English Princess* on 7 March 1667 viz:

> little Mis Davis did dance a jig after the end of the play, and there telling the next day's play; so that it come in by force only to please the company to see her dance in boy's clothes; and, the truth is, there is no comparison between Nell's dancing the other day at the King's house in boy's clothes and this, this being infinitely beyond the other.

When Moll performed again in August 1667 in the production of *Love Tricks* Pepys again remarked that her dancing had saved the play 'a silly play, only Mis's dancing in a shepherd's clothes did please us mightily'. Shortly before this performance Lady Castlemaine, the King's mistress, surprised him by announcing that she was with child, upon which he declared that it could not be his as he had not lain with her for the past twelve months! The father was Lady Castlemaine's latest lover Harry Jermyn. The remark provoked a furious response from the lady and she left the Court in high dudgeon. The split was permanent and prompted Charles to return to the marital bed in an effort to procreate some legitimate children! But the Queen did not conceive until the end of February 1668. In the interim Charles sought consolation with one of his wife's maids of honour Winifred Wells who unfortunately was unable to hold his attention for long and he quickly turned to the ladies of the theatre for a replacement.

Moll's performance in *Love Tricks* was quickly followed by others as Mrs Millicent in *Feign'd Innocence* and Ariel in *The Tempest* before rounding off the year as Celania in *The Rivals*. But it was her performance in the latter that captured the King's interest, in particular her rendition of the song: *My Lodging it is on the Cold Ground*, which soon after 'raised her from her bed on the cold ground and into a bed royal'.

By January 1668, the King's interest in Moll was common knowledge in Court circles and whilst at a performance of *The Wildgoose chase* at the King's Theatre Pepys heard the news that Moll was leaving the

Duke's Players because the King was in love with her. Later in the month Moll attended a performance of *The Indian Emperor* at the Cockpit in Whitehall and her presence was noted with the following comment:

'among the rest Mis Davis, who is the most impertinent slut… in the world; and the more, now the King do show her countenance, and is reckoned his mistress, even to the scorne of the whole world; the King gazing on her, and my Lady Castlemayne being melancholy and out of humour, all the play, not smiling once. The King, it seems, hath given her a ring of £700, which she shews to every body, and owns that the King did give it her; and he hath furnished a house for her in Suffolke Street most richly, which is a most infinite shame…' It seems she is a bastard of Collonell Howard, my Lord Barkeshire, and that he doth pimp to her for the King, and hath got her for him.

Suffolk Street was situated just off the Haymarket and Moll lived here from 1667 until October 1673 when she purchased a house in St James's Square for £1,800; she remained there until 1687 and received a pension of £1,000 per annum.

As previously mentioned the King's renewed attention to his wife resulted in the discovery in April 1668 she was with child but this was quickly followed on the 7 May by the announcement that she had 'miscarryed of a perfect child, being gone about ten weeks; which doth show that she can conceive, though it be unfortunate that she cannot bring forth.' Three weeks later at the Cockpit theatre in Whitehall the Queen attended a performance of *She Wou'd If She Cou'd* in which Moll repeated her performance as Gatty but with unfortunate results:

Mrs Davis was there; and when she was to come to dance her jigg, the Queene would not stay to see it, which people do think it was out of displeasure at her being the King's whore, that she could not bear it. My Lady Castlemaine is, it seems, now mightily out of request, the King coming little to her, and she mightily melancholy and discontented.

It would be her last performance and by the end of the month she had retired to her house in Suffolk Street, richly furnished for her by the King, where the following year Pepys did see 'her coach come for her to her door, a mighty fine coach'.

At the end of 1668 Moll attended a performance of *MacBeth* at the Duke's Playhouse. Among the audience was Pepys who commented that:

> ... it vexed me to see Moll Davis, in the box over his [the King's] and my Lady Castlemaynes head, look down upon the King and he up to her; and so did my Lady Castlemayne once, to see who it was; but when she saw her, she blushed like fire; which troubled me.

Lady Castlemaine took her revenge by taking the actor Charles Hart as her lover but had to pay heavily for the favour. Moll meanwhile had to share the King's bed with her rival Nell Gwyn. Indeed he appears to have favoured Nell above Moll for a considerable time after the latter left the stage and she suffered the indignity of being almost totally eclipsed by her rival.

In May 1669 the Queen was once again reported to be with child but miscarried the following month and from this moment on Charles appears to have abandoned all hope that she would give him a legitimate child. Ever the realist Charles therefore returned to his pleasures and by the end of the year Nell was carrying his child. If Moll had any children by the King at this time they did not survive infancy.

Moll and Nell were not the first actresses to enjoy the King's favour, according the Pepys Mrs Weaver (Elizabeth Farley) had that distinction shortly after the Restoration. Like Nell and Moll this lady's origins are shrouded in mystery but it is clear from surviving records that she was performing on the stage as early as 1660 when she is listed as one of the original actresses of the King's Company which was formed by Thomas Killigrew, brother of Lady Shannon, a one time mistress of the King. She was initially chosen for the title role in Richard Flecknoe's play *Erminia* at the Vere Street theatre and this was followed by appearances in *The*

Royall King and as Biancha, an unrepentant adulteress, in the revival in 1663⁄4 of John Ford's play *Love's Sacrifice*. Exactly when she became the king's mistress is unknown but by May 1661 she claimed that she was the wife of Mr Weaver, a gentleman of Grays Inn but it was not until September 1662 that her deception was discovered and reported by Henry Dobson viz:

> one Eliz: Farley hath gone by the name Eliz: Weaver wife to a gent of Grayes Inn to defraud her creditors and now being discovered that she is none of his wife altho she hath had a child by him and having no other shift for the defrauding of her creditors but merely being sworne one of his Maties servants...

Unfortunately her stage career, such as it was, was interrupted on at least two occasions by childbirth. The first produced a daughter Elizabeth who was baptised 20 May 1661 at St Andrew Holborn as the child of James and Elizabeth Weaver; it is just possible that the child was in fact the King's. A second pregnancy followed in 1664 when she 'of her own accord brought in all of her parts and... wou'd act noe more' and announced she was leaving the stage. 'Big with child' it was reported that her condition offended 'women of quality' and indignant that her parts had been given to others she 'continued her resolution to goe'. Hence forth she reverted to calling herself 'Mrs Farley'. The list of her creditors included Mr Weaver, Miles Lovett, Robert Kerby and numerous others. Despite this she continued to perform and made appearances as Sylviana in *The Siege of Urbin*, Servlina in *Thomaso* and Alibech in John Dryden's *The Indian Emperor* all during the 1664/5 theatre season. The latter an heroic tragedy was a sequel to *The Indian Queen* first performed in 1665; when it was performed again in 1667 Mrs Marshall took the part of Alibech.

Like Moll, Elizabeth did not perform during the years of the Plague and the Great Fire. In fact she did not perform again until 1671 when she played the part of Mrs Martha in Wycherley's *Love in a Wood*. Her last performances were in 1678 as Eudoria in Leanerd's

The Rambling Justice and the whore in D'Ufrey's *Trick for Trick* but thereafter she fades from the pages of history. Clearly Elizabeth's relationship with the King was never on the same footing as that of her rivals Moll and Nell and she was just a brief diversion. But she must have had some redeeming qualities in order to attract him in the first place.

Whilst temporarily eclipsed by her rival Nell Gwyn, Moll waited patiently for the King to resume his visits to her in her house in Suffolk Street but in 1670 another rival appeared on the scene to challenge their position, the beautiful Louise de Keroualle, maid of honour to the King's sister the Duchess of Orleans. Louise had arrived in England with the Duchess in the May of 1670 and immediately made an impression of Charles who begged his sister to allow her to remain. Taken aback the Duchess refused and her beautiful maid of honour returned with her to France shortly afterwards. During the visit Nell gave birth to the King's son in her lodgings in Lincolns Inn Fields but within the month Charles received the news that the Duchess had suddenly died and he was grief stricken.

After a bungled attempt by the Duke of Buckingham to bring the beautiful maid of honour back to England in order to become Charles's mistress the task was eventually accomplished by Ralph Montagu, the English Ambassador in France and upon her arrival she was immediately given a post as one of the Queen's maids of honour. Thereafter Charles dedicated himself to the seduction of this innocent flower of the French aristocracy but she did not surrender her virtue until the winter of 1671 just a few months before Nell presented Charles with another son. Moll meanwhile was completely out of the running and it was not until January 1673 that Charles resumed his visits. Nine months later the result was a fine, strong and healthy daughter, who would be the King's last child.

Moll returned to acting for a very brief spell in February 1675 when she appeared in a production of John Crowne's court masque *Calisto* portraying the River Thames in the prologue and the shepherdess Sylvia in the musical interludes. The role was originally intended for a man but Crowne's choice of a female was well received by the audience because of Mrs Davis's 'graceful motions and admirable singing'. The masque was produced for the Princesses Mary and Anne who played the title roles of Calisto and her friend Nyphe but the court ladies chosen to play the remaining roles proved to be so inept that Moll and Mrs Knight were invited to participate with Mrs Betterton directing the remainder of the cast. Amongst the musicians was James Paisible, a French oboe player who would later marry Moll.

After this performance the whole court was abuzz with the race between the Duchesses of Cleveland (formerly Lady Castlemaine) and Portsmouth (Louise de Keroualle) to have their sons ennobled by the King. The Duchess of Cleveland was determined that her son Henry should be made a Duke before Portsmouth's son but in the end the former was outwitted and lost the race. Nell's eldest son was made an Earl the following year but as with all of the King's daughters there was no title for Moll's three year old daughter. In 1676 the Duchesses of Cleveland and Portsmouth, Nell and Moll were all eclipsed by the arrival of the beautiful Duchess de Mazarin who promptly became the King's mistress and kept that position until she foolishly fell in love with the young Prince de Monaco in the summer of 1677. Thereafter the King returned to the arms of the Duchess of Portsmouth and Nell.

Moll's future husband James Paisible, came to England from France in September 1673 in the company of the composer Robert Cambert, with the intention of staging French-style operas. Unfortunately the project failed but James found employment in the Court Masque *Calisto* in which Moll also appeared and in 1677 had sufficient influence to stage a comedy-ballet written by Mme de la Roche-Guilhen entitled *Rare en tout* at Whitehall on the King's birthday. He also acquired the patronage of the Earl of Rochester who asked his friend Henry Savile to introduce him to Charles 'so that the King may hear his tunes when he is easy and private, because I am sure they will divert him extremely'. Charles was delighted with his compositions and the same year he received a court post. But according to St Evremond Paisible was 'a great and slothful musician... with manners that savoured of a well-bred man, and expressions which he must have leant in his little library'.

The next we hear of Moll is in a Court satire of 1681 where it was implied that she had become the mistress of Baptist May, keeper of the King's Privy Purse, who kept her at the King's expense but given the Exchequer's record of non-payment of pensions it is much more likely that her contact with him was purely financial. Either way her last recorded performance was in John Blow's opera *Venus and Adonis* when she played the part of Venus and her daughter sang the part of Cupid.

In September 1683 Moll's visits to Baptist May to secure her daughter' future finally bore fruit and she was awarded an annuity of £1,500 per annum, which together with her annuity of £1,000 gave her a very reasonable income of £2,500 per annum. But her good fortune did not last beyond the King's sudden death in March 1685. However, the change of sovereign resulted in James Paisible being appointed a court musician shortly after his marriage to Moll in December 1686 but again fate intervened and within two years James II had retired to France and the Paisible's felt obliged sell up and follow him. They remained in France until 1693 returning only after the naval battles of Barfleur and La Hogue had finally destroyed any hope that James II might have had of being restored to his kingdoms.

On his return Paisible was appointed composer to Prince George of Denmark, the husband of Princess Anne and whilst in that position produced a number of instrumental pieces for the theatre, in particular Colley Cibber's *Love's Last Shift* (1695), Southerne's *Oroonoko* (1695), Mrs Pix's *The Spanish Wives* (1696) etc. but his best known work was *The Queen's Farewell* (1695), a sombre piece written for Queen Mary's funeral. His musical skill was acknowledged by several of his contemporaries notably Francois Raguenet who declared that 'the famous Mr Paisible need not give place to any (Masters) at Paris and Zacharias Conrad von Uffenbach who recorded that his 'equal is not to be found.' But perhaps the best assessment of his abilities is the following by a modern historian viz:

Paisible's attractive theatrical music, consisting largely of French-style dances, was good enough to have been mistaken for Henry Purcell's. During the 1690's Paisible was one of the leading composers in England integrating elements of the French and Italian styles-in his case, in a rather quixotic manner. His thirteen mixed-style recorder sonatas were probably the most virtuosic music written for the instrument up to that date, giving some idea of the impact he clearly made as a performer.

On the death of Prince George in 1708 Paisible received a pension of £100 per annum a very welcome addition to his meagre income. But early in the same year Moll also died. Prior to her death Paisible had taken a mistress who gave him several children only one of whom survived and when he also died in 1720 he left just sixty guineas in gold, small change indeed.

Margaret Hughes

Like her contemporaries Nell Gwyn and Moll Davis, Margaret (Peg) Hughes was a beautiful and very talented actress. Her portrait at Coombe Abbey, painted in the style used by Sir Peter Lely to portray a courtesan, reveals a woman of great charm, with dark sparkling eyes, a beautiful milk white complexion and an expression of lively intelligence. But like Nell and Moll her origins are shrouded in mystery. All we know for certain is that she was a member of the King's Company which was formed by Thomas Killigrew shortly after the Restoration and her first recorded performances were in 1668 at the Theatre Royal in Bridges Street, which had an audience capacity of between 700 to 1000.

Of her family little is known except that an unnamed brother was killed in 1670 and she had a sister Judith, allegedly born about 1658, who became the mother of the infamous General Henry Hawley, who was soundly beaten by the Jacobites at the battle of Falkirk in 1746. Judith's husband Francis Hawley, a colonel in the army came from a very respectable family and was a grandson of William Fiennes, Lord Say and Sele.

Why Peg chose to appear on the stage is unknown but it is possible that financial reasons forced her to make the choice but whatever the reason her appearances were infrequent and her influence minimal. It has been suggested that she first appeared in Desdemonda in the revival of Shakespeare's *Othello* but her first recoded appearances were in the plays *The Virgin Martyr* and *The Mulberry Garden* in 1668 when she was allegedly the mistress of Sir Charles Sedley. Unlike some Restoration actresses Peg's talents enabled her to alternate between tragedy and comedy. *The Virgin Martyr* a sacred Jacobean tragedy, written by Thomas Dekker and Philip Massinger, whose central theme was the martyrdom of St Dorothea of Caesarea, being a classic example. This was followed by an appearance as Theodosia in John Dryden's Comedy *An Evening's Love* which was performed at the King's Theatre in Drury Lane. Pepys did not like the play it being heavily influenced by Corneille's comedy *Le Feint Astrologue*, Calderon's *El Astrologo fingido* and Scudery's novella *Ibrahim*. Also in the production was Mrs Ann Marshall as Aurelia, Mrs Knep as Beatrix and Nell Gwyn as Donna Jacinta. Mrs Knep, an indifferent actress, who was liberal with her favour, included Pepys and Sir Charles Sedley amongst her conquests.

Six months later in January 1669 Peg played the part of Panura in John Fletcher's Jacobean tragi-comedy *The Island Princess* with Mrs Marshall playing the part of Quisara and Mrs Corey as Quisana. The play based on the subject of the European Discovery of the East Indies was heavily influenced by French and Spanish sources but for all that Pepys thought it 'a pretty good play, many good things being in it – and a good scene of a town on fire'. Peg's next appearance in that year was in James Shirley's comedy *The Sisters* as Angellina, a play based on the intrigues of the Court of Parma in which Nell Gwynn also appeared as Pulcheria. Her final appearance was in June in Dryden's tragedy *Tyrannick Love* in which she played the principal role of St Catherine, Nell Gwyn playing the part of Valeria, Rebecca Marshall, Berence and Mrs Knep, Nakar and Felicia.

Peg's affair with Prince Rupert is alleged to have begun during Queen Catherine's visit to Tunbridge Wells to take the waters. As only two visits are recorded by Pepys in July 1663 and again in July 1666, we can only assume that it must have been the later date. If true then she was already an actress some two years before her first recorded appearances in 1668. However, it is possible that the Court visited the town at a later date and Pepys did not record the event. Either way Rupert quickly became enamoured of Peg and took her under his protection; he also employed her brother was one of his servants; her last performance was in *The Sisters* towards the end of 1669.

Peg was not the Prince's first mistress. At various times in his life his name was linked with Mary Villiers, Duchess of Richmond; Frances Bard, daughter of Viscount Bellomont, and Catherine Scott, sister of Lord George Goring, one of Rupert's fellow officers. By Frances Bard, he had a bastard son Dudley Bard, who was born about 1666 but killed at the siege of Buda in 1686

The Prince's friendship with Mary Villiers, who possessed a delicate and almost ephemeral beauty, began during the 1st Civil War and was already common gossip by 1645. As well as being the daughter of the infamous Duke of Buckingham, the cherished royal favourite of James I, the duchess could boast of royal descent via Anne, sister of Edward IV and kinship with the famous and the still powerful Howard clan which included the notorious and infamous Lady Somerset and her sister Lady Knollys She was also cousin to Charles II's mistress Barbara Villiers.

According to Madame Dunois, Mary was 'extremely beautiful, and of a mien and presence very noble and Majestic' and was 'gay, spirited and unconventional; courageous and quick-witted'. At the age of twelve she was married for the first time to Charles, Lord Herbert. A widow at the age of fifteen she then married the King's cousin James Stuart, Duke of Richmond but did not bare him any children until the end of 1649 when she produce a son and heir. Prince Rupert was not the father as he was on the high seas making for Kinsale harbour when the child was conceived. When the Duke died in 1655 the Duchess married Tom Howard, a kinsman.

Although Rupert's relationship was clearly nothing more than friendship, Clarendon 's assessment of him is proof of that, his relations with Lady Catherine Goring were much more suspect. This lady acquired a very unsavoury reputation for gallantry during the 1st Civil War, which almost equalled that of Barbara Villiers who 'was credited with a host of lovers'. The daughter of the Earl of Norwich and sister of Lord George Goring, one of Prince Rupert's fellow officers and a very capable cavalry officer, Lady Catherine possessed great charm but no morals. When her husband petitioned for a divorce in 1656, he alleged that she had 'eloped from him, and at Oxford, and other places, had children by other men'. His statement was backed up by several witnesses including a soldier who had served with the Roundhead forces who declared that:

> about nine years since he was desired to waite upon this lady to putney to the head quarters for a protection where she meeting with one of the King's chaplaines took an occasion to be a little with him. She had lockt her door to her and the german peeping in at the key hole saw her clothes upp and the chaplaine upon her thrashing in his long cloak.

A woman servant also testified that she had been familiar with Colonel Tom Howard, who would later become the lover of Lucy Walter and described the occasion thus:

> One night he had left his waxe Poll burning on the table, wch sett all on fire. I rose to put out the fire & saw them both in naked bed together... I could not endure it. I would lay noe longer in her chamber. Soe another maid there till she and I fell out. When I told her what I heard of her abroad of her, my lady would answ: she cared not what they said of her.

The son that has been attributed to Prince Rupert and Lady Catherine was Thomas Scott, who was born about 1643, presumably at Oxford. For many years Edward Scott, Lady Catherine's husband, would not acknowledge the child and only eventually did so with great reluctance. The marriage had already broken down by 1646, when Lady Catherine 'startled Kentish society by taking forcible possession of Nettlestead House and defying her husband to dislodge her. He, however, succeeded in starving her out, and when the siege was raised she escaped by a window'. Rupert's relationship with the lady was by all accounts very brief, she believing that variety was the spice of life. Another twenty years would pass before the Prince's name was again linked with a member of the fair sex.

Prince Rupert's next affair was in 1665/6 when he became involved with Lady Frances Bard, the daughter of Viscount Bellomont, a lady of singular charm and beauty who also possessed much wit. The prince's sister the Electress of Hanover wrote of her that 'She is an upright, good and virtuous woman' and 'there are few like her; we all love her!' In her religion Lady Frances was a catholic and ardent supporter of the Jacobite cause but despite this and her attempts to enlist the Electress's support, they remained very good friends.

The Prince appears to have been held in great esteem by Lord Bellomont and his family, indeed his only son and heir was christened Charles Rupert, which suggests that he might have been the child's godfather. However, Lord Bellomont, who was a scholar and traveller as well as a gallant officer, died tragically in a sand storm whilst travelling to India as Charles II's Envoy to the Great Moghul in 1656, leaving a widow and four young children. Exactly when the affair began is unknown but it was conducted with great secrecy. Even the Comte de Gramont was unaware of it!

Rupert was therefore no stranger to the opposite sex but his reputation as a lover was lamentable. According to Gramont:

> he was valiant and hardy even to rashness; but his nature was subject to certain eccentricities which he would have been ill pleased to have had to reform. His genius delighted in mathematical calculations, besides which he had some talent for chemistry. He was courteous almost to excess when politeness was not strictly necessary, yet overbearing to the point of brutality when circumstances demanded a more civilized mode of behaviour. He was a large man and his general bearing all too ungracious. Plain and severe even when he sought to show softness, his physiognomy, when he was in one of his evil humours, wore the expression of a true reprobate.

After their performances in Dryden's tragedy *Tyrannick Love* Nell Gwyn and Peg left the stage and settled into new roles as the acknowledged mistresses of the King and his cousin Prince Rupert. Thereafter Peg 'and Prince Rupert were as constant to each other as any man and his wife were in England' but no children followed until much later, unlike Nell who produced a son within the year.

Peg would never appear in another play written by Dryden, in fact she did not return to the stage until 1676 and there are precious few references to her in the intervening years. The first occured in June 1670 when her brother, who had been taken into Rupert's service, was killed after an argument. The event was recorded by Lady Chaworth thus: 'One of the King's servants hath killed Mr Hues, Peg Hues' brother, servant to Prince Robert upon a dispute whether Mis Nelly or she was the handsomer now at Windsor'; a Mr Hewes, perhaps another brother, was amongst the mourners when Rupert died twelve years later.

Prior to taking Peg as his mistress, Rupert was made Governor and Constable of Windsor Castle and took up residence in the Round Tower; he also had a house in Spring Gardens, Whitehall and another in Beech Lane, Barbican. According to his earliest biographer 'He took extraordinary delight in the Castle... bestowing no small part of his time and Art in Beautifying and adorning it, being now one of the finest Ornaments the Kingdom has, and is preferred by his Majesty above any of his Palaces'.

When his mistress finally presented him with a daughter, Rupert's happiness seemed complete but suddenly in 1676 Peg returned to the stage to act for the Duke's Company. Only lack of money could have forced her to take this course of action and her decision to appear under the auspices of a rival company can only be explained by the sorry state the Theatre Royal was then in.

The new Theatre Royal which had opened in 1674 was designed by Sir Christopher Wren and paid for by public subscription; the money to provide new scenery and costumes was raised by the actor-shareholders. The original built in 1663 was destroyed by fire in 1672 together with all the stock of scenery and costumes and the company was forced to move temporarily into the recently vacated Lincolns Inn Theatre, previously inhabited by the Duke's Company.

The 'exciting and elaborate scenery' of the old Theatre Royal plus its success in devising a new style of comedy had contributed significantly to box office takings during Peg's first years as a player there. When the play 'Tyrannic Love' was staged in 1669, in which Peg appeared as St Catherine:

the company commissioned a scene of Elysium... from the painter Isaac Fuller [which took him] six weeks to produce, and, after much litigation, the company paid him £335. 10s. The play [then] ran for 14 consecutive days, according to Fuller – an almost unheard of run and took £100 per day... compared with the usual receipts of £40 or £50.

The new style of comedy developed over a period of time in such plays as 'The English Monsieur', 'All Mistaken' by James Howard and *The Wild Gallant*, *Secret Love* and 'An Evening's Love' by Dryden, in which Peg had played the part of Theodosia, also ensured the Company's continuing success.

Unfortunately, however, on Peg's return in 1676 the theatre's prospects were not so bright. By 1674 Killigrew 'had pawned his building shares, his interest in the acting shares and his patent in return for cash (and) in spite of such concern for the actors welfare as the provision of a company prostitute, his relations with the actors deteriorated'. The senior players Hart and Kynaston were also in open revolt and Killigrew was forced to hand over his interests to his son Charles, who proved to be almost 'as bad a manager as his father'. And the situation got much worse when 'actors stole costumes and props... some of the best younger actors ran off to Scotland (and) performances were given intermittently and to small audiences (whilst) new plays were almost entirely restricted to parodies of the rival company's successes'.

As a result it is easy to see why Peg chose to return to the stage as a member of the Duke's Company which in 1671 had moved into the new Dorset Garden Theatre 'the grandest of the Restoration theatres'. During the 1675/6 season Peg appeared in seven plays. The most successful of these productions was *The Rover* which was adapted from Tom Killigrew's play *The Wanderer* and by all accounts a vast improvement on it. Peg's fellow actresses were Ann Marshall in the role of Angellica Bianca and Elizabeth Barry as Helena, sister of Florinda and the plot

1. George (Villiers), 1st Duke of
Buckingham. Peter Paul Rubens.

2. Ninon DeL'Enclos. Pierre Mignard.

3. Marie Mancini, Princess Colonna.
Pierre Mignard.

4. Barbara Villiers, Countess of Castlemaine.
Sir Peter Lely.

5. Mrs Jane Middleton. Sir Peter Lely.

6. Frances Stuart, Duchess of Richmond. Sir Peter Lely.

7. Margaret, Lady Denham. Sir Peter Lely.

8. Miss Warmestry.

9. Nell Gwyn. Sir Peter Lely.

10. Margaret (Peg) Hughes. Sir Peter Lely.

11. Louise de Keroualle, Duchess of Portsmouth. Sir Peter Lely.

12. Lady Byron. Sir Peter Lely. (By kind permission of Philip Mould).

13. Louise, Duchess of Portsmouth. Mary Beale. (By kind permission of Philip Mould).

14. Hortense, Duchess de Mazarin. Jacob Ferdinand Voet. (By kind permission of Philip Mould).

15. Elizabeth, Lady Kildare. Studio of Sir Peter Lely. (By kind permission of Philip Mould).

16. Frances, Duchess of Richmond William Wissing. (By kind permission of Philip Mould).

17. Mary (Moll) Davis. Sir Peter Lely. (By kind permission of Philip Mould).

18. A Courtesan. Mary Beale. (By kind permission of Philip Mould).

19. A Courtesan formerly called Nell Gwyn. Studio of Sir Peter Lely. (By kind permission of Philip Mould).

20. Lady called Nell Gwyn. Studio of
Sir Peter Lely. (By kind permission of
Philip Mould).

21. Mrs Maria Fitzherbert. Sir
Joshua Reynolds. (National Portrait
Gallery).

22. Amelia, Countess of Yarmouth after Peter van Hogh. (National Portrait Gallery).

23. Honourable Mrs Anne Vane after John van der Bank. (National Portrait Gallery).

24. Mrs Maria Fitzherbert. (National Portrait Gallery).

25. Alice Keppel. (National Portrait Gallery).

26. Daisy, Countess of Warwick. (National Portrait Gallery).

27. Thelma, Lady Furness. (National Portrait Gallery).

revolved around the amorous adventures of a group of Englishmen in Naples during carnival time. Eventually, however, the King's and Duke's Companies merged and a united company was formed which gave its first performance in 1682.

After the season was at an end Peg retired once again from the stage and never returned. During the interval she had given Rupert a daughter and the remainder of her life was now devoted to her education. Ruperta was probably born in June 1673 and before Rupert's death in 1682 it was his ardent wish that she should marry the King's bastard son by Nell Gwyn. Unfortunately, however, the King had other plans, and the match did not take place. Nevertheless Rupert's desire for a match between the two Royal Houses of Stuart and the Palatinate, whether legitimate or illegitimate continued unabated.

The next opportunity occurred in December 1680, when Rupert's nephew, George Louis of Hanover, paid a visit to England in order to woo the Princess Anne. On his arrival he was given an apartment in Whitehall and one of his first tasks was to pay his uncle a visit: 'I went to see Uncle Rupert, who received me in bed for his ailment in his leg often keeps his to his bed. He has to take care of himself'. George did not return to Hanover until March 1681 but despite paying his respects to the Princess Anne, nothing came of the proposed marriage alliance. Nevertheless he 'found Anne charming and would have been much honoured if a match had been proposed'. A marriage alliance between the two protestant branches of the Royal Family had much to recommend it but instead the princess went on to marry the prince of Denmark. During his visit George also met Peg and her unmarried sister Judith and many years later Lady Suffolk recounted that 'He was supposed to have an intrigue with Mrs Hawley... and afterwards when he came to the crown, he always took particular notice of her son, General Hawley...' As Judith did not marry Francis Hawley until 1684 and General Henry Hawley was not born until 1685, the imputation that the latter was George's son is therefore untenable.

Although increasingly bedridden Rupert was still able on occasions to attend official functions but he was still beholden to Peg in many ways and shortly before his death wrote to his youngest sister, the Electress

Sophia that 'What you have been told about Mme Hews is very true. She took great care of me during my illness and I am obliged to her for many things' and concluded by saying that 'as for the little one (Ruperta), she cannot resemble me, (for) she is turning into the prettiest creature. She already rules the whole house and sometimes argues with her mother, which makes us all laugh'.

When Rupert eventually died in 1682, he was not a wealthy man. But there was sufficient ready money left to pay his debts and provide for Peg and her daughter. In an iron chest his executors found 1,694 guineas, £1,000 in silver and numerous pieces of jewellery including a great pearl necklace, later sold to Nell Gwyn for £4,520 plus a large cabinet worth £8,000. With some of the proceeds Peg was able to purchase from the nephew and heir of Sir Nicholas Crispe, the magnificent mansion in Fulham that was later known as Brandenburg House where she lived for the next ten years until she was forced to sell it in 1693 to Timothy Lannoy and George Treadway. To his bastard son by Frances Bard, he left 'in addition to his house at Rhenen the legacy of his mother (but also) all money owed to him by the Emperor, the Elector Palatine, or any other person or persons whatsoever not naturall borne subject of the King of England'.

At her father's death Ruperta was about nine years old and did not marry until she was twenty two. Her choice was Colonel Emanuel Scrope Howe, Groom of the Bedchamber to William of Orange, her senior by some ten years. The marriage produced five children but only three survived to adulthood. In 1705, Brigadier-General Howe was appointed Envoy-Extraordinary to the Court of Hanover a post he held until his death in 1709. During his residence there he unwittingly became embroiled in the very sensitive discussions that were taking place around the question between the Whigs and Tories on the future Hanoverian succession. Like her father Ruperta was not always the most tactful person when wanting to make a point and when she 'filled her letters to London with reports of Hanoverian indifference' on the subject of the succession, the Whigs, the Electress Sophie's firm supporters roundly accused Sophie of 'having become the tool of their political enemies' the Tories. Howe meanwhile brought some calm to the situation by assuring her of 'Her Majesty's kind intentions towards herself and her family' but the presence of Rupert's ex-mistress Frances Bard, a known supporter of King James, at the Hanoverian Court did nothing to allay the fears of the Whigs. Eventually, however, the situation was resolved to everyone's satisfaction and upon her husband's death Ruperta returned to England.

When Peg eventually died in 1719, her remaining goods and chattels, were administered by her sister Judith and not her daughter Ruperta. Her remains were buried in the parish church of Lee in Kent and many years later Judith was also buried there.

ISABELLE-ANGELIQUE, DUCHESS DE CHÂTILLON

As the winter of 1648/9 progressed into a new year Isabelle-Angelique, Duchess de Châtillon faced an uncertain future. Civil War was raging in France and the news had just arrived that her husband had died from the wounds he had received during a skirmish at Charenton, between the forces of the Prince de Conde and the rebels of Paris. The Duke was mortally wounded and his body carried to nearby Vincennes where he died the following day.

The Duchess received the news with comparative indifference as he was a far from faithful husband and she a far from faithful wife. In fact the Duke had gone into battle wearing the garter of his mistress, Madamoiselle de Guerchy, on his arm. She was just one of many women he had loved, including the beautiful Ninon de L'Enclos before she embarked on her career as the most famous *female galante* ever! The little grief that the Duchess did show was according to a contemporary 'counterfeit grief, after the manner of ladies who love themselves too well to care for any one else'.

But it was not the death of her husband that worried her it was the knowledge that she was with child and unsure of its paternity! Was it the fascinating Duc de Nemours or her husband? When the child, a boy, was born in early July 1649, the Duchess resolved her dilemma by simply naming the child after its legal father. Exactly when de Nemours became Isabelle's lover is uncertain, but it was clearly after her marriage in 1645. Charles Amadeus, Duc de Nemours, was the husband of Elisabeth de Bourbon-Vendome, granddaughter of Henry IV 'Le Grand' and thus cousin by marriage of Charles II, who later became Isabelle's lover. At one point Isabelle was carrying on intrigues with three different admirers at the same time, Nemours, the Prince de Conde and Charles! When the Duc was killed by his brother-in-law the Duc de Beaufort, the brother of his wife, in a duel a few years later in 1652 and the Prince de Conde eventually lost interest, she was left with just one.

Charles II, then Prince of Wales, first met Isabelle in the spring of 1648 at a Court Ball given in his honour by his cousin La Grand Mademoiselle but he left shortly afterwards for Holland and it was only on his return in the June of the following year, that he was able to renew his courtship. In the interval he took an English mistress Lucy Walters, who bore him a son before he left again in 1650 with the intention of invading England and during his adventure he was crowned King of Scotland at Scone. The outcome is history. After being defeated at the battle of Worcester by Oliver Cromwell, he fled back to the safety of France and the arms of the Duchess de Châtillon.

Isabelle de Montmorency-Bouteville was the daughter of Francois (de Montmorency), Comte de Luxe – who was executed in 1627 for duelling with the Marquis de Beuvron, leaving a young widow with two infant children. At the tender age of fourteen she entered the household of Mme de Longueville, the Prince de Conde's sister and the latter immediately became infatuated with her. But he did not become her lover, an honour he shared with the Duc de Nemours, until after the death of her husband.

Her beauty was a glory to behold but she was not the first member of her family to become a royal mistress. That honour went to her cousin Francoise, the daughter of the Marquis de Thury and maid of honour to Marguerite de Navarre, first wife of Henri IV 'Le Grand', who became the latter's mistress before he ascended the throne of France. Just why Isabelle should have chosen to become the mistress of the Duc de Nemours, a member of the House of Savoy, and later the Prince de Conde, a Prince of the Blood, is unclear. As a widow of

Gaspard de Coligny and daughter of the House of Montmorency she had every prospect of marrying well for a second time, although it would be another fourteen years before she chose to do so. Her choice was instructive. Christian Ludwig of Mecklenburg-Schwerin was a member of a sovereign princely house and a considerable step up in rank for Isabelle. If she could not marry Charles Stuart, and become Queen of England, then she would have the next best thing. There were no children of the marriage but it was written in the marriage contract that she could return to France whenever she wished. For the Duke it was deemed a mes-alliance because they were not of equal rank but it was tolerated by his subjects.

As cousin of the famous Duc de Montmorency, who was executed for high treason in 1632, Isabelle and her brother stood to inherit a sizeable fortune but on his death it was seized by the crown and distributed amongst the unfortunate Duc's sisters, the Princess de Conde, and the Duchesses d'Angouleme and de Ventadour. The Princess de Conde received the largest portion but King Louis XIII, retained possession of Chantilly and Dammartin, because of the excellent hunting to be had there. Isabelle and her brother Francois-Henri (subsequently Duc de Luxemburg) received nothing, a bitter blow, but in time Isabelle would have her revenge on the Princess.

The Princess de Conde, Charlotte de Montmorency, Isabelle's kinswoman, was a great beauty in her youth. At the age of sixteen she was commanded by Henri IV to marry his cousin the Prince de Conde, but it was apparent to all that this was simply in order to made her his mistress. Charlotte, however, had other ideas and with her husband's assistance fled the country in order to avoid the King's attentions. Henry was distraught and furious that his plans had come to naught especially as he had charged himself with all of the expenses of the young Prince's education and therefore felt that the prince was forever in his debt and honour bound not to oppose his plan.

There was no more lovely girl at court than the young princess:

> She was then sixteen years old – said Cardinal Bentiviglio, the Papal Ambassador... and her loveliness was adjudged by all men to accord with

the fame therof. She was very fair; her eyes and all her features full of charm; an ingenous grace in all her gestures and in her manner of speaking. Her beauty owed its power to itself alone, since she did not bring to its aid any of the artifices of which women are wont to make use.

The King, then fifty-five years old, was still as amorous as he had been at twenty and initially convinced himself that his interest in the young beauty was purely paternal. At the time she was betrothed to another, a handsome young nobleman from Lorraine, Francois de Bassompierre – a redoubtable lady killer, high in the King's favour. When Henry realised he was in love with the young beauty, he informed the distraught young man that he was breaking off the engagement:

Baron, I wish to speak to you as a friend. I am not only in love, but distracted about Madamoiselle de Montmorency. If you marry her and she loves you, I shall hate you. If she loved me, you will hate me. It were better that the marriage were broken off, lest it should mar the good understanding between us, and destroy the affection I entertain for you. I have decided to marry her to my nephew, the Prince de Conde and to keep her near the person of my wife. She will be the solace and support of the old age upon which I am about to enter. I shall give her to my nephew, who is only twenty, and prefers hunting a thousand times to ladies society; and I desire no other favour from her than her affection, without pretending to anything further.

When the King's passion became ever more violent, the Prince de Conde remonstrated with him and violent scenes took place between them until he abruptly left the court taking his wife with him and fled to the Spanish Netherlands. The rest is history.

Isabelle, an imperious young beauty, was forced for many years to watch while the princess enjoyed the fruits of the inheritance that she believed was hers, but despite making a splendid marriage to the Duc de Châtillon she remained unhappy and to console herself cast around for a suitable distraction. During the course of her life she achieved much notoriety as the most accomplished coquette of her time, who appreciated to the full her many attractions and disdained to turn away any of her admirers! Even the poet Charpy wrote verses about her and the devastating effect she had the young beaus that gathered around her.

Louis de Bourbon, Prince de Conde (known as 'La Grande' Conde for his famous military victories), the third of Isabelle's lovers was of a completely different mettle to his rivals. Like Isabelle's husband, he was closely related to his lady love, his mother being the niece of the Connetable Henri de Montmorency. In order to prepare him for the position he would inevitably hold at court Conde was given the best possible education. In character he was fearlessly brave, quick witted and full of energy and determination. But he was also haughty, overbearing, selfish and indifferent to the needs or sufferings of others. However, these major defects in his character were made up to some extent by his great military gifts.

The Prince de Conde and Isabelle became lovers after the birth of her son in early 1649. The event was shortly followed by the death in 1650 of the Dowager-Princess de Conde, the Prince's mother, at Isabelle's residence of Châtillon-sur-Loing, whence she had retired. In her last days the Princess had fallen much under the influence of Isabelle who now saw an opportunity to be revenged for being disinherited:

> The Duchesse de Châtillon – observed Lenet-who was the most astute woman in the world, had so well understood how to employ her adroit and subtle mind and her agreeable and insinuating manners as to make herself so completely mistress of the princess-dowager, that she saw only with her eyes and spoke only with her mouth.

The result was that the dowager-princess bequeathed to Isabelle nearly all of her jewellery and the revenues for life of several of her estates. Hoping to profit from the situation, the Prince de Conde's young wife opened an unaddressed letter sent by the Duc de Nemours to Isabelle, urging her to take possession of the properties left her by the dowager-princess. On being confronted with the contents by the Princess, Isabelle simply dismissed it as a forgery and as the Prince de Conde was still totally enamoured of her, he ordered his wife to allow Isabelle to take possession of the properties.

The House of Montmorency was declared by Henry IV to be the premier Noble House of Europe after the Bourbons and provided many able military commanders, including Francois, Isabelle's brother who increased the family's fame by becoming a Marshal of France and leading the armies of Louis XIV to many great victories. As a young man he shared in all of the misfortunes of his cousin and childhood companion the Prince de Conde and as a reward for his loyalty the prince arranged for his marriage in 1661 to one of the wealthiest heiresses in France, Madeleine de Luxemburg-Piney.

Sadly Francois's reputation has suffered over the centuries mainly due to St Simon's portrayal of him in his Memoirs viz:

> A noble name, courage, unbridled ambition, and great capabilities, accompanied by love of intrigue and dissolute living, enabled him to overcome the drawbacks of what was at first sight an astonishingly repulsive exterior. For, although no one could credit this who ever met him, one did become accustomed to the sight of a hump that was medium big in front but very thick and monstrously pointed behind, with all the usual accompaniments of such deformities. Nobility and charm of manner transfigured him in his most ordinary gestures.

Without a doubt Francois appears to have been Conde's greatest pupil and although inferior to Conde and Turenne, he was far superior to Marshal Tallard and the Duc de Villeroi, Louis XIV's other generals.

Despite her tarnished reputation, Charles II became infatuated with Isabelle and pursued her at every opportunity and gave her the nickname of 'Bablon'. As previously related, they met for the first time at a ball at the French Court in the spring of 1648 whilst Charles was paying court to his cousin Le Grand Mademoiselle. His interest did not go unnoticed by his prospective fiancée and his suit of his cousin did not progress as a result of it. It is not known for certain when the Duchess finally succumbed to the young prince's advances, but after a short time he left for Holland and did not see her again until he returned in June 1649.

By this time, she had lost her husband, given birth to a child over whose paternity there was a question mark, and had engaged in two affairs, one with the Duc de Nemours and another with the Prince de Conde.

Charles's renewed courtship of Isabelle did not escape the attention of Edward Hyde, his chancellor or indeed of Le Grand Mademoiselle, whom Charles was courting once again for her vast fortune! To complicate matters even more, Charles began an affair with Lady Elizabeth Boyle, a daughter in law of the Earl of Cork, which resulted in a daughter Charlotte. Charles's pursuit of 'Bablon' infuriated La Grand Mademoiselle who in her characteristically forthright manner declared:

> It pains me to see you dancing and tricotet and amusing yourself, when you ought to be there (in England), either risking your head or putting a crown on it. You are not worthy of a crown if you do not want to seize it at the point of a sword, and at the risk of your life.

Clearly she had forgotten that that is exactly what Charles had done when he had invaded England only to be defeated at the battle of Worcester!

To console himself for Mademoiselle's rejection of his suit, he decided to capitalise on his popularity with the younger French nobles. Invitations to hunt, play billiards play tennis, attend parties, concerts and plays came in a steady stream and he entertained them all with stories of his adventures. Meanwhile, Isabelle, who was becoming increasingly enamoured of the young man, began to contemplate marriage with her young lover, but for the moment chose to continue the relationship as a romantic *amour courtois*. But fate intervened to separate them when Cardinal Mazarin requested that Charles leave France as a direct result of pressure from Oliver Cromwell.

He left the country in July 1654 after the Cardinal had promised to pay his debts and expenses for the journey, having spent his last night on French soil at the Duchess's country retreat of Merlou. His mother cried and the Venetian Ambassador wrote in his dispatches 'He has the sympathy of all France'. A few days after his departure, Hyde, received the unwelcome news that Charles had secretly married the Duchess.

It was of course untrue as was the rumour that he had married his other mistress Lucy Walters.

Charles never saw 'Bablon' again and her influence on him has not been fully appreciated. She was his first French mistress and clearly encouraged his interest in French culture, in particular poetry and music; his favourite instrument was the violin. Charles, for his part, loved all things French and acquired a marked taste for the plays of Moliere and the antics of the famous 'Scaramouche' and his band of Italian players whilst he was in exile. When he returned to England, he continued to favour French wines, French music and even persuaded Claude Sourceau, a French tailor, to settle in England.

One of his first acts at his restoration, was to reform 'The King's Music' in accordance with the latest French fashion. In exile he had spent much of his leisure time dancing and continued to take a great deal of pleasure in this form of exercise through out the remainder of his reign. By 1666, however, Charles was bored with French music and thereafter employed a company of Italian musicians including two castrati. Charles also became a great admirer of the guitar and work of the Italian virtuoso Francesco Corbetta.

Having achieved her ambition of becoming the mistress of a Prince of the Blood, plus a King in exile and marrying a sovereign prince, 'Bablon' now stood aside and made way for a younger generation of her close kin who reached even more dizzy heights of celebrity and fame, most notably the Comte de Guiche and his sister the Princess de Monaco.

Armand de Gramont, Comte de Guiche, was the nephew of Isabelle's cousin, the Comte de Gramont and considered by many to have been one of the handsomest men in France. Indeed his undeniable good looks, haughty manner and impulsive character attracted the attention of Philippe, Duc de Orleans, the brother of Louis XIV, and before long he became a great favourite of that unfortunate prince and his wife Henrietta, the sister of Charles II.

De Guiche, a great-grandson of Diane d'Andouins, a mistress of Henri IV, found the role of royal favourite sat very comfortably on his shoulders. The Duchess of Orleans was quite taken with him and foolishly arranged meetings in her private apartments where he came disguised as a fortune teller. In order to divert attention from the object of his passion, de Guiche, who was bi-sexual, promptly laid siege to the heart of one of Henrietta's maids of honour. His choice of the lovely Louise de la Valliere was singularly unfortunate, because it put him on a collision course with the King, who was just beginning to take an interest in the 'tall, shapely, extremely pretty' maid of honour himself. But in order to divert suspicion from his own interest in Henrietta. De Guiche, despite being banished from court, still managed to have letters sent to Henrietta via Madame de Montalais, a member of her household.

La Valliere, whose 'fresh almost incandescent beauty, springtime colouring, memorably soft voice – so sweet that no one who heard it ever forgot it - and shyness' so captivated Louis that she became the first of his 'Grand Passions'. Henrietta was naturally extremely annoyed that the King no longer paid her the same attention and turned to De Guiche for solace, leaving her maid of honour to her fate! Eventually De Guiche was banished to Holland for his intrigues but not before almost compromising Henrietta's good name.

The Princess de Monaco, a ravishing brunette, was married to Louis Grimaldi and had left France for self imposed exile in Monaco a few weeks before Charles II was restored in 1660. Five years later she returned to the French court to take up a position as superintendent of Henrietta's household. Within a short time, however, her beauty began to attract the attention of the French King, who found himself competing for her affections with the Marquis de Puyguilhem, the Princess's cousin, who had loved her since childhood. To rid himself of his rival, Louis banished him from court, but the affair with the Princess did not proceed as planned and within a few months it was over. However, she retained the post of superintendent of Henrietta's household until 1668 and then became a dame of honour to the Duc's second wife.

The Marquis de Puyguilhem, more commonly known as the Comte de Lauzun, achieved a notoriety and fame that completely eclipsed that of his cousins De Guiche and the Princess of Monaco. A Gascon, ambitious and eccentric, he came from an ancient family and on his mother's side was a great-grandson of the Marechal de la Force. 'One of the smallest men God ever made' he was wiry and sharp featured and possessed a wit that brought women flocking to his side. Since childhood he had been in love with his cousin the Princess de Monaco who returned his passion, but their families would not allow them to marry. When the Princess became the King's mistress, Lauzun became enraged and reminded her of the letters she had written to him, which he threatened to show the King. Louis responded by imprisoning him for a short time in the Bastille. It was the first of several visits.

In the winter of 1669/70 the French court became aware that the King's cousin, 'La Grand Mademoiselle', was in love and the object of her affections none other than the Comte de Lauzan! This extraordinary turn of events would bring loss of office, imprisonment and utter ruin on de Lauzan, because it was clear to all that the King would never allow such a marriage. Mademoiselle's vast wealth and lands could not pass out of the hands of the royal family. A husband of royal blood must be found! The King proposed his brother, the Duc d'Orleans, who had just lost his wife Henrietta, but Mademoiselle turned down the offer and managed to obtain the King's promise that she could marry her intended, only for him to go back on his word.

Although distraught, Lauzan behaved with great dignity and refused the King's offer of to make him a duke and marechal of France. But he destroyed the good impression he had made by calling Madame de Montespan, the King's mistress, a liar and common whore, because she had not supported him in his efforts to marry Mademoiselle. The King's reaction was swift, Lauzan was arrested and accompanied by a company of musketeers imprisoned in Pignerol, an isolated castle in the Alps near Turin, where he remained for the next ten years!

So ended, temporarily, the career of the man described by St Simon as 'full of ambition and caprice... wishing always to go too far, never content with anything, proud in his dealings, disagreeable and malicious by nature'.

Fate, however, was eventually kind to Lauzan, and on being released from prison, he married, and in 1688 was sent by Louis XIV to England to assist King James in his endeavour and to see that his wife and child were safely conveyed to France, following the invasion of William of Orange. But he never saw Mademoiselle again; she died in 1693 followed by Isabelle in 1695 and thus ended a remarkable chapter in the life of the Duchess de Châtillon and her near kin.

Louise-Renee de Penancoët de Keroualle, Duchess of Portsmouth

Louise-Renee de Penancoët de Keroualle, Charles II's last and greatest love, was not the first member of her extended family to become a royal mistress. That honour went to Anne de Pissejeu, Duchess d'Etampes and Francoise de Foix, both mistresses of Francois I. They were followed by Renee de Rieux, Louise's great-aunt Le Belle Chateauneuf 'a ravishing blond of twenty summers' when she became the mistress of the bi-sexual Henri III of France in 1572/3. 'With wonderful blue eyes and a complexion of lilies and roses... She passed for the most perfect beauty of the Court, and one could pay a lady no higher compliment than to say that she resembled her'.

La Belle Chateauneuf was followed by other more distantly related family members most notably Jacqueline de Bueil, mistress of Henri IV plus the Princess de Soubise and Madame de Montespan, mistresses of Louis XIV. In the eighteenth century Louise's kinswomen the three de Mailly sisters, Louise-Julie, Pauline-Felicite and Marie-Anne, each in turn became a mistress of Louis XV. In addition, the Chevalier de Lorraine, a cousin, became the male favourite of Philippe, Duc d'Orleans, brother of Louis XIV. The Princess de Soubise and Madame de Montespan, contemporaries of Louise, acquired vast fortunes during their time as royal mistresses and it was probably their spectacular success that inspired Louise to follow their example.

The story of La Belle Chateauneuf however, illustrates all too clearly the fragility of the royal mistress's position at court, for within a short time she found she had a rival in the person of Marie de Cleves, first wife of the Prince de Conde, and it was not long before she was replaced in her royal lover's affections.

To compensate his ex-mistress for her loss, Henri determined to find her a husband, although she was not consulted on his choice. The prince eventually decided on a very wealthy citizen named Duprat de Nantouillet, but the choice was singularly unfortunate as he did not match his intended bride in social rank; Renee was after all descended from the Royal House of France and the Ducal House of Brittany and kin to her ex-lover Henri.

Surprisingly Duprat declined the honour of marrying the ex-mistress of a Prince of the Blood, and furious at the slight, Henri conspired with his brother Charles IX to revenge himself on the unfortunate man. The brothers thereupon invited themselves to his house and after the banquet, the guests broke into his coffers and carried away all of his silver and plate! Shortly afterwards whilst walking in the street, Duprat happened to meet Madamoiselle de Chateauneuf on horseback. When she realised that this was the man who had refused her hand in marriage, she promptly set about him with her riding whip.

A few years later, on the occasion of his marriage to Louise de Lorraine – who bore a striking resemblance to his deceased mistress Marie de Cleves - Henri now King of France, attempted for a second time to find Renee a husband. His choice of Francois de Luxembourg, at one point a suitor for the hand of the fair Louise de Lorraine, was much more in keeping with the lady's rank. When the King approached him, he addressed him in the following manner 'Cousin, I have married your mistress; but I desire that in exchange, you should marry mine'. He followed this by saying 'I desire that you espouse her immediately' hinting very strongly that if he did not do so, something very unpleasant would befall him. Francois 'begged very humbly that the King grant him a week's respite' and on being given three days promptly took horse and rode without a break for the frontier.

Eventually Renee married a Florentine named Antinoti, who was superintendent of the galleys at Marseille. However, the marriage did not last, because 'having detected him in a compromising situation with another demoiselle, she stabbed him bravely and manfully with her own hand'. Shortly thereafter she married a second time another Florentine Philippe d'Altoviti, self-styled Baron de Castellane, but a few months later he was killed in a brawl with Henri d'Angouleme, Grand Prior of France, a bastard son of Henri II of France.

Louise Renee de Penancouët de Keroualle, was born in September 1649 in her family's chateau in Brittany, the daughter of the Siegneur de Keroualle, a descendant of the ancient Breton nobility. He was not a wealthy man, but his wife was related to some of the most noble and ancient families in France. Marie de Ploeuc, the niece of Le Belle Chateauneuf, came with a very respectable dowry plus a pedigree festooned with descents from the Royal Houses of France and Brittany and the illustrious House of de Rohan. In the absence of large family estates and a dowry, it was these royal descents that gave Louise connections with some of France's most ancient and noble families.

In character, Louise bore no resemblance at all to her great-aunt, the beautiful and fiery Renee. The latter's scandalous life was a source of embarrassment to the family, especially as it did not benefit in any way from her brief reign as a royal mistress. It was therefore with some trepidation that Louise's parents allowed her to take up the position of maid of honour to the Duchess of Orleans at the French court.

Had they known of the sexual proclivities of the Duke, and how unhappy the Duchess was in her marriage and the intrigues she became involved in, they might very well have recommended Louise enter a convent instead.

Louise's introduction to the French court was a direct result of the influence of the Duc de Beaufort, the family's patron and Monsieur de Chaulnes, the Governor of Brittany. On their recommendation, she was appointed a maid of honour to Henrietta Anne, Duchess of Orleans, the sister-in-law of Louis XIV. Beaufort, a grandson of Henri IV of France and his mistress Gabrielle de Estrees, was a 'Frondeur' and took a very active part in the Revolt of the Parliaments against the crown in 1648, for which he was imprisoned in the dungeon of Vincennes. He was adored by the fish wives of Paris because he learnt to speak their language, but he had a reputation for duelling and killed his brother-in-law, the Duc de Nemours – a rival of Charles II for the favours of the enchanting Duchess de Châtillon – in a duel in 1652. Beaufort, who never married, was killed in action shortly after Louise's appointment during a French expedition to Canada in 1669; Louise's brother Sebastian was seriously wounded in the same expedition.

The French historian Saint-Simon accused Louise's parents of placing her in the Duchess's household in an attempt to become Louis XIV's mistress, but Louis had just taken Madame de Montespan as his mistress and had eyes for no other. The real reason was to find a suitable husband, and at one point it looked as if they would achieve a splendid match with the Comte de Sault, eldest son of the Duc de Lesdiguieres. But due to the lack of a sizeable dowry, it never took place.

In the 1660's the French Court was not yet centred on Versailles but on the Royal Palaces of Fontainebleau, St Germain-en-Laye, the Louvre and to a lesser extent Compiegne. The Duchess and her entourage, however, spent the summer months at St Cloud, the Orleans family home, and the winter at the Palais Royal, and it was here that Louise learnt the etiquette and ways of the French Court.

The cause of the Duchess's unhappiness was her husband's preference for his own sex. By the time that Louise became one of her maids of honour, the Duc had taken as his favourite, the blond cherub faced Chevalier de Lorraine, Louise's cousin, a 'magnificent gigolo and breathtakingly handsome member of the House of Guise' who 'had a treacherous and ruthless nature'. At parties the court was often treated to the sight of the Duc 'hanging girlishly on to the arm of the Chevalier, a dainty figure with a waist undeniably as small as Madamoiselle de Fiennes'; the latter one of the Duchess's maids of honour was also the Chevalier's mistress. Louis XIV tolerated his brother's preference for his own sex, but still remained concerned about the possibility of him becoming a rival. When he approached the Chevalier on this very issue, the latter replied 'Sire, Monsieur is a good man, he loves Your Majesty; believe me, he would never do anything to displease you'. 'Will you stand surety for him' asked Louis. 'I will, Sire' replied Lorraine. 'I am very glad of it' replied the King.

Shortly after Louise had entered the Duchess's household, Monsieur discovered that his wife was having secret talks with Louis, who planned to send her to England to negotiate a treaty with her brother Charles II, perhaps the most important man in her life. Irritated beyond measure, however, by the behaviour of the chevalier de Lorraine in the proceedings, Louis lost patience and had him arrested and despatched to the country were he was imprisoned in the Chateau d'If. Monsieur, distraught, demanded his immediate release, but Louis stood firm. When he was finally released, the chevalier took himself off into voluntary exile in Rome, where he promptly carried on an affair with Cardinal Mazarin's niece, the Princess Colonna, an old flame of Louis XIV.

In addition to the torment inflicted upon her by her jealous husband, the Duchess was forced to endure the spectacle of her brother-in-law seducing several of her maids of honour. Among these were Louise de la Baume de la Blanc, Mademoiselle de la Valliere, who was Louis's first 'Grand Passion' and Madame de Montespan. Within a few years, however, of taking Louise as his mistress, he had a brief affair with the Princess de Monaco, superintendent of the Duchess's household, whose brother, the Comte de Guiche, had been a favourite of Monsieur before he met the Chevalier de Lorraine. A third affair with, Madame de Ludres, maid of honour to Monsieur's second wife, was over almost a quickly as it had begun. Such behaviour therefore was unlikely to inspire Louise's parents with the belief that she would be in safe hands as a member of the Duchess's household!

Fortunately Louise was not tempted to follow the example of Madamoiselle de Fiennes and company, but she had to be on her guard as her beauty had already attracted attention: 'My eyes were delighted with her, the poet Charles Robinet exclaimed. 'Your new maid of honour is as sweet as she is beautiful... A girl of great intelligence'.

As the prospect of a good marriage faded Louise faced an uncertain future but just as the situation began to look desperate, fate stepped in and offered exciting new prospects. In July 1668, Charles II wrote to his sister the Duchess of Orleans that he desired to 'make a stricter alliance with (his cousin the King of) France than there has been hitherto'. Six months later he wrote again telling her of his desire to 'enter into a personal friendship with the king and unite our interests so far for the future as there may never be any jealousies between us'. The Duchess who acted as an intermediary between the two kings was finally ordered to travel to England in 1670, and under cover of a royal visit, ensure the treaty was signed and returned.

Louise accompanied her mistress to England, where her beauty made such an impression on Charles that he requested she remain in England, even offering to make her a member of the Queen's household. 'This is the jewel that I covet' he is alleged to have told her! The Duchess refused but on her death a short time after, Louise returned to England on the orders of Louis XIV in the hope that she would become Charles's mistress, and thereby would be able to spy for him. Charles II who loved all things French, asked the Duke of Buckingham, a childhood companion and cousin of his previous mistress Barbara Villiers, to travel to France and offer Louise the post of maid of honour to his wife Queen Catherine. Buckingham, however, left Louise stranded at the port of Dieppe, where she was rescued by the English Ambassador, Ralph Montagu, who arranged for the King's yacht to take her to Dover. 'Mademoiselle Keroualle hath bin at Dieppe these ten days' wrote the Ambassador 'and hears nothing of the yacht that the Duke of Buckingham, Mr Godolphin tells me, was to send for her'. Louise never forgot the slight.

Charles II was renowned for his voracious sexual appetite. At the age of fifteen he lost his virginity to his old nurse Mrs Christabella Wyndham, who in her youth had been 'a celebrated beauty'; Madame de Beauvais performed a similar service for Louis XIV. Upon his Restoration, Charles returned the honour by conducting an affair with Mrs Wyndham's daughter-in-law, Winifred, who remained his mistress on and off for a good number of years.

Although Louise successfully established herself as Charles's principal mistress, her position was always under threat from the likes of Nell Gwyn and to a lesser extent by Mary Davies, both successful actresses, whose charms had made a considerable impact on Charles and who provided him with ample proof of his intimacy with them by producing several children. The most serious rival was Nell Gwyn, because Charles could not resist her wit and charm. The situation is best summed up by Madame de Sevigne:

The Duchess could not forsee finding a young actress in her path by whom the King is bewitched... He shares his attentions, his time, and his health between them both... The actress is quite as proud as the Duchess of Portsmouth; she spites her, makes faces at her, assails her, and often carries the King off from her. She boasts of those points in which she is preferable, that she is young, silly, bold, debauched and agreeable; that she can sing, dance and play the part de bonne foi.

Of course, Louise was very different from Nell. She was French, Catholic, and born into an ancient family of great pride but little fortune. Whilst Queen Catherine was no threat to her, 'barren, ugly, squat and dull as she was', both Nell and Barbara were, if only because they had both provided the king with children.

Nell, who much enjoyed teasing Louise, also ridiculed her pride in her ancestry:

this Duchess acts the person of quality; she pretends that she is related to everyone in France. No sooner does any grandee die than she puts on mourning. Ah well! if she is such a great lady, why did she descend to become a catin? She ought to expire with shame; for myself it is my profession; I don't pique myself on anything else...

Before long Louise had her own finely furnished set of lodgings in Whitehall and Charles visited her every morning at 9 a.m., sometimes staying until 11 a.m.. For a long time she played 'hard to get' but eventually when staying at Euston in Suffolk, the home of the Dukes of Grafton, she finally succumbed to Charles's persistent declarations of love and she became his mistress. Almost nine months to the day, their son followed and titles and lands were showered upon her, from which she was able to draw an annual income of £10,000. But even then, she was not content with this, and she asked for and was granted the estate of d'Aubigny in France.

The birth of her son in 1672, seemed to set the seal on Louise's success, but unlike her predecessor the Duchess of Cleveland, she drew the line at producing a child every year. Indeed almost immediately after her son's birth, Charles began to visit one of his old mistresses, Moll (Mary) Davis and the result of this re-union was a daughter born the following year. To add insult to injury, Charles caught the pox and passed it on to Louise. The French Ambassador Ruvigny recorded the event and informed the French Foreign Minster:

> While the King [Louis XIV] was winning provinces, the King of England was catching a malady which he has been at the trouble of communicating to the Duchess of Portsmouth. That prince is nearly cured, but to all appearance the lady will not soon be rid of the virus.

The lesson was not lost on Charles and thereafter he did not sire any more illegitimate issue.

In 1673 the Duke of York, Charles's brother, wished to remarry but only made one stipulation, his intended must be beautiful! This irritated his brother Charles so much that he told him:

> The more or less of beauty that a wife has, contributes nothing to, and takes nothing from, the happiness of marriage, and in a week one gets so accustomed to her face that it neither pleases nor displeases one.

Sensing an opportunity to advance the interest of her friend the Duchess d'Elbeouf, Louise suggested the Duchess's fourteen year old daughter Marie Francoise as a suitable candidate. She even went so far as to obtain a portrait of the young lady. The French Ambassador, Colbert de Croissy, was furious as Louis XIV favoured the widow of the Duc de Guise, but James thought her ugly. Mademoiselle de Elbeouf was the great-grand daughter of Henri IV of France and his mistress Gabrielle d'Estrees, and a distant relative of Louise via the de Rieux family. A legitimate union between herself and the Royal House of Stuart would be a coup indeed, but fortune did not favour the project and the Duke married the Princess of Modena instead.

In 1676 after a number of years as the King's principal mistress, Louise suddenly found her position seriously threatened by the arrival of the celebrated beauty Hortense Mancini. 'She is the most beautiful woman

I have ever seen' declared the Comte de Gramont. Her arrival was engineered by the English Ambassador, Ralph Montagu, who rode out of London to greet her; a short while afterwards he performed a similar service for Charles's ex-mistress Barbara, Duchess of Cleveland when she left to settle in France. Before long the new French Ambassador, Honore de Courtin, was reporting back to his master the King of France:

> The arrival of the Duchess Mazarin has caused a great stir... The King of England appears to have been attracted by her beauty, and though the affair has so far been conducted with some secrecy, it is likely that this growing passion will take the first place in the heart of that prince.

Hortense's arrival and the Duchess of Cleveland's departure ushered in an incredible year for the King's mistresses present, past and future for in the early part of the year Louise suffered a miscarriage and to recover took the waters at Bath. This was followed by the news that the Duchess of Cleveland had taken as her lover, the Archbishop of Paris, twenty-five years her senior. Francois de Harlay de Champvallon, was the grandson of Jacques de Harlay de Champvallon, lover of Marguerite de Valois, the first wife of Henri IV. The Archbishop's family, although not an ancient one, was singularly favoured by Henri IV when he took as his mistresses two of the Archbishop's cousins, Charlotte de Essarts and Jacqueline de Bueil.

The noise that Barbara's affair caused in England and France was quite remarkable but it was trumped by Hortense when Charles discovered that the young Prince of Monaco had become infatuated with her! Charles, aggrieved and jealous that the young prince should even dare to approach her, and astonished that Hortense had not rejected his advances outright, responded by stopping payment of her pension. Antoine de Grimaldi was just sixteen years old and the son of the celebrated Princess de Monaco, who had briefly been the mistress of Louis XIV. Louise meanwhile had returned from taking the waters at Bath positively glowing with good health: 'Her skin has grown again so fair and fresh that I cannot imagine how Charles, palled as he is with beauty, will be long in her company without becoming once more her slave' exclaimed Courtin the French Ambassador. Hortense's brief ascendancy was over and Louise once more took her place as the King's principal mistress.

Meanwhile in France Madame de Montespan, a distant kinswoman of Louise, was facing a similar crisis in her relationship with Louis XIV. The King, who was now in his late thirties, suddenly indulged in a series of brief affairs, that caused his mistress great anguish and concern. Athenais de Rochechouart, whose exquisite beauty and wit had totally captivated the King eight years previously, took the only action available to her and promptly retired to take the waters at Bourbon. The King's sister-in-law, the Duchess of Orleans, described his predicament thus: 'Everything was grist to his mill, provided it was female: peasant girls, gardeners' daughters, chambermaids, ladies of quality, provided that they pretended that they were in love with him'. In rapid succession he bedded Madamoiselle de Grancey, the Princess de Wurtemburg, Madamoiselle des Oeillets, Madame de Ludres and even Madame de Montespan's own nieces, the Duchesses of Nevers and de Sforce! But it was only a temporary setback for the reigning mistress, for on her return, Athenais appeared more radiantly beautiful than ever and when he was informed of her arrival, Louis ran to meet her.

Louise's reign as Charles's principal mistress lasted for fourteen years, which was an incredible achievement, despite being punctuated by many other liaisons, quite apart from acting as the eyes and ears of Louis XIV. However, Louise almost lost her power and influence when she allowed herself to be compromised over her association with a notorious womaniser the Chevalier de Vendome, also known as the 'Grand Prior'. The Chevalier, a relative of Louise and the grandson of Henri IV by his mistress Gabrielle de Estrees, had a reputation as an evil, depraved and dissolute man. The diarist St Simon described him as a 'lair, swindler, thief, frivoller' and a 'dishonest man, even to the marrow of his bones'. He was also the nephew of Hortense Mancini, Louise's former rival, and by a very curious twist of events she quickly fell in love with him! His royal connections were an obvious attraction but his charm and courtly graces were such than within a short time there were stolen meetings in her private apartments and secret letters passing between them. However, it was not long before Charles was informed of the situation and ordered the Chevalier to depart the kingdom and never return. Charles who blamed the Chevalier and not Louise, sought to make amends by asking the French King to grant her the title of Duchess d'Aubigny and the right to sit on a *tabouret* before the Queen of France.

Sadly Louise did not learn from her mistake. After she returned to France on the death of Charles in 1685, she became involved with the celebrated Duc d'Elbeouf, another descendant of Henri IV and his mistress Gabrielle. Henri de Lorraine, was much younger than Louise with a reputation as bad as the Chevalier de Vendome, 'A liar, a cheat abounded to vice' who (according to St Simon) 'spent his youth as a scourge to every family through his lewd behaviour to women and his frequent boast of favours he had not received'.

HORTENSE MANCINI

She was not French but Italian and when she was eleven years old a fortune teller told her: 'Your husband will be very rich, and he will adore you, but you will not love him and 'You will have many lovers and a happy life'. And so it came to pass.

Hortense Mancini was born in Rome, the niece of Cardinal Mazarin, chief minister of Louis XIV during his minority. She came to France at the age of six with her sister Marie, brother Philippe and mother Hieronyma and was immediately lodged in an apartment at the Louvre; Hortense's elder sister Olympe had arrived with her brother Paul six years earlier in 1647. On her arrival Hortense acquired her first admirer, Philippe, Duc d'Anjou, Louis XIV's thirteen year old younger brother, who became passionately attached to her and would not let her out of his sight.

At first it was Olympe a 'brunette with a long face and pointed chin; small but (with) sparkling eyes', according to Madame de Motteville, who made the greatest impression on the french court – she was intensely disliked by her mother who very early on recognised her disagreeable and selfish nature – but eventually it would be Marie and Hortense, both dark beauties, who made the most lasting impact. All three achieved the distinction of being loved by a king. Olympe and Marie by Louis XIV and Hortense by Charles II; Philippe their younger brother allegedly practised the 'italian vice' and achieved the dubious distinction of being the first to corrupt the young Duc d'Anjou. Philippe, created Duc de Nevers by his uncle the cardinal, went on to marry Madame de Montespan's niece and when 'Le Montespan's' reign as royal mistress was over she encouraged her royal lover to take Philippe's wife as his mistress whilst he turned a blind eye to the whole proceedings.

Diane Gabrielle de Thianges inherited the famous Mortemart beauty and wit in full measure. 'Few women' exclaimed St Simon 'have surpassed her in beauty. Hers was of every kind, with a singularity which charmed' and even when she died at the age of sixty she was 'still perfectly beautiful'. But the Duchess did not succeed in her endeavour to become Louis's mistress and for consolation turned her attention to Louis's cousin the Prince de Conde, commonly known as Monsieur Le Duc. The latter son of 'La Grand Conde', the victor of Rocroi, was desperately enamoured of her and had been much addicted to gallantry since his youth. Despite his small stature 'which resembled a gnome rather than a man' he was very successful in his love affairs. To his mistresses he was gallantry personified but to his wife, a cousin of Charles II, he was a tyrant.

Once his nieces were established in France the Cardinal busily set about arranging splendid marriages for them to prominent members of the French aristocracy. Laura married the Duc de Vendome, Anna-Maria, the daughter of the Cardinal's sister Margharita Martinozzi, married the Prince de Conti, Olympe, the Comte de Soissons and Marie, the italian Prince Colonna. Despite her disagreeable nature – 'wilful and obstinate' was the Cardinal's verdict – Olympe became a great favourite of the young Louis XIV and it was not long before the Cardinal realised that she must be quickly married in order to protect her good name. The candidate for her hand in marriage Prince Eugene de Savoy-Carignan, was a member of the House of Savoy and an excellent choice 'an honest man' according to Madame de Motteville 'and, above all, a good husband'.

After her marriage Louis visited the Hotel de Soissons, Olympe's Parisian town house, every day:

> 'It was into this important and brilliant whirlpool' said St Simon 'that the King first of all threw himself and where he acquired that air of politness and gallantry that he has maintained all his life, and which he has learnt so well to combine with propriety and majesty. The intrigues and adventures which, King though he was, he became involved in at the Comte de Soissons whirlpool left very baneful impressions on his mind'.

At the birth of her first child Louis stood as godfather but within a year he had fallen in love, much to the annoyance of Olympe, with Marie, her younger sister. Louis's feelings for Marie were much more intense and for the first time in his life he was genuinely in love.

Madame Mancini did not love her eldest daughter 'She has an evil nature' she declared 'My husband, who was a famous astrologer, said that she would cause great misfortune'. On her deathbed she requested that the Cardinal put her in a convent. Within a short time Louis was addressing Marie as 'My Queen' and together they read plays and novels. 'They were like two lovers in a romance' declared Le Grand Mademoiselle. But it did not last because the Cardinal and Queen Mother had other plans for Louis who, despite declaring to the Cardinal that he wished to marry Marie, was forced marry the Spanish Infanta.

Whilst Louis was pursuing Marie, Olympe had taken a new lover the Marquis de Vardes, the son of one of Henri IV's mistresses. Francois Rene du Bec, was a fascinating scoundrel, good looking, brave, an accomplished gallant, whose amours were legion. The affair lasted a number of years during which Vardes also attempted to gain the affections of Henrietta, Duchess d'Orleans, the sister of Charles II. After a short spell in the Bastille for refusing to marry Louise de la Valliere, Louis's mistress, and making disparaging remarks about the Duchess of Orleans, Vardes was exiled to Montpellier for twenty years and replaced in Olympe's affections by the Marquis de Villeroy and he in turn by numerous others. Villeroy, who became one of Louis's best friends, went on to win many victories for France against the King's enemies.

Hortense arrived in Paris in 1653, a year later Charles II left for Germany with a modest train of gentlemen and servants and the promise from Cardinal Mazarin that he would pay his debts and expenses for his journey. They never met and it would be another twenty-two years before their paths crossed again. Charles had been a pensioner of France since his arrival in 1646 except for a brief period when he left for Scotland to try and win back his kingdoms. But now the Cardinal was forced to bow to pressure from the new ruler of England, Oliver Cromwell and request that Charles should leave France forever. Before leaving he asked his current mistress the Duchess de Châtillon to marry him but her concern over matters of court precedence should she become his wife delayed matters so much that he did not pursue it further. He left with 'a very ill opinion of both men and women, and did not think that there was either sincerity or chastity in the world'.

Meanwhile Hortense continued her education in Paris and grew to be an exceptionally beautiful and alluring young woman. Reports of her beauty spread far and wide and when the Cardinal sought a husband for her elder sisters, Olympe and Marie, the candidate he chose refused to wed either but on seeing Hortense exclaimed 'If I might marry her, I would not care if I died three months later'. At the time Hortense was only nine years old! Several years later when she was only twelve years old, Charles sent word to the Cardinal that he wished to marry Hortense but his proposal was rejected out of hand the Cardinal declaring 'he does me too much honour, for as long as the King's cousin remains unmarried he must not think of my nieces'. To another of Charles's courtiers the Cardinal declared 'I can do nothing for His Majesty'. Hortense knew nothing of the proposal until after the Restoration.

When Hortense finally married in 1661, just a few months short of her fifteenth birthday, it was to her original suitor the only son of the extremely wealthy Duc de la Meilleraye. They were married in the Cardinal's private chapel and ten days later he died and she inherited a sizeable fortune of twenty-eight million livres plus the Palais Mazarin! Shortly after her marriage Louis began to frequent the Palais Mazarin informally on his own and on other occasions with his mother and wife. But his visits soon aroused the jealousy of her husband and Louis also found that he had competition in the form of the Chevalier de Rohan who was a great admirer of Hortense. Louis was drawn to parties at the Palais as they out shone anything that Olympe had provided at the Hotel Soissons. In addition Hortense was extremely amusing and very outspoken a trait that Louis professed to abhor but secretly admired especially in a woman. 'I should have died if she had said that to me' he once said after overhearing one of her conversations with an old admirer.

Everyone believed that Louis and Hortense were lovers but Madame de lafayette's shrewd assessment of the situation was much more accurate and to the point 'Her beauty' she remarked 'together with the advantage of a husband in no sense lovable... might easily have involved [Louis and Hortense] in a passion, had not Monsieur Mazarin... removed his wife from the King's proximity'. Louis had now shown extraordinary favour to three of the Cardinal's nieces but none of the relationships had lasted. It was now time to move on and he did so but his choice surprised everyone for it was none other than his sister-in-law, Henrietta, Duchess of Orleans. To divert attention from the object of his desire he courted one of her maids of honour Louise de la Valliere and the rest is history.

During the course of their marriage it became evident to Hortense that her husband was paranoid and deranged and after many years of persecution and harassment and after bearing him four children, three daughters and a son, she deserted him. Such an action was fraught with dangers. Many years later Hortense fully recognised the seriousness of her situation when she declared to her companion St Evremond 'a wife ought not to leave her husband'. In her defence Mme de Sevigne wrote 'one recognizes that she is justified, when one sees Monsieur Mazarin'. Retention of her vast fortune which had been dissipated by her husband over the years was not an issue but the stigma of leaving her husband and abandoning her children would effectively ensure that she was shunned by aristocratic society. That she determined to take such action was proof of the seriousness of her situation and news of it soon reached the Courts of Europe. 'The suddene retreat of Madame Mazarin' declared Charles II 'is as extraordinaire an action as I have heard. She has exceeded Lady Shrewsbury in point of discretion by robbing her husband 'adding with a final word of admiration 'I wish her a good journey'.

The Chevalier de Rohan, and old admirer, his page Couberville and her brother Philippe accompanied Hortense on her flight from France to Italy. During the proceedings she took a violent fancy to de Rohan's page and the result was a child that was born in Italy and then put out to nurse; news of the event caused a sensation in France. Six months after the child's birth she returned to France with her brother to celebrate his forthcoming marriage to Madame de Montespan's niece. Louis promised her a pension of 24,000 livres a year if she wished to return to Rome and without a moment's hesitation she accepted. However, on her arrival she discovered that her sister Marie wished to leave her husband Prince Colonna! The Prince, tired of her love affairs with the Chevalier de Lorraine, the favourite of the Duc d'Orleans, and the Duke of Brunswick-Lunenburg (the father of George I) whilst on a visit to Italy, had a reputation for poisoning his enemies. Unable to persuade her to remain Hortense accompanied her but when they arrived at Marseilles they parted and she set off for Savoy where the Duke, another old admirer, had offered her sanctuary.

Hortense remained in Savoy, as the Duke's guest, for three years much to the annoyance and chagrin of his wife a 'beautiful, fascinating and intelligent but dissolute and unscrupulous woman' who was prone to gallantries of her own as befitted a great-granddaughter of Henri IV and Gabrielle de Estrees. There is no evidence that Hortense ever became the Duke's mistress but on his sudden death in 1675 of a heart attack, she was promptly asked to leave the country by his widow.

Whilst she was in Savoy Hortense's activities were closely watched by a small political faction in England headed by George, Duke of Buckingham and Ralph Montagu, formerly England's Ambassador to France. The reason for their interest was obvious, they wished to oust their monarch's present mistress the French born Duchess of Portsmouth and replace her with a new mistress who would be more amenable to their designs and who better than Hortense. Montagu on a brief visit to Savoy encouraged Hortense to make her way to England and settle there. When she finally made up her mind to do so she used the excuse of wanting to visit her cousin, the new Duchess of York. Countess Pratoneri a member of the Duchess's household wrote to the Duke of Modena 'I believe we shall shortly have the Duchess of Mazarin in England, which is very displeasing to their Royal Highnesses, but it is impossible to prevent... She will come'.

Her arrival in London in breeches and boots was dramatic and Montagu arranged for a house to be taken for her in Covent Garden Piazza. Within a short time she was meeting Charles two or three times a week at the Duchess of York's apartments in St James's Palace. The woman that Charles had wanted to marry for a share of the Cardinal's fortune now stood before him not as a supplicant in search of a pension but as a beautiful and fascinating woman in her own right. 'She is very beautiful' he declared 'and I would rather talk with her than with any other. But I will not allow myself to be won over' he exclaimed. She did not ask for a pension but he gave her an allowance of £4,000 per annum and thus at one stroke solved her present financial problems. When the King of France refused to interfere in her efforts to regain her fortune Charles took up her cause. 'It seems to me' remarked the French Ambassador 'that the King of England takes the interest of this lady more to heart than he did... And that he may well become passionately attached to her'.

Indeed he did. Parties were arranged at Whitehall and he visited her every night only returning in the small hours of the morning. The Duchess of Portsmouth was beside herself with anxiety and grief at the thought of her beautiful rival. 'You must get her back at all costs' the French Ambassador wrote frantically to Louis 'She is dangerous to France, because of her beauty and her resentment toward Your Majesty'.

Within a year of her arrival in England Hortense had acquired another admirer the young Prince of Monaco. Antonio Grimaldi was the eldest son of Luigi, Prince of Monaco and his wife the beautiful Elizabeth Charlotte de Gramont, who had briefly captured the attention of Louis XIV. Despite his youth, he was only fifteen years old, he fell passionately in love with her and her part Hortense was equally smitten by the young man but the affair resulted in the loss of her pension. Charles was not about to be cuckolded by anyone least of all a young foreign prince.

But Hortense's personality and beauty also attracted members of her own sex. Shortly after her arrival she befriended Lady Sussex, Charles's bastard daughter by the Duchess of Cleveland, who was then heavily pregnant with her first child and often in ill health. Charles who was very fond of his daughter was delighted when Hortense took an interest in her health:

> 'The King' declared the French Ambassador 'goes nearly every day to visit Madame de Sussex, whom Madame de Mazarin is nursing. I happened to be there the day before yesterday when he came. As soon as he came Madame Mazarin went and whispered to him with a great air of familiarity, and she kept it up all the time the conversation was general, and never called him Your Majesty once... I remain convinced that it is not without foundation that the most enlightened courtiers believe that the King their master desires to profit by his opportunities'.

Even Montagu, who had suggested that she come to England, fell in love with her:

> 'Monsieur de Montagu, who had a mind to arrange an affair between the King and Madame Mazarin, has himself fallen into her toils, and malicious tongues say that he is being unfaithful to the ravishing Madame Middleton with whom he has been in love with for a long time', declared the Ambassador.

Meanwhile in France, Hortense's children and their cousins, Olympe's children, were giving cause for concern. Luigi Tommaso, Olympe's eldest son, 'a pleasure-loving spendthrift' scandalised the whole family by falling in love and marrying the daughter of one of the Prince de Conde's equerries, for which 'mesalliance' he was promptly disinherited by his mother and grandmother. But his mistake was nothing in comparison to his sisters, Madamoiselles de Carignan and Soissons. 'Their conduct for a long time was so indiscreet and their debauchery so scandalous the M de Savoie could no longer tolerate what he heard of them', with the result that Madamoiselle de Carignan was arrested and placed in a convent and her sister exiled to Brussels, where the Elector of Bavaria also placed her in a convent. But it was the second son, the Chevalier de Savoie who scandalised the whole of Europe.

This young man, who was just twenty-four years old when he came to London in 1683, fell passionately in love with his aunt Hortense and promptly challenged her latest lover Baron de Banier – a Swedish nobleman – to a duel and killed him! Hortense was grief stricken and Philippe was hurried out of the country in order to avoid further scandal. Her life seemed to be filled with great tragedy of which this was only the latest example. In the same year her eldest daughter Marie Charlotte ran away from her convent with the Duc d'Aiguillon, came to London and bore him a child. The marriage did not last and on her return to France she became the mistress of the Prince de Conde who, according to Saint Simon, 'spent millions upon her' only to discover that she was betraying him for the Comte de Roucy.

Only Prince Eugene, Olympe's youngest son, made a mark in the world. He was originally intended for the church but preferred the military life, 'his nose spoils his face' and 'he is always dirty and has lanky hair which he never curls' declared the Duchess of Orleans. When his mother fled France in 1680 he was put under the care of his grandmother the Princess de Carignan but even in his youth he preferred the company of his own sex. When Louis XIV refused his request for a commission in the French Army, he fled to Vienna and offered his sword to the Emperor and the rest is history.

But it was the sons of Laura, Duchess of Vendome, Hortense's elder sister who made the biggest noise in the world. The eldest Louis-Joseph was a gifted and brave general who believed that he 'derived his talents from a more distant source' i.e. from his great-grandfather Henri IV and his mistress Gabrielle de Estrees. Louis XIV had an enormous regard for his grandfather Henri IV and thought that by elevating Vendome it would help in his efforts to promote his own bastards, the Duc de Maine and Comte de Toulouse.

Unfortunately, however, Vendome's great military gifts were accompanied by many grave defects of character all of which were duly recorded in great detail by the diarist Saint Simon. 'The King' exclaimed

Saint Simon 'tolerated in M de Vendome what he never would have pardoned in a Son of France'. He practiced the 'Italian vice', a trait he shared with his uncle the Duc de Nevers, and was shamelessly immoral, overbearing, with a ravenous pride. He was also intolerably insolent towards the legitimate princes but 'willing to treat all other persons as equals'. His younger brother Philippe (the lover of the Duchess of Portsmouth) was famous for his amorous escapades and according to Voltaire 'These two princes, neglected their persons to a degree of which the lowest of men would have been ashamed'.

Nevertheless Saint Simon had to admit that he did have some redeeming qualities: 'He had a very noble countenance and a distinguished bearing. He was naturally graceful in his movements and in his speech, possessed much innate wit, which he never cultivated; spoke easily, supported by a natural boldness; knew the world and the Court and was above all an admirable courtier'.

Despite Montagu's and Buckingham's hope that Hortense would completely supplant the Duchess of Portsmouth as Charles's mistress, this never happened. Hortense's own temperament and endless string of affairs, so reminiscent of the Duchess of Cleveland, ensured that she never became Charles's sole mistress. She had to share his bounty with Portsmouth and Nell Gwyn but it did not worry her in the least!

When death finally came to Hortense it was sudden and mercifully painless. To the very end she retained her beauty and vitality. 'Everybody from England speaks of the Duchess of Mazarin's beauty' declared Ninon de l'Enclos in 1699 'just as they talk of Mademoiselle de Bellefonds (Hortense's grand-daughter) which is now in the bud'. The legacy she left her family was not one of tangible riches but a free spirit that continued to manifest itself in her children and descendants over many generations.

The tradition of supplying a mistress for the royal bed also persisted. In addition to her daughter Marie Charlotte, who became the mistress of Henri Jules, Prince de Conde, her granddaughter Armande became the mistress of the Prince's son and successor Louis Henri, who for a brief period was Regent of France during the minority of Louis XV. But the most spectacular example was the three daughters of Armande, Louise

Julie, Pauline Felicite and Marie Anne each of whom in turn became the mistress of Louis XV!

Shocking as the details of her life may appear it is well to remember that Hortense's desertion of her husband and abandonment of her children was the act of a desperate woman. Contemporary attitudes on how a wife should behave in seventeenth century France centred around the image of the docile wife and the overwhelming ideology of her subordination in both elite and popular culture.

Unfortunately however, her husband's jealousy and eccentric and potentially life threatening behaviour over the years forced Hortense to act otherwise and expose herself to enormous adverse ridicule and shame and the near certainty of severe financial hardship because he had total control over her property and income. In addition she was denied any contact with her children. That she was willing to submit to all three is testimony to her desperate situation and the legal bias in favour of her husband's rights as opposed to her own.

Having said all of the above, it is doubtful if Hortense's amoral character would have been satisfied within the bounds of matrimony and thus it was inevitable that she would look to the role of royal mistress as being a way out of her financial difficulties. In many ways she was her own worst enemy who brought many of her woes upon herself.

4

THE HANOVERIAN PERIOD

The Guelphs & Fitzroys

With the death of Queen Anne in 1714 and the accession of George, Elector of Hanover to the kingdom of Great Britain the coveted role of *mistress en titre* became virtually obsolete until it acquired a new lease of life under George IV. However, it did enjoy a brief blaze of glory before doing so under George I who despite being portrayed as a dour and humourless character did seek amusement and relaxation outside of marriage with a variety of mistresses but remained devoted to just one, the Duchess of Kendal.

The prince acquired his first mistress, Marie Catherine Leonore von Meysenburg-Zuschen, at the age of seventeen. Marie was five years his senior and the younger sister of Clara Elisabeth von Meysenburg-Zuschen, his father's mistress. The von Meysenburgs were of undistinguished ancestry but George Philip von Meysenburg-Zuschen, the father of the two girls, had ambitions to find good marriages for them in France. Unfortunately he was unsuccessful but during their visit his daughters acquired enough of French culture to become celebrities on their return to the Court of Hanover.

During their visit to France Louis XIV was in the early years of his 'Grande Passion' for Madame de Montespan and it would not be stretching the imagination too far to speculate that the two sisters were greatly influenced by her example. Ernst August, the future Elector, was clearly smitten by Clara's freshness, gaiety and newly acquired Parisian style of dress and speech. If they could not find husbands then they would have to make their mark in the world by other means. The route they chose was not for the faint hearted and the role of royal mistress was fraught with dangers but sensing that here was an opportunity not to be missed Clara quickly captured the heart of Ernst August and also acquired a husband in to the bargain, Baron von Platen! The scene was now set for the long reign of 'La Belle von Meysenburg' as 'Mistress en Titre' until the Ernst Augusts' death twenty-five years later. But it was not long before she acquired a unsavoury reputation as 'One of the worst harpies the world has ever known' with 'no redeeming qualities ... unscrupulous, ambitious and shamelessly corrupt'.

Clara was not the Elector's first mistress, that honour appears to have gone to the Marchesa Paleotti, by whom he allegedly had a son. She was followed by the Princess Colonna, Marie Mancini, Louis XIV's first love. The affairs took place during his numerous visits to Italy prior to 1664. Maria Cristina Paleotti, was the great-granddaughter of Robert Dudley, lover and favourite of Elizabeth I and at the time of her affair with Ernst August she was a young bride of sixteen. Prior to her marriage she had scandalised Roman society by allowing herself to be seduced by the Prince Colonna; the result was a bastard daughter. Such was her reputation that when the Marchese Paleotti, a nobleman of undistinguished ancestry, asked for her hand in marriage her father Carlo Dudley, self styled Duca di Northumbria gladly accepted the offer.

Marchese Paleotti was a widower of only a few months, whose first wife was murdered, along with her father, by order of a certain Count Suzzi, who suspected the Marchese of being in love with his wife. The Marchesa Maria Cristina a learned and quick witted woman and a great beauty was passionately interested in music and poetry. A couplet composed in 1665 describes her thus: 'A face of beauty, and a breast of snow, wit on her lips, her cheeks with health aglow'. She had large blue eyes, splendid black hair, and something childlike and angelic in her personality, which, at forty years of age, caused her to be taken for the sister of her daughters. Her exploits never ceased to fill Italy with the noise of her name – to such a degree that, to this day, she is often cited as one of the most astonishing 'aventurieres' of the seicento a period which had the privilege of being richer than any other in adventurers of both sexes.

The Princess Colonna, a sister of Hortense Mancini, once sought as a bride for Charles II was abandoned by her first love Louis XIV and subsequently made an arranged marriage with the Prince Colonna, head of one of Rome's most aristocratic families. The marriage was an unhappy one, which produced three children, one of whom was alleged to have been by Ernst August. To combat her husband's neglect and the tedium of her situation the princess ran up huge gambling debts and took lovers, but like her sister Hortense, she eventually abandoned her husband and children and fled back to France only returning to Italy after her husband's death.

As a seemingly respectable married woman Clara von Meysenburg was now able to conduct her affair with Ernst August with impunity and within several years had given birth to a son and daughter, both of whom were almost certainly her lover's children; in recognition of her birth the daughter was granted the Arms of the House of Brunswick with a baton sinister. Maria Catherine meanwhile had also found a husband, Johann, von dem Bussche zu Ippenburg, an Officer in the Hanoverian Army, whose brother was Governor of George Ludwig, later George I; several children were born of the marriage including two daughters and a son and it is quite possible in view of her affair with George Ludwig that he might have been the father of the two daughters, the son married George I's bastard daughter.

George Ludwig's affair seems to have come to an end shortly before he married his cousin Sophia Dorothea in 1682 and thereafter until he took Ermengarde von der Schulenburg as his mistress in 1691, he remained a faithful husband. But disaster was about to strike the Electoral household and within a short time Sophia Dorothea in retaliation for her husband's infidelity took a lover Count Philip von Konigsmark. It was a very dangerous move on the princess's part which eventually led to her lover's death.

Konigsmarck 'a reckless patrician, a dandy, a rake, a gallant comrade, accomplished courtier and fortune's favourite' arrived in Hanover in early 1688 and served as a volunteer in the Elector's army until May 1689 when he became a commissioned officer. He very quickly became a firm friend of George Ludwig, Sophia Dorothea's husband. But it was the Countess von Platen (*nee* Clara von Meysenburg) who first engaged his interest and within a short time of his arrival they are alleged to have become lovers. However, the truth was probably much more simple. Konigsmarck may simply have presented himself to the Elector's mistress as a matter of course as no doubt any foreign ambassador would have done when he first arrived at the Electoral court.

Whatever the truth Konigsmarck soon found that the Elector's daughter-in-law was much more to his taste. The Konigsmarck family's reputation for gallantry was well known. Indeed his brother Charles had been involved in a great scandal during a visit to England in the early sixteen eighties when he was tried for the attempted murder of Thomas Thynne, his rival in the affections of Lady Ogle whom he wished to marry. Aurora, their younger sister, a famous beauty, defied convention by remaining unmarried before becoming the mistress of Augustus the Strong, Elector of Saxony and mother of the famous Marshal Saxe, one of France's greatest military commanders.

As a close friend of George Ludwig, Konigsmarck was often in the Princess's company and during that time was able to exercise his famous charm and from the outset it was obvious that she was quite smitten by the dashing guards officer. In time Konigsmarck began to correspond with her but initially she did not respond although she eventually relented. Her decision to act thus was in retaliation to her husband's public display of his regard for his mother's new maid of honour Ermegarde Melusine von Schulenburg. Unfortunately Sophia Dorothea's portrayal of the injured wife irritated the Electress Sophia who had endured her own husband's infidelities for over thirty years.

Within a short time George Ludwig's 'Grande Passion' for Ermengarde produced a child; she would eventually bear two more daughters, thus bringing George's total of bastard children to five. Ermengarde was the daughter of Gustaf Adolf, Baron von der Schulenburg and came from a well connected noble family but she never married. She was not a great beauty but was 'kind, well educated, intelligent and shrewd' and above all discreet. Sophia's views on her son's conquest were very explicit 'Do you see that mawkin?' 'You would scarcely believe that she has captivated my son'. Her predecessor the Countess von dem Busshe meanwhile had lost her position as George Ludwig's mistress some years previous and afterwards had returned to her husband by whom she had two further children.

Meanwhile Sophia Dorothea was falling head over heels in love with Konigsmarck and her letters to him reveal what an unhappy young woman she was. As her passion grew she began to sacrifice all prudence. Konigsmarck on his part was relentless in scolding the timid young woman and perpetually insisting on a meeting and declaring that he will kill himself if she persisted in refusing to receive him.

Sophia Dorothea, although intimidated by Konigsmarck's tactics was touched by his alleged sufferings and exhorted him to marry, undertaking to find him a wife. 'I will marry if you order me to' he answered 'but on condition that you swear to me on your oath that you will always cherish the affection you have seemed to show me. I am starting for the Morea' he continues' and I hope I shall never come back.' Then he adds: 'When wilt thou have pity on me. When shall I overcome thy coldness? Wilt thou ever keep from me the rapture of tasting perfect joy. I seek it in thy arms, and if I may not taste it there I care for naught else. No! if I may not be happy with you I will not be happy at all.' Alarmed, Sophia Dorothea implored him not to rush to his death. To which he answers: 'Since you ask me to stay, I will do so with joy. My greatest happiness is to pay you my court... Courage, Madame; see me for once — no more — half a quarter of an hour.' Eventually he received the final favour. 'Last night,' he writes on 9 November 1692, 'makes me the happiest and the most satisfied man in the world. Your kisses showed me your tenderness, and I could not doubt your love.' From there onwards her fate was sealed.

George Ludwig's reaction to his wife's infidelity was swift. Konigsmarck disappeared on the night of 15 July 1694 and was never seen again, presumed murdered. George and Sophia Dorothea were then officially divorced and she was forced to spend the rest of her days in confinement at Ahlden.

When George Ludwig became King of Great Britain in 1714, he arrived in the country with him his mistress Ermengarde and their three bastard daughters who were immediately installed in St James's Palace.

He was quickly followed by his bastard half sister Sophia Charlotte and her children, her husband having arrived with George.

In 1716 Ermengarde was created Duchess of Munster, in Ireland and three years later Duchess of Kendal in England whilst Sophia Charlotte had to wait until 1721 before being created Countess of Leinster in Ireland and then the following year Countess of Darlington in England. Unsatisfied with these honours both ladies also sought foreign titles from the Emperor Charles VI; Ermengarde was made Princess of Eberstein in 1722 whilst Sophia Charlotte became Countess von Kielmansegg in 1723.

The Duchess of Kendal did not enjoy a trouble free reign as *mistress en titre*, there were rumours that whilst in Hanover George I had seduced the wife of Count von Platen, who was possibly his bastard half brother. The lady in question Sophia Carolina Eva Antoinetta von Offelin, had married Ernst August, Count von Platen in 1697 and bore him several children before separating from her husband prior to the accession of George I. Her last child Frederica Louise was born in 1713 and the ten year gap between this child and her previous child has given rise to the rumour that George I was her father. However, the Electress Sophia always denied that the Countess was her son's mistress.

Shortly before his death in 1727, George I is also alleged to have taken an English mistress viz: Anna Maria Brett. The source for this rumour was Lady Suffolk, mistress of George II, who recounted the story to Horace Walpole during one of the many visits to her home. Miss Brett was according to Walpole 'very handsome, but dark enough by her eyes and complexion and hair for a Spanish beauty' and was 'lodged in the palace under the eyes of Bathsheba' his name for the Duchess of Kendal. The affair appears to have begun shortly after George received news of the death of his wife Sophia Dorothea in 1726.

Miss Brett was the daughter of Lieutenant-Colonel Henry Brett by his wife Anne, Dowager Lady Macclesfield, the daughter of Sir Richard Mason. In view of her mother's reputation, she had previously been the mistress of Henry Fitz Roy, 1st Duke of Grafton (bastard son of Charles II and Barbara Villiers) and Richard Savage, Earl Rivers (cousin of Catherine Sedley, Countess of Dorchester, mistress of James II), by whom she had two bastard children, it is not surprising that the daughter should follow her mother's example, the only difference being that the daughter remained unmarried during her affair. Miss Brett's reward for her brief reign was two annuities totalling £900 for the remainder of her life.

With the sudden death of George I in 1727 and the accession of his son and heir George II, a new era of royal mistresses was ushered in. George II's principal mistresses were Henrietta, Lady Suffolk, Mary, Dowager Countess of Deloraine; described by Lord Hervey as 'one of the vainest as well as one of the simplest women that ever lived' with 'one of the prettiest faces ever formed' and Amalia Sophia von Wendt, Countess of Yarmouth. Lady Suffolk and Lady Deloraine belonged to the powerful Howard clan that had supplied royal mistresses to Britain's Monarchs over many generations and the Countess of Yarmouth, was the grand daughter of George I's first mistress Marie Catherine Leonore von Meysenburg.

The characters of the three women were very different. Whilst Lady Suffolk was loyal, discreet and won universal admiration for her patience in the face of much abuse by her royal lover, Lady Deloraine was a woman of spirit who was not afraid to embarrass and humiliate the King if the occasion demanded it. Indeed her impulsive nature would eventually prove her ruin when one evening in 1742 she pulled the King's chair from beneath him as he went to sit down. Whilst being amused at Lady Deloraine's misfortune when she had been subjected to the same jest he did not find it so funny when Lady Deloraine returned the favour. As a result Horace Walpole records, 'the monarch... was so hurt and so angry that the Countess is disgraced and her German rival remains in sole and quite possession'. Lady Yarmouth on the other hand was more devious and clever and had had lovers before the King with others during her reign as *mistress en titre*.

Thus the tradition of certain families supplying our monarchs with mistresses continued. But it would be the Royal Princesses of the Guelph family over the next few generations who would provide the surprises in this continuing story. The first of these Princess Amelia, the daughter of George II and his wife Caroline of Brandenburg-Anspach, was born in 1711, therefore just sixteen years old when her father became King. She was a witty and personable young lady and when plans for her marriage to her cousin Frederick the Great came to naught, she resigned herself to a life time of celibacy but fate decreed that although she would be denied a husband, she would not lack admirers. The first of these was the Duke of Grafton, her father's Lord Chamberlain. As the grand daughter of the ill fated Sophia Dorothea the princess's actions were perfectly understandable but thankfully neither the princess or the Duke allowed themselves to make the same mistake of having a full sexual relationship! Nevertheless Amelia resembled her grandmother in many ways and was described by one contemporary as, 'charming, with a winning smile that few could resist, and an engaging manner that heightened her not inconsiderable beauty'.

Charles Fitz Roy, 2nd Duke of Grafton, the grandson of Charles II and Barbara Villiers, was old enough to be the princess's father. Well past middle age, plump and portly he nevertheless managed to captivate the princess with the hereditary Stuart charm and whilst paying court to Amelia also paid court to Lady Burlington, Lady of the Bedchamber to Queen Caroline, who also became infatuated by him! Lady Burlington, a descendant of Mary Carey, mistress of Henry VIII, was extremely jealous and followed the duke everywhere. All the ladies of the court found him uncommonly attractive but only Amelia shared his passion for the hunt and twice sometimes three times a week they would join the chase often outdistancing the other courtiers in order to meet at a secret rendezvous. On one occasion at Windsor they failed to re-appear and on their return after dusk explained that they were forced to take refuge in a private house in Windsor Forest. The Queen, understandably, was extremely angry but was prevented from reporting the incident to the King by Sir Robert Walpole the jealousy of Lady Burlington prevented them from meeting more often.

The skill that the Duke displayed in avoiding any direct confrontations between his two loves was truly remarkable but he did find Lady Burlington's attentions rather tiresome. Indeed it is alleged that Lady Burlington once cried over him in public and regulated her life so that she could be near him as much as possible. The Earl of Winchelsea, Lady Burlington's uncle was very pointed in his disapproval of her conduct: 'Besides his debts and difficulties, he (Lord Burlington) has the incumbrance of a wife, my niece, the wickedest, mischievous jade upon earth. I can easily pardon the lady her coqueting and her intriguing… But lying and making mischief, abusing everybody, imposing upon her husband and exposing him only to show her power, does deserve some correction and some wholesale severity, such as sending a lady down into the country'.

Lord Hervey was much more direct in his disapproval 'My Lady… choosing rather to mortify her pride than her inclination, and, sacrificing the great lady to the woman, consulted her heart and not her character, her lover and not her husband, in this difficulty; and while she laudably in reality gave up everything to her passion, she seemed so meanly to have considered only per pin-money and her interest. It was plain from hence how differently the Steward's staff operated on the husband from the effect the Chamberlain's staff had on the wife; for as his Lordship's affection to the one was the occasion of his quitting the Court, my Lady's attachment to the other was the reason of her remaining there'.

The affair did not end there as Lady Burlington's daughter a creature 'of the softest temper, vast beauty, birth and fortune' conceived as overwhelming a passion for the Duke's son Lord Euston, as her mother had done for the Duke many years before and in a wild moment married him. Unfortunately, however, she was dead six months later the victim of her husband's 'extreme brutality the details of which are almost too revolting to be believed', according to a contemporary.

The Princess Amelia arrived from Hanover in 1715 at the age of seven, with her grandfather George I and parents George Louis, the Electoral Prince and his wife Caroline. Freidrich Louis, Amelia's eldest brother remainder in Hanover and did not arrive until 1728, after the death of his grandfather. At the time of her arrival Ermengarde Melusine von Schulenburg was her grandfather's *mistress en titre*. In an attempt to emulate his father George Louis took an English mistress, Mrs Howard (later Countess of Suffolk) who retained that position until she retired from Court in 1734; she was followed by the widowed Countess of Deloraine, who was Governess to the Princesses Louisa and Mary, sisters of Princess Amelia.

Several years prior to Lady Deloraine becoming George II's mistress, her cousin the Honorable Anne Vane, daughter of Lord Barnard, became the mistress of Prince Frederick and in quick succession bore him two bastard children who unfortunately died as infants. The Prince who was loathed and intensely disliked by his parents had been left behind in Hanover on the accession of his grandfather George I in 1714 and grew up bereft of all parental supervision or love.

When he finally arrived in England in 1728 it was only to find that his parents affections were firmly fixed on his younger brother William, Duke of Cumberland. Indeed on his arrival his father declared to Sir Robert Walpole 'I think this is not a son I need much to be afraid of'. Nevertheless the Prince made a favourable impression on most people that he met. Lady Bristol, one of his mother's ladies of the bedchamber declared him to be 'the most agreeable young man it is possible to imagine' with 'the most obliging address that can be conceived'.

Mistress Vane, 'the beautiful Vanella', was one of Queen Caroline's Maids of Honour and court gossip had already linked her name with Lord Harrington and the bi-sexual Lord Hervey, grandson of Lady Betty Felton, one time mistress of the Duke of Monmouth; Lord Hervey was also a cousin of Elizabeth Villiers, Countess of Orkney, mistress of William III, and Lady Deloraine. The affair with Prince Frederick began in the autumn of 1731 and when five months with child she left Court and took up residence in Soho Square with a pension of £3,000 per annum; the son that she bore in the June of 1732, died at the age of three from convulsions and was buried in Westminster Abbey.

Eventually the Prince's affair convinced his father George II that it was time he had a wife and an official was sent out to the Courts of Europe in search of a suitable bride. In time the list was reduced to the sixteen year old Princess Augusta of Saxe-Gotha and the marriage hastily arranged. Unfortunately the character of the Prince did not measure up to careful scrutiny or inspire confidence. Indeed Lord Egmont wrote of him that 'He has no reigning passion; if it be, it is to pass the evening with six or seven others over a glass of wine and hear them talk of a variety of things, but he does not drink. He loves play, and plays to win, that he may supply his pleasures and his generosity, which last is great, but so ill-placed that he often wants the wherewithal to do a well-placed kindness, by giving to unworthy subjects... He can talk gravely according to his company, but is sometimes more childish than becomes his age. He thinks he knows business, but attends to none... He is extremely dutiful to his parents, who do not return it in love, and seem to neglect him by letting him do as he will, but they keep him short of money'.

In the mean time the King had grown tired of Lady Deloraine and during a visit to his beloved Hanover had fallen in love with Amelia Sophia von Wallmoden, the grand daughter of his father's first mistress Maria Catherine von Meysenburg and her husband General Johann von dem Busshe. 'A young woman of the first fashion at Hanover' according to Lord Hervey, Amelia was twenty-nine years old and a married woman with two young children. The King brought her to London on the death of Queen Caroline in December 1737 and installed her with her husband in St James's Palace. In her entourage she brought her youngest child, Johann Ludwig, an infant of just one year who was almost certainly the fruit of her affair with the King. Amelia was not a great beauty. Viscount Townshend described her as 'a brunette with fine black eyes, very well shaped, not tall or low, has no fine features but very agreeable in the main'. The King certainly found her very agreeable and shortly after her arrival she was divorced by her husband and in recompense created Countess of Yarmouth.

With so many examples of marital infidelity before her it is not surprising that Princess Amelia should seek to follow the same path as her father and brother. But there is no firm evidence that she lost her virginity to the Duke of Grafton. The affair, such as it was, was already in full swing by the July of 1729, when her 'undisguised flirtation' was noted at a dinner party at Richmond by Peter Wentworth, Lord Strafford's brother. The Princess's choice was an unfortunate one as Queen Caroline had 'a thorough aversion to the Duke for the liberties he took with one of her great blood'. Indeed the Duke was famous for his insouciance and his cousin Lord Waldegrave records that 'he had a particular manner of talking to his master on all subjects, and of touching upon the most tender points which no other person ever ventured to imitate'. He also had 'the greatest penetration in finding out the foibles of men that ever I knew' declared Horace Walpole 'and wit in teazing them' and 'He understood the Court perfectly and looking upon himself as of the Blood Royal, he thought nothing ought to affect him but what touched them'. Lord Hervey's tribute was no less illuminating 'By coming very young into the great world, being of great quality, and formerly very handsome, he had always kept the best company; and by living perpetually at Court he had all the routine of the style of conversation which is a sort of goldleaf, that is a great embellishment when it is joined to anything else, but makes a very poor figure by itself'.

Grafton, a widower for at least three years standing entertained no thoughts of re-marriage and it is very unlikely that George II would have agreed to a union between his daughter and the son of a Royal Bastard, however illustrious his origins. The stigma of contracting a *mesalliance* was just too great! Besides the Princess was still young and would surely find a husband from amongst one of the many German Royal Houses. Despite the Princess's infatuation she was not promiscuous by nature, unlike her father and during the whole affair displayed an admirable mixture of coquetry and restraint that keep the Duke perpetually enthralled. This type of behaviour was all the more puzzling considering her implacable hostility to her father's mistress Lady Suffolk. Indeed the Princess was the major cause of Lady Suffolk's downfall when she reported to the King that his mistress had conspired with Lord Bolingbroke to over throw his first minister Sir Robert Walpole. It was also hinted that the relationship between Lady Suffolk and Lord Bolingbroke was of an intimate nature rather than just friendship. The King's reaction was to declare that he would 'never speak to her or see her again in private' and he made good his threat. When Queen Caroline tried to prevent Lady Suffolk from leaving court in disgrace George declared 'What the devil did you mean by trying to make an old, dull, deaf, peevish beast plague me when I had so good an opportunity of getting rid of her'.

With her grandmother's example before her it is understandable that Princess Amelia was reluctant to consummate her passion for the Duke.

But this did not prevent her niece the Queen of Denmark, her brother Frederick's daughter, from abandoning all discretion and indulging in a scandalous affair with her husband's chief physician Johann Friedrich Struensee and bearing him a child; the Queen briefly imprisoned in Denmark and then exiled to Hanover died suddenly of scarlet fever at the age of twenty-three. George III was mortified and ashamed by the conduct of his sister so reminiscent of her great-grandmother but it was the behaviour of his brothers the Dukes of Gloucester and Cumberland that hurt him the most.

Unwilling to look for wives from amongst any of the Protestant Royal Houses of Europe, the Dukes preferred to seek partners from amongst the English Aristocracy. The Duke of Gloucester who 'was of a quiet, retiring disposition, (and) weak in health' had enjoyed an income of £12,000 per annum since the age of twenty-one and initially keep 'carefully away from women and gambling'. Indeed there is no record of him being involved with any member of the fair sex until he fell in love with the beautiful widowed Countess of Waldegrave. His choice was most unfortunate and one that was least likely to appeal to his brother the King, whose favourite sibling he was because the Countess was the bastard daughter of Sir Edward Walpole and his mistress, a former milliners assistant. Despite the stigma attached to her birth however, the Countess was very well connected being the grand-daughter no less of Sir Robert Walpole, Britain's first Prime Minister; there were even rumours that Sir Robert's wife had briefly been the King's mistress. In addition she was cousin of Lady Kildare, one time mistress of Charles II, Ann Vane, mistress of Frederick, Prince of Wales and Lady Deloraine, mistress of George II.

As a bastard the Countess was extremely fortunate to wed as her first husband the Earl Waldegrave, formerly tutor to the King, who at forty-four was twice her age. The marriage which in most aristocratic families would have been taboo was accepted by the Earl's family without any fuss. The bride's undoubted beauty plus the knowledge that the Earl was a great-grandson of King James II via his bastard daughter Henrietta, Lady Waldegrave were undoubtedly major factors in accepting it. Unfortunately the Countess's new found happiness did not last as within four years her husband died suddenly of smallpox leaving her in impecunious widow with three small daughters. Within a year of his death, however, fortune began to smile once more in the shape of the King's younger brother the Duke of Gloucester, whose marked attentions were beginning to be noticed by polite society. Unwilling to become his mistress the Countess eventually married her prince in private with only her private chaplain present but she would pay a heavy price for her ambition. Many years later the Duke would express his regret for what he did with the words 'I am indeed severely punished for my juvenile indiscretion'.

The strains placed upon the Duchess's marriage by the refusal of the King (George III) to recognise it and accord her the status of HRH were considerable and later when the couple quarrelled over the details of the education of their daughter the Duke wrote to his brother that 'if she lets the children from this time alone, and behaves more respectfully to me before the world, she may still remain in my house'. The Duchess's nemesis came when her husband began an affair with one of her ladies in waiting, the ambitious and impecunious Lady Almeria Carpenter, daughter of the Irish Peer Lord Tyrconnel. Lady Almeria, who was indisputably the legitimate daughter of her father, was a kinswoman of the notorious Barbara Villiers, Duchess of Cleveland, mistress of Charles II. Described as 'one of the most beautiful women of her time, but to whom nature had been sparing of intellectual attractions' the lady remained the Duke's constant companion for the remainder of his life.

The Duke of Cumberland, Gloucester's younger brother fared no better in his marital choice of Mrs Anne Horton, who although of respectable ancestry; she was the daughter of Simon Luttrell, Earl of Carhampton, was still unequal in rank to her husband. According to Horace Walpole she 'had the most amorous eyes in the world and eyelashes a yard long; coquette beyond measure, artful as Cleopatra, and completely mistress of her passions and projects'. The King refused to acknowledge the marriage or receive them at Court. Fortunately there were no children of the union.

The end result of these transgressions was the Royal Marriage Act of 1772 which forbade any member of the Royal Family to marry without the King's permission. However, this did not prevent the King's daughter, Princess Amelia, from falling in love with the Honorable Charles FitzRoy, great-grandson of the Duke of Grafton, who had commanded the love of her great-aunt Amelia, the daughter of George II. Twenty years her senior and described as 'a dull, sedate, reserved soldier, only interested in little apart from his profession' he nevertheless became her 'general factotum and confidant'. The intensity of her passion was evident for all to see. Expressions such as 'My ever blessed and beloved angel' and 'My ever beloved angel' together with 'Ever your own very own' and 'For ever your affectionate wife and darling' regularly appeared at the end of her letters to him together with the initial A.F.R (Amelia Fitz Roy). Although there is no record of a marriage she wrote 'for years I have considered myself his lawful wife, though suffering all the trials of that, without ever enjoying my rights'.

As for Fitz Roy it would appear that his vanity but not his heart was touched by her devotion. When she died she left all she had to him but her brother the Prince of Wales persuaded Fitz Roy to resign as residuary legatee and all of her effects remained in the family including the £4,000 debt that she owed him. That his regard for her was not of the same nature can be judged by his conduct during her last illness when Lord Glenbervie recorded that 'The Court ladies have observed that for some time past General Fitz Roy has treated her with great harshness, or even brutality. At an earlier period personal familiarities had frequently been observed to pass between them'. Her last words to her sister Mary, who was also said to be much in love with the General, were 'Tell Charles I die blessing him'.

HENRIETTA HOWARD, COUNTESS OF SUFFOLK

When George Augustus, the thirty-five year old Electoral Prince of Hanover and Prince of Wales decided to take a mistress he chose one of his wife's maids of honour, an Englishwoman Mrs Henrietta Howard. Weary of the trials and humiliations she had suffered at the hands of a vexatious and brutal husband and eager to escape from the relative poverty in which she found herself, Mrs Howard willingly accepted the honour with gratitude and looked forward to a more secure future.

But Mrs Howard was no ordinary mistress for 'not only did she possess in a superlative degree all that could charm the senses, but also intelligence, culture and exquisite tact and understood to perfection the art of pleasing'. She had great need of these qualities because the prince was far from being the perfect lover. According to Horace Walpole 'No established mistress ever enjoyed less of the brilliancy of the situation than Lady Suffolk' (as she became). The prince for his part 'was sullen and silent in public, and imperious in his sudden, often inexplicable, enthusiasms and hatreds in private'. The reason for this fractious nature was the indifferent treatment he had received from his father during his early years.

Similarly the treatment Mrs Howard had received from the hands of her 'wrong-headed, ill-tempered, obstinate, drunken, extravagant and brutal' husband, also affected her deeply and instilled into her an overwhelming desire to escape from him. But given the severe penalties that could be inflicted on a wife for deserting her husband this was a very difficult task. The Prince's offer therefore seemed to be the ideal solution. However Mrs Howard was not the stuff from which mistresses were made and throughout the entire relationship sought to maintain a respectable front to her association with the prince; 'Indeed from the propriety & decency of her behaviour (she) was always treated as if her virtue had never been questioned, her friends even affecting to suppose that the connection (with the prince) had been confined to pure friendship'. The strain, however, of maintaining such a façade was considerable and contributed greatly to her ill health in the coming years.

Like her contemporary the ravishing and captivating Madame de Prie, mistress of the Prince de Conde, a French Prince of the Blood and cousin to Louis XV, Mrs Howard used her obvious charms to amuse the prince but she was unable to influence him in the way that Madame Prie was able to with her lover. Indeed whereas Madame Prie 'never gave him advice except after being asked for it' and in effect 'disposed of him as a slave' Mrs Howard was unable to do so because of the Prince's intractable temperament. Indeed 'her situation was such as would have been insupportable to anyone whose pride was less supple, whose passions less governable, and whose sufferance less inexhaustable'.

Unlike the Prince de Conde who 'consecrated himself to her (his mistress) body and soul Mrs Howard found herself in almost the same position as she had endured with her estranged husband and whatever gallantries the Prince might indulge in the Court soon realised that 'the person of his Princess (wife) was dearer to him than any charms of his Mistresses'. This unfortunate situation was exasperated even more by the fact that Mrs Howard cherished intellectual ambitions and was a fierce critic of the patriarchal ideology of the subservience of women to men. Nevertheless despite all of these restrictions Mrs Howard made the best of her situation and within a short time of becoming the Prince's mistress was holding private supper parties in her apartments which attracted politicians such as the Earl of Chesterfield, Viscount Bolingbroke, Lord Peterborough, the Duke of Argyll, his brother Lord Ilay, the Duke of Dorset, Sir Spencer Compton and the poets Pope and Gay. The Prince, a jealous man by nature, disapproved of these gatherings and often flew into a violent rage when he discovered such persons calling upon his mistress.

As the daughter of a English Baronet and with a substantial dowry Miss Hobart had every reason to expect that she would make a good marriage. However, fate dealt her a blow from which she never truly recovered. At the age of nine, her father Sir Henry was killed in a duel and shortly afterwards her mother also died. Bereft of parental supervision at such a tender age Henrietta's position was further compromised by the discovery that her father had died heavily in debt. In order to keep the family together the trustees of her father's remaining estate appealed to her step-grandmother the Countess of Suffolk for support and protection. Although it was the only course open to them, it would prove to be a mistake for which Henrietta would suffer for the remainder of her life.

The Hobarts, of Blickling, Norfolk came from good gentry stock with no record of any connection with past royal mistresses or favourites. However, Sir Henry, Henrietta's father was renowned for non payment of his debts and the prosecution of his neighbours. In his politics he was a 'Whig' as one would expect from a grandson of John Hampden, the patriot. A good marriage to Elizabeth, daughter of Sir Joseph Maynard, who brought with her a dowry of £10,000, enabled Sir Henry to live reasonably comfortably for a short while but he was eventually forced to sell large parts of his estate in order to pay his growing debts. Although much loved by his wife and children Sir Henry's lack of financial acumen and inability to retain his ancestral estate provided his daughter with a valuable object lesson in how not to manage her affairs.

Apart from Sir Henry the only other member of the Hobart family to achieve any kind of notoriety was one of his innumerable kin, a Miss Hobart who was maid of honour to Catherine of Braganza. This young lady had the misfortune to be mentioned in the Memoirs of the Comte de Grammont, where she is depicted in a less than flattering light. According to the memoirs she 'had a good figure, an air of great deliberation, much wit, and an intelligence which was well-informed if discretion was not its strong point'. 'Her imagination was lively though uncontrolled; her glances were ardent though the eyes from which they proceeded were not calculated to inspire passion. Her heart was susceptible; but rumour had it, that it was susceptible only to the charms of her own sex'. Henrietta Hobart by contrast was a lady of cultivated intellect - an inheritance no doubt from her grandfather Sir Joseph Maynard, a renowned jurist – with pleasant and amiable manners, fine chestnut-brown hair, large clear eyes and a milk white complexion.

It was whilst she was under the protection of her step-grandmother, the Countess of Suffolk, that Henrietta met her future husband Charles Howard, a younger son of the Earl of Suffolk. The Howard family were renowned in the annals of English History but since the reign of James I had lost all power and influence at Court. The Suffolk line was descended from a younger son of the 4th Duke of Norfolk and included amongst others the notorious Lady Somerset who poisoned Sir Thomas Overbury, Lady Elizabeth Felton, mistress of the Duke of Monmouth and Elizabeth, Lady Orkney, long time mistress of William of Orange; Lady Orkney, was Charles Howard's first cousin but the connection did little to increase the family's fortunes.

To curry favour with King James I, the 2nd Earl of Suffolk took a Scottish bride Elizabeth Home, daughter of the Earl of Dunbar whilst his son the 5th Earl married the daughter of Baron Castle Stewart, a distant kinsman of that monarch. The result of these unions was an assortment of issue that displayed wild extremes of behaviour. The 5th Earl 'A gentleman who was never yet in business, loves cocking, horse matches, and other country pursuits' was a political cypher and his sons had decidedly anti-social tendencies. Charles, the third son was addicted to drinking, gambling and whoring and was described by a contemporary as 'wrong headed, ill-tempered, obstinate, drunken, extravagant, brutal', all of which, unfortunately, he managed to conceal most of the time beneath a veneer of charm and respectability.

The marriage of his younger son to the orphaned daughter of a Norfolk baronet, with a dowry of £8000, despite her father's extravagance, was a very agreeable prospect for the Earl of Suffolk and in turn Henrietta's marriage into the powerful Howard clan was for her a considerable step up in rank. It also connected Henrietta with several past royal favourites and mistresses as previously mentioned; her successor in her royal lover's affections was the Countess of Deloraine, her husband's cousin. Many years later Lord Chesterfield was to remark 'How she came to love him, or how he came to love anybody, is unaccountable...'.

George's attempt to acquire a mistress was not however governed by passion but by 'a silly idea he had entertained of galantry being becoming' to which he 'added the more egregious folly of fancying that his inconstancy proved he was not governed; but so awkwardly did he manage that artiface that it demonstrated more clearly the influence of the Queen' The cause of the prince's erratic and sometimes inexplicable behaviour was neglect – his father George I had never displayed any paternal affection for him and had prevented him from taking any active part in affairs of state. This enforced idleness bred a fierce resentment which was reinforced by his father's treatment of his mother, who after a brief love affair with Count Konigsmarck was placed under house arrest for the remainder of her life.

During the early years of her reign as the Prince's mistress Henrietta sort relief from her abusive husband and cold, unfeeling lover by forming friendships with courtiers such as Lords Chesterfield, Bolingbroke and Peterborough. A more fascinating and mercurial set of individuals it would be difficult to find. Chesterfield, the grandson of Barbara Villiers first love, and also the great statesman William Saville, Marquess of Halifax, 'was very short, disproportioned, thick and clumsily made; had a broad, rough-featured, ugly face, with black teeth, and a head big enough for a polyphemius' according to Lord Hervey. But he had 'more conversable entertaining table-wit than any man of his time'. He also '... affected following many women of the first beauty and the most in fashion' and was therefore a must at Henrietta's intimate supper parties.

Despite the high regard and affection that Lord Chesterfield's grandfather had for the Duchess of Cleveland (nee Barbara Villiers), his grandson the third Lord pointedly refused to extend the same courtesy to the Duchess's grandson, the Duke of Grafton, in his role as Lord Chamberlain. Indeed he openly ridiculed Grafton's notorious pride in his royal descent declaring: 'I foolishly imagined that well-born meant born with a sound mind in a sound body; a healthy, strong constitution joined to a good heart and a good understanding. But I never suspected that it could possibly mean the shrivelled, tasteless fruit of an old genealogical tree'. But Chesterfield subsequently repented of his folly in speaking out when he married, an illegitimate daughter of George I, thus falling victim to the same pride as Grafton in possessing a royal connection, albeit a bastard one.

Lord Bolingbroke, who had previously served the exiled Stuart pretender James Francis Edward Stuart, was perhaps the most fascinating of all her admirers. In his youth he led a 'riotous life' which had greatly 'alarmed his relatives', was fond of the bottle and very ardent in his pursuit of the opposite sex; to one of his friends Thomas Coke, MP, he wrote 'Really Tom, you are missed; whoring flags without you'. On another occasion 'He himself bragged that in one day he was the happiest man alive, got drunk, harangued the Queen, and at night was put to bed to a beautiful young lady, and was tucked up by two of the prettiest young peers in England, Lords Jersey and Bathurst'. Of him Lord Chesterfield later recalled 'I am old enough to have heard him speak in Parliament, and I remember that, though prejudiced against him by party, I felt all the force and charm of his eloquence'. He then went on to add:

All the internal and external advantages and talents of an orator are undoubtedly his; figure, voice, elocution, knowledge and above all the purest and most florid diction, with the justest metaphors and happiest images.' His manner of speaking in private conversation is just as elegant as his writings. Whatever subject he either speaks on or writes about, he adorns it with the most splendid eloquence.

Praise indeed! When Henrietta met him, Bolingbroke had returned to England and left the pretender's employ forever. True to form he continued with his riotous way of living in the hope perhaps of emulating the exploits of his cousins the celebrated rake John Wilmot, Earl of Rochester and Barbara and Elizabeth Villiers.

Lord Peterborough, a relative of Bolingbroke, via the Howard family had been employed by successive monarchs in various military and diplomatic posts and had a reputation as a wit and gallant. He was also renowned for his erratic and unpredictable behaviour so much so that the poet Pope remarked: 'It was impossible that a man of so much Wit as he shew'd cou'd be fit to command an Army, or do any other Business'. Horace Walpole described him as 'one of those men of careless wit and negligent grace who scatter a thousand bon-mots and idle verses'. To Jonathan Swift he was 'the ramblingest, lying rogue on earth'. But despite this he managed during his career to become 1st Lord of the Treasury under William of Orange before falling out with that monarch. Like Bolingbroke he flirted with Jacobitism and was sent to the Tower of London for alleged complicity in the plot of Sir John Fenwick to assassinate William. Trevelyan, the historian, summed him up in the following words: '... quarrelsome, boastful, light-minded, over busy with tongue and pen, changing his plans and his friends as readily as he shifted his shirt, sudden in resolutions but unable to hold a course... leaving the tasks of yesterday half done.' However, it was for his exploits in the 'War of the Spanish Succession' that he was chiefly remembered and the conduct of his wife Carey Frazier, who prior to their marriage had firmly set her sights on supplanting the Duchess of Portsmouth to become the mistress of Charles II. But despite her obvious charms she did not succeed.

Such then were the characters of some of the courtiers who patronised Henrietta's private supper parties in the hope of once again gaining access to state affairs. All had been dismissed from their posts after the accession of George I and henceforth formed part of the Tory opposition to future royal policy. Queen Caroline, however, was well aware of the fact that Henrietta's rooms were being used as 'the seat of a political faction' and increasingly prevented her husband from visiting his mistress for three of four days at a time. The prince, who had now succeeded his father as George II, was also becoming extremely impatient of his mistress and despite the fact that she was now the King's mistress as opposed to a mere prince, the change in status brought Henrietta little benefit.

At the time of her marriage in 1706 Henrietta brought with her a dowry of £6,000 which was administered by trustees appointed by her uncle John Hobart. Charles Howard, her husband, was not allowed access to the money but he was able to get his hands on the interest and as this constituted a sizeable portion of their combined income it was not long before they were seriously in debt. Her husband's continual violence towards her, his drunkenness and frequentation of London's many houses of ill repute was the main reason why she sought to obtain a post in the household of Sophia, the Electress of Hanover, who it was expected would succeed Queen Anne. In the event she obtained the promise of a post as lady in waiting to Princess Caroline, the wife of Sophia's grandson George Augustus.

Henrietta's success was followed by that of her husband who obtained the post of Groom of the Bedchamber to the future George I. All of this was a result of Henrietta's determination to find some financial security in the face of her husband's reckless extravagance but her salary of just £300 a year was a far cry from the situation she would have wished to be in. Nevertheless it was a beginning and as her husband received a sum of £500 per annum the future look more promising. Despite the belief that she would immediately benefit financially and materially from becoming George II's mistress, it was not until some time into their relationship that she was rewarded for her compliance. The sum she received £11,500 worth of stock, jewellery and furnishings was poor recompense for her status as the King's favourite.

Despite her obvious beauty and intellectual accomplishments the union did not produce any royal bastards. In this respect Henrietta followed the example of Lady Orkney (nee Elizabeth Villiers) and thus perhaps deserves the title of royal favourite rather than royal mistress. With the death of her husband in 1733 and the end of her relationship with George II the following year, Henrietta was finally free of spend the rest of her life as she wished but to the surprise of many she chose once again to enter the state of matrimony. Her choice, George Berkeley, was totally unexpected.

According to Lord Hervey 'Mr Berkeley was neither young, handsome, healthy, nor rich, which made people wonder what induced Lady Suffolk's prudence to deviate into this unaccountable piece of folly'. Berkeley, was the younger son of Charles, 2nd Earl of Berkeley and his wife Elizabeth Noel. The Earl who suffered in later life from dropsy was 'intolerably lazy and somewhat covetous' according to Jonathan Swift. A deeply religious man his three children were totally unlike him. They were according to one modern historian 'characteristic Berkeleys, opposed to conventional respectability and careless of the world's opinion, their actions stamped with the unmistakeable impress of personality, sometimes agreeable, sometimes unpleasant, but always dangerously close to folly'.

The character of the elder brother James Berkeley was captured by Lord Hervey in the following words: 'He was haughty and tyrannical, but honourable, gallant, observant of his word, but equally incapable of flattering a prince, bending to a Minister, or lying to anybody he had to deal with.' Lady Betty, George's sister 'possessed a marked individuality' with 'the power to attract men of superior intellect, and when committing her thoughts to paper, was infinitely more interesting'. But it was James's offer to kidnap the Prince of Wales (later George II) and then spirit him away on a ship to any other part of the world that earned him everlasting fame. The incident would seem to be a direct result of the strong antipathy that George I felt for his son and eventual successor. Indeed their relations were so bad that on one occasion the King placed his son under house arrest because he was alleged to have challenged the Duke of Newcastle to a duel.

Fortunately, however, Henrietta's second venture into marriage was a great success and they really did live happily ever after. But the conflict that she encountered in her first marriage marked her for life. Her husband had subjected her to a reign of abuse which she bore with remarkable calm and patience but for all that she was still powerless to bring the marriage to an end. It would be many years before she even sought a judicial separation and it was only her position as mistress to George II that protected her from further abuse. 'Self preservation is ye first law of nature' she declared 'are married women then ye only part of human nature yt must not follow it?' When he demanded that she return to him, she countered by saying 'I have but too good reason to fear worse treatment than I believe the law of England allowes, and in such cases I have always heard a wife is protected' In the end she won her freedom but at a terrible cost, her son was taken away from her and she never saw him again.

The Loves of Florizel (George IV)

George IV's appetite for the fair sex was legendary and by the age of twenty-one his name was a by word for lechery on London's social scene. No other monarch can match his record for promiscuity, not even Charles II! In character he resembled his grandfather Frederick, Prince of Wales and like him was shamefully neglected by his parents in preference to his younger brother the Duke of York.

Although by the age of sixteen he was 'proficient in the classics, mathematics, natural philosophy (sacred, profane and modern), and could speak French, German and Italian' it was very apparent to the King that he did not possess those qualities that were needed for the difficult task of being a constitutional monarch. As a result he slipped in to a life of dissipation and vice from which he never managed to eradicate himself but still some how managed to retain his reputation as the 1st Gentleman of Europe.

Denied the companionship of children his own age, young George grew up with a marked tendency for self delusion and play acting and a complete indifference for the feelings of others. Indeed the Duke of Wellington later recorded that he possessed 'a most extraordinary talent for imitating the manner, gestures, and even the voices of other people, so much so that he could give you the exact idea of anyone however unlike they were to himself'. When his tutor Dr Richard Hurd, Bishop of Lichfield was asked for his opinion of the Prince's character he replied that 'He will either be the most polished gentleman or the most accomplished blackguard in Europe', but it was the opinion of most of his contemporaries that he was 'possibly an admixture of both'.

As a young man George showed a marked preference for companions with 'a spice of vice in their nature' such as the Whig politician Charles James Fox, the painter Richard Cosway, Sheridan, the playwright, 'Beau' Brummell, Jack Payne and Lord Coleraine but it was his uncle the Duke of Cumberland who introduced the Prince to 'most of the vices of the rich and corrupt few'. Fox and Lord Coleraine were the worst offenders the latter in particular for his 'pursuit of the wives and daughters of common citizens' and together with his drinking companions the Dukes of Norfolk (renowned for his coarseness, drunkenness and aversion to soap and water), Queensberry (known as Old Q) and Rutland (whose wife became the mistress of the Duke of York, the Prince's brother), he soon became according to the Bishop of Llandaff '.... a man occupied in trifles, because he had no opportunity of displaying his talents in the conduct of great affairs'. As a result the Prince soon became the butt of many social and political satires.

Like his fellow monarch Charles II, George was not always particular about his choice of female companions among whom could be numbered the beautiful actress Mary 'Perdita' Robinson and the courtesan Grace Dalrymple Elliott but when he did take the trouble to be more selective he always chose ladies with breeding such as Anna Sophia Hodges and Lady Melbourne (rumoured to have been the mistress of his brother the Duke of York) all of whom, however, were just a prelude to his 'Grande Passion' for Maria Fitzherbert.

Unlike Mrs Robinson and Grace Elliott, Mrs Hodges, Lady Melbourne and Mrs Fitzherbert all came from respectable families. Indeed Mrs Hodges and Mrs Fitzherbert were cousins and came from ultra-royalist

Catholic families. But even so they were complete opposites in character. According to contemporary accounts Mrs Hodges 'had all the properties of (the goddess) Diana – except her chastity'. Married at the age of fifteen in 1782 she quickly became disillusioned with her husband and looked elsewhere for fulfilment as the Prince's mistress. Neither the marriage or her affair produced any children but when she subsequently took up with Charles William Wyndham, brother of the Earl of Egremont, she gave birth to three bastard children. Such behaviour was surprising given her social standing but an examination of her ancestry provides a partial explanation.

Among her relatives she could count Winifred Wells, allegedly a long time mistress of Charles II; Lady Byron, another mistress of Charles II during his exile; Goditha Price, mistress of James II; Eleanor Needham, mistress of James, Duke of Monmouth and Catherine Sedley, mistress of James II. She was also descended from Lady Felton, mistress of the Duke of Monmouth and was a cousin of Barbara & Elizabeth Villiers, mistresses of William of Orange and Charles II.

Mrs Hodges affair with the Prince appears to have lasted for about a year from the spring of 1783 to May 1784 and first caught the Prince's attention when mounted for the chase; her mother was deemed to be the best horsewoman in England. Mr Hodges, who was a willing party in the proceedings allowed the Prince to visit his wife every day at their lodgings in Pall Mall but his brother-in-law, a groom of the bedchamber to the Prince, was appalled by their behaviour and threatened to take her out of town 'for he didn't choose his sister should be talked of in such a manner'.

As with so many of his relationships the Prince quickly became bored with his latest conquest. Indeed during the affair he appears to have pursued and laid siege to Lady Melbourne a famous Whig hostess and friend of the Duchess of Devonshire, who listed Charles James Fox, George Canning, Charles Grey and Lord Byron amongst her admirers. A vivacious beauty with a 'commanding figure, exceeding the middle height (and) full of grace and dignity' she married at the age of eighteen a husband renowned as a 'Paragon of Debauchery' who within ten months of the marriage took Sophia Baddeley, the celebrated actress as his mistress.

Elizabeth Milbanke, a cousin of the notorious rake Sir Francis Blake Delaval, intimate friend of Edward, Duke of York, uncle of the Prince of Wales was eminently fitted to occupy the position of *mistress en titre*. Although not a direct descendant of a royal mistress, she was a lady with a past and none of her children, except the first, appear to have been by her husband, two being by Lord Egremont and the third allegedly by Henry Frederick, Duke of Cumberland; the child she bore in 1784, christened George, was almost certainly the result of her brief affair with the Prince of Wales. Her name was associated with the Prince from 1782 to 1786 during which time the only benefit she gained was the appointment of her husband as a Gentleman of the Bedchamber to the Prince.

Like her rivals Mrs Hodges and Maria Fitzherbert, Lady Melbourne was not the only member of her family to enjoy the fruits of royal favour. Lady Milbanke, her mother had, albeit briefly, been pursued by the Duke of York, son of George II, who also paid court to her cousin Lady Stanhope, whilst another cousin Lady Tyrconnel, became the mistress of Frederick, Duke of York, brother to the Prince of Wales.

Despite her promiscuous behaviour Lady Melbourne believed that 'affairs of the heart must not be the cause of open scandal but must be treated with discretion. Scandal was to be avoided; discreet unfaithfulness within marriage (however) was acceptable'. She was without doubt 'a woman of acute intelligence', who knew how to use her lovers to forward her social ambitions and the advancement of her family. Lord Byron, the poet, described her as 'the best friend I ever had in my life and the cleverest of women'; later he would marry her niece.

Lord Egremont, the father of Lady Melbourne's first two children, was renowned for his amorous exploits and his friendship with the Prince of Wales. He was in many ways the image of his father, who according to one contemporary was an habituee of the flesh pots of Covent Garden and 'an unexampled instance of debauchery who had more than once acquired instead of a virgin, a Verole'. Among his many conquests were the actress Mrs Lattimore, the courtesan Nancy Fetherstone and the most famous of all the harlots Betsy Careless 'A peerless beauty... the Gayest, most Charming, Wittiest of all the Courtezans around Covent Garden'.

Despite engagements to Lady Mary Somerset in 1774 and Lady Maria Waldegrave in 1780, Egremont preferred the charms of his many mistresses among whom were Lady Melbourne, Elizabeth Ilive and the actress Elizabeth Fox. The affair with Lady Melbourne produced at least two bastard children, perhaps three, whilst Mrs Ilive, whom he later married had four and Mrs Fox (who subsequently had an affair with the Prince of Wales and bore him a son) another four. The Earl was according to Greville, the diarist 'remarkably acute, shrewd and observant and in his manner blunt without rudeness and caustic without bitterness'. But he was unsuited to political life preferring to 'revel unshackled in all the enjoyments of private life, both physical and intellectual, which an enormous fortune, a vigorous constitution and literary habits placed in abundant variety before him'.

Mrs Fitzherbert by contrast was 'sweet by nature' with a modest demeanour plus a pink and white complexion, hazel eyes and luxuriant fair hair, who would never consent to being just the Prince's mistress like her cousin Mrs Hodges. The Prince's passion for her was extraordinary and they were eventually wed by an Anglican minister with her father and brother as witnesses. Given that this was in direct contravention of the Royal Marriage Act it is surprising that Mrs Fitzherbert was prepared to marry according to the rites of the Church of England.

The marriage lasted for nine years until he abandoned her for Lady Jersey and although Mrs Fitzherbert had produced a son, who survived only a few hours, by her second husband she bore no surviving issue from her union with the Prince; she was reputed to have been with child shortly after her marriage but if true it did not result in a live birth.

True to form, however, the Prince soon lost interest in his 'wife' and sought distraction elsewhere most notably with Elizabeth Billington and Anna Maria Crouch, both singers and ladies of great beauty. But the relationship finally ended in 1794, when he took a violent fancy to the 'beautiful but unprincipled' Countess of Jersey, a grandmother of forty-one years; her husband, George Bussey Villiers, Earl of Jersey, a cousin of Barbara Villiers, was a great-grandson of the famous Duke of Marlborough and son of 2nd Earl of Jersey, lover of Marlborough's daughter the Duchess of Montagu.

Frances Twysden, was just seventeen years old when she married the Earl of Jersey in 1770 and in 1778 after bearing her husband several children embarked upon an affair with the Duke of Devonshire, whose wife was a close friend of the Prince. The Duke was quickly followed by Mr Fawkener, a Clerk to the Privy Council (said to be the father of one of her daughters) until she eventually captured the attention of the Prince. She had first attracted his attention in 1782 but initially resisted his advances declaring 'If he is in love with me I cannot help it. It is impossible for anyone to give another less encouragement than I have.'

The Earl of Jersey's marriage to the only daughter of an impoverished Irish Bishop caused much surprise in polite society, given his distinguished ancestry and connections it was hoped that he would have made a much better match. But despite her seemingly modest origins he appears to have been genuinely attached to her and 'when all the world had deserted her' continued to show her 'undiminished and unremitting kindness'.

Despite her relatively modest origins, Lady Jersey had some impressive family connections including kinship with the notorious Barbara Villiers and Elizabeth Villiers, Countess of Orkney, mistresses of Charles II and William of Orange; Goditha Price, mistress of James II and Mary Boleyn mistress of Henry VIII. Like her rival Lady Melbourne, Lady Jersey was a member of the 'Devonshire House Set' and a close friend of Georgiana, Duchess of Devonshire. She was intelligent and witty but according to her contemporaries never happy 'without a rival to trouble and torment'. Of her success one wag reported 'Lady Jersey has at last accomplished her ardent desire to be admitted to the Queen's Parties at Windsor'.

Lord Jersey, dubbed 'the Prince of Maccaronies' by Elizabeth Montagu because of his foppish dress and behaviour, was a close friend and kinsman of the 3rd Duke of Grafton, whose grandfather the 2nd Duke had captured the heart of the Princess Amelia, daughter of George II. The association did not benefit either individual despite Grafton's brief tenure as Prime Minister. Indeed Lord Jersey was not given any post in the Duke's cabinet and had to wait under Lord Rockingham's ministry before being appointed Vice-Chamberlain.

By the time of her affair with the Prince Lady Jersey must have thought that her childbearing days were over but it is alleged that at the age of forty two she bore the prince a son who died as an infant. Undaunted by the experience the 'vivacious, wilful and beautiful' mother of ten moved into Carlton House with her new lover and took full advantage of her new situation. When the Prince decided to marry his cousin Princess Caroline of Brunswick, his new love secured the post of Lady of the Bedchamber. Many years later the Duke of Wellington declared that Lady Jersey had had a major part in the Prince's choice of bride hoping that her 'indelicate manners, indifferent character, and not very inviting appearance' would disgust the Prince and strengthen her position as the new royal favourite.

During her reign as the current royal favourite, Lady Jersey's position was never seriously challenged but her behaviour towards the Princess of Wales came under severe criticism from courtiers and the public alike. When the Princess declared to the Prince that she knew Lady Jersey was his mistress, he protested loudly and rather disingenuously, that she was 'a woman whom I declared on your arrival not to be my mistress, as you so indecorously term her, but a friend to whom I am attached by the strong ties of habitutude, esteem and respect'. Not content with this Lady Jersey sent her husband to the King in an effort to restore her good name but when he declared that she 'had been a most faithful and virtuous wife' the King could not contain his mirth.

When the relationship came to an end it was sudden and without warning. The Prince sent his private secretary Colonel John McMahon and Edward Jerningham to negotiate with her but matters dragged on for some considerable time before an agreement was reached. The reason appears to have been the Prince's interest in Mrs Eliza Crole, an actress and previously mistress of the Earl of Egremont, who gave him a son.

Bewildered and distraught, Lady Jersey sought consolation elsewhere and took as her next lover the Earl of Carlisle, in his youth a leading rake and gamester but now a serious politician and former Lord Lieutenant of Ireland. Frederick Howard, 5th Earl of Carlisle, cousin of the poet Lord Byron, belonged to a junior branch of the powerful

Howard family and was a kinsman of the Earl of Jersey. True to form Lady Jersey, at forty-seven, presented him with a son Frederick, who did not survive infancy. But the affair did not prosper and shortly afterwards she retired to the continent to avoid her creditors; despite her reign as a royal favourite there were no compensating financial benefits. Indeed when her husband died in 1805, she was left without 'sufficient income to support (her) rank' and although she asked the Prince to grant her a pension it was her son who came to her aid.

After the breakup with Lady Jersey, the prince once again returned to the familiar arms of Mrs Fitzherbert and for another six years remained relatively faithful. However, in 1806 he was seen to be in pursuit of Lady Hertford, a matron of forty six, 'very handsome' of large proportions but described by one contemporary as 'the most forbidding, haughty, unpleasant-looking woman'. 'She had a frigid bearing' exclaimed the Comtesse de Boigne and 'a pompous mode of speech, was pedantically accurate in her choice of words, with a manner both calm and cold... a great lady in every sense of the word'. The Prince became besotted with her and the association lasted for eight years.

It was now twenty-nine years since the Prince gave himself up to a life of pleasure and debauchery and predictably it had taken a heavy toll on his health and temper. Indeed he had now reached the point in his life where 'during the later years..., a quiet indulgence of certain sensual enjoyments seemed the sole object of his existence'. He 'was essentially a lover of personal ease' but without any redeeming qualities and according to Robert Huish, his biographer, 'notwithstanding the principles inculcated in his youth... his subsequent conduct proved that he rather upheld the men than valued their principles, and that he repudiated their principles as soon as he had abandoned the men'. On his death his obituary declared that 'no act of the King's life seems to have been guided by any principle but that of self-gratification'.

It had not always been so. As a young boy he was taught the 'virtues of simplicity, hard work, punctuality and regularity' and beaten regularly by his tutors if he displayed any 'sign of laziness, laxness or untruthfulness'. Unfortunately this strict regime failed to eradicate the major flaws in his character and he grew up with a positive aversion to hard work. Instead he preferred to be esteemed for 'the elegance of his address and the gentlemanliness of his manner' and readily admitted that he was 'rather too fond of wine and women'.

He was therefore singularly ill-prepared to take over the role of Regent when his father finally fell a victim to madness in October 1810. The prospect filled him with dread and drew the comment from one of his contemporaries that during the day he was forced to make '... frequent applications to the liquor chest' in order to brace his nerves up to the mark of facing the difficulties he will soon have to encounter. Fortunately Lady Hertford, who possessed considerable political acumen, was on hand to give him the support and confidence he needed to fulfil his new role.

Isabella Anne Ingram Shepherd, was the eldest daughter and co-heir of Charles Ingram, Viscount Irvine and his wife Frances Shepherd, bastard daughter of Samuel Shepherd, MP of Exning. Unlike Lady Jersey, Lady Hertford bore her husband only one child who eventually succeeded to the title and having performed her duty of providing an heir sort entertainment and pleasure elsewhere.

The Prince and Lady Hertford first came into regular contact when Mrs Fitzherbert sought her help over the custody of Minnie Seymour, the orphaned daughter of Lord Hugh Seymour, Lord Hertford's brother, who had by various ways and means come into the custody and care of Mrs Fitzherbert prior to the death of her mother. So grateful was he that his attentions to her soon became public knowledge and Lady Bessborough noted that he 'frets himself into a fever... to persuade (Lady Hertford) to live with him publickly!

Unlike all of his previous favourites, Lady Hertford was a considerable heiress in her own right but her mother's bastardy sat very ill on her conscience. In fact it was not the only incidence of bastardy in her family. Mrs Machell (nee Warmestry), Lady Hertford's great-great-grandmother, was a maid of honour to Catherine of Braganza, the wife of Charles II and before her marriage to John Machell, had carried on a intrigue with Lord Taaffe, the result of which was a bastard child; the whole episode being recorded in the 'Memoirs of the Count de Gramont'.

The combined income of the Hertfords, Lord Hertford alone received £70,000 per annum from his Irish estates, made them financially independent and thus able to indulge in their passion for the decorative arts, something they had in common with the Prince of Wales. The Prince also took a very keen interest in their only son Lord Yarmouth, a noted libertine and the model for Lord Steyne in *Vanity Fair*, who was according to one modern historian proof 'that even after the lapse of a hundred years ancestral strains can be powerful enough to reassert themselves; so powerful indeed, that in this able and consummate roué the spirit of Charles II, and that of his mistress, the Duchess of Cleveland, lived again, their concupiscence unabated'.

As with so many of the Prince's friends, Lord Yarmouth's character did not stand up to careful scrutiny. He was in the opinion of one noted modern art historian 'not a likeable man' but 'a wayward son, a wretched husband, a feckless Irish landlord, a Tory autocrat abusive of reform, and an example of undisguised debauchery', all of which was in sharp contrast to the exquisite sensibility that he showed when purchasing pictures for his art collection in the sales rooms of London and Paris.

Whilst his mother maintained her position as the latest royal favourite, Lord Yarmouth was showered with gifts and offices and the Prince delighted in 'the accuracy of his judgement and his discrimination' in the choice of pictures for his art collection but when his mother was displaced by another in 1819, all of this came to an end.

Maria Anne Fitzherbert

Maria Anne Smythe was born in Hampshire on 26 July 1756 into a good and respectable Catholic family, the eldest child of Walter Smythe, of Brambridge and his wife, Mary Ann Errington. Educated by the Ursuline Nuns in Paris she possessed a cosmopolitan style and elegance that could only be obtained from frequent contact with Royal Court of the Bourbon Kings of France, a quality that her future lover George IV found most attractive.

At the age of seventeen she married Edward Weld, of Lulworth

Castle, Dorset, a rich Catholic landowner sixteen years her senior but after only three months, the young groom fell from his horse and died leaving her a widow. In 1778, she married Thomas Fitzherbert, of Swynnerton and Norbury in Staffordshire, 'a tall, powerful man inclined to run to fat to counteract which he ate sparingly and took violent exercise'. The marriage produced a son who died young, but when her husband died suddenly shortly after the anti-Catholic Gordon Riots she inherited the family home in Mayfair together with an annual income of £2,500.

Maria was not a conventional beauty but she had a flawless complexion offset by an prominent aquiline nose and a character that radiated a very becoming serenity and gentility accompanied by an air of quiet common sense and sensitivity which attracted all and sundry. She was according to Lady Hester Stanhope 'sweet by nature and who even if they are not washed for a fortnight are free from odour'.

As already stated Mrs Fitzherbert, was a cousin of the notorious Mrs Hodges, who for a brief time in 1783 was mistress of George IV, when Prince of Wales and later Charles Wyndham, brother of Lord Egremont. Mrs Hodges affairs were so notorious that they brought considerable shame upon the Smythe family but the latter already had several skeletons in the family cupboard. A careful examination of the antecedents of the Smythe family reveal that, true to form, they were already connected to several royal mistresses including Winifred Wells, a mistress of Charles II.

Mrs Wells was one of Catherine of Braganza's original Maids of Honour, but she did not become the King's mistress until after he had caste aside Lady Castlemaine in 1667. Winifred is credited by Samuel Pepys with having aborted the King's child at a court ball in 1662/3, which was allegedly taken up by the King in his handkerchief for subsequent dissection in his laboratory. Winifred later went on to marry Thomas Wyndham, one of the King's equerries and bore him two children; the son, Charles, was made a page of honour to James II and followed him into life-long exile and served in Captain Dorrington's regiment in the armies of the King of France. In addition to Mrs Wells, Maria was also related to Catherine Sedley, mistress of James II and the notorious Lady Shrewsbury, mistress of the 2nd Duke of Buckingham.

The exact circumstances surrounding Maria's meeting with the twenty-two year old Prince of Wales, are unclear. One version states that they met at the opera in 1784 and the prince immediately fell in love with her. Another recalls that the prince saw her accompanied by her husband whilst driving in Park Lane. The truth would appear to be that in 1784 Maria was persuaded by her kinsman, Lord Sefton and his wife to accompany them for a London season and from the moment he saw her the Prince became besotted but despite all of his entreaties she refused to become his mistress.

In desperation the Prince offered her marriage but she rebuffed his advances. Undaunted he stabbed himself with a knife, feigning suicide and declared that 'only her presence would save him'. Aware that this might be 'some strategam derogatory to her reputation' she 'resisted, in the most peremptory manner… saying that nothing should induce her to enter Carlton House'. But eventually she agreed to visit him and almost fainted at the sight of the Prince looking 'pale and covered with blood.' When he declared 'that nothing would induce him to live unless she promised to be his wife' she reluctantly allowed him to place a ring on her finger but on her return she immediately fled to the continent. For a year she travelled through France, Holland, Germany and Switzerland all the while pursued by messengers from the Prince. The strain on her family was immense and her father had several heart attacks before she agreed to return and marry the Prince but he did not die until several years later.

Although the ceremony may have been legal in the eyes of the Catholic Church, under the terms of the Act of Settlement of 1701, the Prince would be deprived of his rights to the succession if he married a Catholic. Moreover, he was well aware that the Royal Marriage Act, passed in 1772, forbade any member of the Royal Family under the age of twenty-five from marrying without the Sovereign's consent and Parliamentary approval, which he was unlikely to obtain. In addition, despite her high connections a legal marriage was out of the question too.

The ceremony was performed on 15 December 1785 by an Anglican cleric the Reverend Robert Burke, who was specially released from debtors prison for the occasion and paid the sum of £500, in the drawing room of Maria's Mayfair home in the presence of her uncle Henry Errington, brother John Smythe and friend Orlando Bridgeman. In her own words Maria had 'given herself up to him, exacted no conditions, trusted to his honour and set no value on the ceremony he insisted on having solemnised.' However, during the coming years the Prince proved to be incapable of remaining faithful to his 'wife' and had a string of affairs with a number of actresses and singers including Elizabeth Billington, Anna Maria Crouch and Marie Hilligsberg.

Mrs Billington, according to one admirer 'the greatest singer England has ever produced', was previously the mistress of the Duke of Cumberland and subsequently of the Duke of Sussex, both younger brothers of George IV but also of the 4th Duke of Rutland. However 'the coarseness of her manners soon disgusted him' and he moved on. Mrs Crouch, 'a vocalist of great beauty', had an annuity of £1,200 settled on her by the Prince, which was cancelled on his marriage. Marie Hilligsberg was a prima ballerina, the daughter of French parents who appeared in many ballets, often in men's trousers. They were, of course, only transient affairs which did nothing to undermine the Prince's loving relationship with his wife!

After nine years of relative bliss the Prince suddenly became enamoured of the forty year old Lady Jersey an affair that lasted from 1794 to 1798 and was quickly followed by another with Elizabeth Fox alias Mrs Crole, whose son George Seymour Crole was the only child that the prince ever acknowledged privately or publicly. Mrs Crole was previously the mistress of George O'Brien Wyndham, Lord Egremont, by whom she had four children. Her son by the Prince was bequeathed £25,000 in the Prince's will, but he eventually received just £10,000 plus an annual pension for life; Mrs Crole received a pension of £500.

The Wyndhams were closely related to the Hervey-Aston's,

Carpenters, Milbankes and Delavals, all of whom provided the Prince and some of his royal cousins with mistresses for the royal bed. Mrs Crole, Lord Egremont's mistress and Mrs Hodges, the mistress of Charles Wyndham, Lord Egremont's brother, both had affairs with the Prince of Wales. In addition Lord Egremont had an affair with Lady Melbourne, another of the Prince's mistresses, whilst Charles Wyndham completed the circle by marrying Lady Jersey's daughter.

To complicate matters even further Lady Melbourne's mother and her cousin Lady Anne Stanhope were both mistresses of the Duke of York. Another cousin Sarah Delaval, who married George Carpenter, Earl of Tyrconnel, was also a mistress of the Prince, and her sister-in-law Lady Almeria Carpenter, a cousin of Lord Egremont, became the mistress of the Duke of Gloucester one of the Prince's uncles; Lady Stanhope's brother-in-law, the Earl of Chesterfield, also married an illegitimate daughter of George I. As descendants of the Howard and Villiers families it is not really surprising, therefore, to find them continuing the family tradition of supplying royal mistresses.

When the Prince eventually tired of Lady Jersey, he begged Maria to return to him and sent his brother the Duke of Kent to plead his cause. Reluctantly she agreed but only after the Pope had confirmed that she was indeed the Prince's wife. To celebrate she invited numerous friends and relations to her 'wedding' breakfast and recounted afterwards that she 'hardly knew how she could summon resolution to pass that severe ordeal, but she thanked God she had the courage to do so'. Despite her initial reservations about returning Maria told Lord Stourton that 'the next eight years were... the happiest of her connection with the Prince'.

But after their reunion the Prince once again proved that he was incapable of remaining faithful to one woman. Between 1800 and 1810 his names was associated with a number of different women including the Comtesse de Mesnard, Mrs Taylor and the Countess of Bessborough. The latter was to quote a contemporary historian 'possessed of marked individuality (who) had the power to attract men of superior intellect, and when committing her thoughts to paper, was infinitely more interesting, because more natural and spontaneous, than the people, much her superior in literary accomplishment, with whom she was corresponding…'. In addition her 'playfulness and wit gave her an eternal youth and a fascination as compelling as it was indefinable (which) atoned for (any) obvious faults which, elsewhere we should be quick to condemn'. Unfortunately, however, the Prince's advances to the lady made no impression whatsoever and she firmly resisted all attempts to get her into the royal bed!

The Comtesse de Mesnard, however, was a different proposition. Contemporary sources are silent on this ladies presumed affair with the Prince. Louise Josephine Nompar de Caumont, was the sister of Anne Jacobe, Comtesse de Balbi, mistress of Louis XVIII, King of France. The two sisters came to England in 1794 but Louise did not return to France until after the King was restored in 1815; the Comtesse de Balbi had returned in 1802 after the Treaty of Amiens. The bastard son that the Comtesse de Mesnard bore in December 1802 was given the names of Francois Louis de la Porte similar to the names borne by the chaplain to the exiled King and his brother the Comte de Artois, who however made no reference to the boy in his will. The obvious conclusion to be drawn from this scenario is that the child appears to have been placed in the care of one of the exiled King's retainers and passed off as his son. Why the Prince of Wales should allow this to happen is a mystery. The only alternative conclusion one can reach is that the child was in fact the bastard son of the exiled King or his brother. Many years later when the child showed an interest in his mother's estate, he received a very hostile reception from his aunt, the Comtesse de Balbi, which is quite understandable if indeed he was the son of her sister by the Comtesse's ex-royal lover!

When the end of Maria's affair with the Prince finally came it was humiliating, for true to his nature the Prince was incapable of remaining faithful to one woman. The new object of his passion was Lady Hertford and Maria soon found herself being used to preserve her good name. He also paid court to Lady Bessborough with protestations of 'eternal love' which she never forgot or forgave; at that time her current lover was Lord Granvill, because his behaviour was so extreme:

> Such a scene I never went through' she recalled as he 'threw himself on his knees, and clasping me round, kissed my neck before I was aware of what he was doing... sometimes struggling with me, sometimes sobbing and crying... vows of eternal love, entreaties and promises of what he would do – he would break with Mrs F and Lady H, I should make my own terms! I should be his sole confident, sole adviser – private or public – I should guide his politics, Mr Canning should be Prime Minister etc, etc.

In face of such base ingratitude Mrs Fitzherbert wrote to the Prince in the following terms:

> The very great incivilities I have received these two years just because I obeyed your orders in going [to Brighton Pavilion] was too visible to everyone present and too poignantly felt by me to admit of my putting myself in a situation of again being treated with such indignity, for whatever may be thought of me by some individuals, it is well known YRH four-and-twenty years ago placed me in a situation so nearly connected with your own that I have a claim upon you for protection.
>
> I feel I owe it to myself not to be insulted under your roof with impunity. The influence you are now under, and the conduct of one of your servants, I am sorry to say, has the appearance of your sanction and support, and renders my situation in your house, situated as I am, impossible any longer to submit to.

However Mrs Fitzherbert did not finally break with the Prince until 1811 when finding that she had not been seated on the Prince's right at a dinner given in honour of the exiled French King Louis XVIII, she immediately left having been told 'You know Madam, you have no place'. The power and fascination that she had previously exerted over the Prince's mind and emotions was now clearly at an end and it was time for her to move on with her life. Those qualities of character that had once held him enthralled and her sweet nature were now no longer strong enough to keep him.

5

THE EDWARDIAN ERA

The King's Loose Box

Like Charles II, Edward VII had three principal mistresses during his life, Lily Langtry, Daisy Warwick and Alice Keppel but his first sexual encounter was at the age of nineteen with the actress, Nellie Clifden, and his subsequent sexual adventures earned him the nickname of Edward the 'Caresser'. In his pursuit of the fair sex he followed the example of his grandfather Ernst II, of Saxe-Coburg-Gotha, who was renowned for his amourous escapades. Ernst, married as his first wife Princess Louise of Saxe-Coburg-Altenburg but neglected her shamefully and when she sought consolation elsewhere banished her forever from the lives of her two young sons and then continued his own irregular life by taking another mistress! When he married a second time it was to a princess of the House of Wurtemburg, who was also his neice but fortunately there were no children from the match. Several illegitimate children resulted from his affairs including a daughter Berta Ernestine, who married her cousin, the illegitimate son of Ernst's aunt the former Grand Duchess Constantine of Russia!

Edward's first mistress of any note was allegedly Jeanne, wife of Charles Guillaume de Talleyrand-Perigord, Prince de Sagan. The affair appears to lasted a good number of years and her second son Paul Louis, born in Paris in 1867, is alleged to have been the Prince's son. Jeanne's husband was a member of the noble french family of Talleyrand-Perigord and a great-grandson of the famous Charles-Maurice de Talleyrand-Perigord, Chief Minister to the Emperor Napoleon. The Princess was one of his regular Paris hostesses, along with the Comtesse de Pourtales 'a celebrated beauty and leader of fashion' and Baronne Alphonse de Rothschild, the sister of Alfred and Nathaniel Rothschld, who were at Cambridge with the Prince. All three of these ladies received long afternoon visits from the Prince in the 1880's but the Comtesse de Pourtales vigorously denied that she was ever the Prince's mistress when the subject was brought up following his memorial service in 1910; 'So ridiculous that everyone considered I had an affair with him!'

The Princess de Sagan was followed by the famous Parisian courtesans Guilia Benini and Hortense Schneider but they were only brief affairs. Hortense Schneider, was famed for her performances of Offenbach operettas. Her relations with Royalty were so intimate as to earn her the title of 'le passage des princes'. Guilia Benini known as 'La Barucci', the self-styled 'greatest whore in the world' received 'an astonishing number of visitors' including the Prince to her home but died of consumption in 1871 when her brother tried unsuccessfully to blackmail him.

Edward's affair with Helen, Lady Forbes, the wife of Sir Charles John Forbes of Newe, was brief but it is alleged that it did produce a daughter, Evie, born in 1868. Lady Forbes beauty was well known, Lord Frederick Hamilton describing her as 'the most perfect example of classical beauty I have ever seen, [with] features as clean-cut as those of a cameo'. Evie was of perfect proportions and became 'for many years one of the best known of society hostesses'. The claim that she was the Prince's child was made by her son Edward James in his autobiography 'Swans reflecting elephants: my early years'. In support of his claim he quoted the 150 or more letters written to his mother from the Prince in which he always addressed her as 'My dear child'. 'Evie' undoubtedly 'enjoyed a relationship of unusual intimacy' with the Royal Family; Queen Alexandra was god-mother to her daughter Alexandra Maud, born in 1896, who was also said to bear a striking resemblance to the Prince of Wales and he was godfather to her son Edward, born in 1907.

In addition to Lady Forbes, the Prince of Wales is also said to have bedded two of her sisters, ie Harriet, Lady Mordaunt and Georgina, Countess of Dudley. Lady Mordaunt, a flirtatious and headstrong young woman, described by Lord Frederic Hamilton as 'a radiant apparition', was the first of the sisters to have had the honour of becoming the Prince's mistress prior to her marriage in 1866. Her only child, a daughter, Violet Caroline was born in 1869 and she declared that the father was either Lord Cole, Sir Frederick Johnstone or the Prince of Wales; the first two were cited as co-respondents in her husband's petition for divorce but not the Prince. The affair caused a great scandal. Many years later in 1891 Sir Francis Knollys wrote that 'Mr Gladstone, who was then Prime Minister took all the indirect means in his power (and successfully) to prevent anything being brought out in the course of the trial that could be injurious to the Prince or the Crown'. The third sister Georgina, Countess of Dudley, 'a celebrated beauty and leader of fashion' did not become the Prince's mistress until 1896, when she was fifty years old! He is alleged to have bedded her after his first Derby win with *Persimmon*.

The Moncreiffe family's record of supplying three royal mistresses, all sisters, for the Prince was unique but it continued into the next generation when Evie's daughter Audrey, briefly became the mistress of Edward VIII, when he was Prince of Wales and Rosemary Leveson-Gower, the wife of Lady Dudley's grandson was also pursued by the Prince. In addition Evie's cousin Ida Stewart-Forbes married Mrs Keppel's brother Sir Archibald Edmonstone, whilst Ida's brother James married Daisy Warwick's half sister Angelina St Clair-Erskine. This tangled web of connections between the royal mistresses was further complicated by Lady Dudley's nephew marrying Winifred (Freda) Birkin, who later won the heart of Edward VIII, as we shall see. Mrs Keppel, of course, is the great-grandmother of Camilla Parker-Bowles. The Moncreiffe sisters were also related to James Hay, one of the male favourites of King James I.

Another royal favourite was the widowed Lady Susan Vane Tempest, *nee* Pelham-Clinton, daughter of the 5th Duke of Newcastle, whom Queen Victoria described as 'really a clever, agreeable, handsome girl'. Lady Susan, a direct descendant of Barbara Villiers, mistress of Charles II was connected in numerous other ways with that famous wanton and many other royal mistresses among them Lady Augusta Murray, who married (?) HRH Augustus, the Duke of Sussex, son of George III, and

Lady Susan Wilson, daughter of the 7th Duke of Marlborough, who was another mistress of the Prince of Wales. When Lady Susan Vane Tempest discovered that she was pregnant by the Prince in 1871 she wrote to him asking for financial assistance in order to buy the silence of her servants. The Prince sent his physician Dr Oscar Clayton to assist her, but nothing further was heard of the child.

Patsy Cornwallis-West, who was the Prince's mistress in 1874, bore a son George, who later married the widowed Lady Randolph Churchill – herself a mistress of Edward VII. Patsy, a grand-daughter of the Marquess of Headfort, was a court favourite and it was said that George had been fathered by the Prince in the woods at Eaton whilst staying with the Duke of Westminster, an estate worker's little girl having 'seen the Prince on top of her'. Patsy's cousin, the 4th Marquess of Headfort, also formed a royal connection by marrying Rose Boote the famous 'Gaiety Girl', who had been a mistress of the Prince before her marriage.

The Prince's preference for choosing a mistress from families that had had provided royal mistresses in the past, was very pronounced. The next example was Lady Aylesford. On this occasion it was Lady Aylesford's husband that provided the royal connection. The 7th Earl of Aylesford (1849-85), was a cousin of Daisy Warwick's husband and Mary Venetia James (*nee* Cavendish-Bentinck), another alleged mistress of the Prince. He was also descended from the 1st Earl of Portland, a favourite of King William III and thus was connected with the Villiers and Howard families.

The Prince's affair with Lady Aylesford took place after her marriage in 1871 and during their time together he wrote a number of 'extremely imprudent letters containing improper proposals'. During that time she produced two daughters, the second of whom Lady Alexandra may possibly have been the Prince's child. However, the affair did not last long and by 1876, Lady Aylesford was romantically involved with Lord Blandford, the eldest son and heir of the 8th Duke of Marlborough, brother of Lady Susan Wilson, another of the Prince's mistresses. Unwisely Lady Aylesford gave the Prince's letters to her new lover, who promptly passed them on to his brother Lord Randolph Churchill, a great friend of the Prince. When Lord Randolph threatened to make the letters public because he was jealous of the Prince's attentions to his wife, the former was furious and Lord Aylesford sued for divorce.

DAISY, COUNTESS OF WARWICK

Frances Evelyn Maynard, more commonly known as Daisy, was born in 1861, the elder daughter and co-heir of Colonel the Honourable Charles Henry Maynard, of the Royal Horse Guards, who was the son of 3rd and last Viscount Maynard. Like Lady Susan Vane Tempest, another of Edward VII's mistresses, Daisy came with impeccable royal connections. She was directly descended from Arabella Churchill, mistress of King James II, by her husband Charles Godfrey and thus was also kin to the 1st Duke of Buckingham, the royal favourite of King James I. Her mother, Blanche FitzRoy, also had a triple illegitimate decent from King Charles II via the Dukes of Grafton (by Barbara Villiers), the Dukes of St Albans (by Nell Gwyn) and the Dukes of Richmond (by Louise de Queroualle). The concentration of such a large genetic input from the aforementioned royal mistresses has not been fully appreciated in previous accounts of Daisy's life and goes along way to explain her impetuosity, steely determination. and passionate nature.

Daisy's father, Colonel Maynard, should not of course be left out of the equation, he had a reputation 'as a brilliant equestrian and a beau sabreur, with a well known fondness for wine and mad cap exploits' qualities that his daughter inherited in full measure. But the Maynard family also hid a very large skeleton in their closet in the person of Ann (abella) or Nancy Parsons, wife of the 2nd Viscount Maynard, the colonel's uncle, who had a very colourful and chequered past before her marriage. Indeed so much so that one historian has described her as the 'the English counterpart of Ninon de l'Enclos'.

Before ending up as Lady Maynard, this unfortunate beauty had passed through the hands of several other noble lords before reaching the altar. But despite being passed from lover to lover:

no coarsening marks were present in her appearance, nor to any appreciable degree had her beauty suffered from the defiling ordeal. Just as her face and figure retained an unspoilt and refreshing seductiveness, so her manners and choice of language were all that could be desired; added to which... she remained essentially religious and serious-minded, which trait... immeasurably increased her charm.

After a bad experience in the West Indies whilst under the protection of a Mr Haughton or Horton, Nancy returned to England in 1763 and settled in London in Brewer Street, Golden Square, where her 'lovely oval face, of the type that haunted Correggio waking and sleeping, the lofty, thoughtful brow, the pensive eyes, the classic nose and, not least, the shapely lines of the graceful form – all these accessories of beauty combined to inspire' the Duke of Grafton with a deep and abiding infatuation, all of which was reinforced by 'the magnetic quality of her personality'.

Augustus Henry Fitz Roy, 3rd Duke of Grafton, was the grandson of the 2nd Duke of Grafton, Lord Chamberlain to George I and II, and so it is alleged lover of the latter's daughter the Princess Amelia. As the descendant therefore of the notorious beauty Barbara Villiers, Duchess of Cleveland and her royal lover Charles II, the Duke was a catch indeed and in true Villiers style the affair was 'conducted with the minimum of secrecy and discretion'. The affair began just as the duchess was about to give birth to her second child and endured to the surprise of all for seven years during which time Nancy 'presided constantly at her lover's table' and 'did the honours with an ease and an elegance that the finest nobility in the kingdom were compelled to admire'. As for the Duke's character it was generally acknowledged that 'harnessing his energies to any task that materially interfered with his personal pleasures and comfort was highly distasteful to him' but despite this he rose to become 1st Lord of the Treasury, i.e. Prime Minister.

When the affair ended Nancy was not short of admirers to take the Duke's place. The Duke of Bedford, was the first and he was quickly followed by the 'remarkably handsome and young' Duke of Dorset of whom the Duchess of Devonshire wrote 'I always have look'd upon him as the most dangerous of men, for with that beauty of his he is unaffected and has a simplicity and persuasion in his manner that makes one account very easily for the number of women he has had in love with him'. Dorset, who was some ten years her junior, immediately took her off to France but failed to marry her, as predicted by the society gossips.

Within a few years the novelty of being the lover of Grafton's ex-mistress had worn off and Dorset left her in order to take up with Mrs Armistead, who would later become the wife of Charles James Fox. Undaunted Nancy immediately captured another beau, Charles, Viscount Maynard and within three years they were wed. The attachment lasted for a good number of years but like all men when her physical charms no longer excited him he sort consolation elsewhere and took a mistress Mme Derville by name, a member of the Paris Opera. Nancy meanwhile is alleged to eloped with one of her husband's servants and then was murdered by her young lover near Fontainbleu in 1814, where her body was left in a ditch minus the family jewels. In the same year as she died Daisy's father Charles Maynard was born.

Whether Daisy was aware of the scandalous behaviour of her forebears is unknown but initially there was no hint that she would emulate their exploits and further scandalise Edwardian society. But as with her ancestor Barbara Villiers, the loss of her father at a very young age, she was only three when he died, and the re-marriage of her mother, appears to have an unfortunate affect on her development. By all accounts her step-father, the Earl of Rosslyn, was 'an intelligent and charming man' and a great personal friend of Benjamin Disraeli, but he was more interested in horse racing than in supervising the upbringing of his step-daughter. Without the firm hand of a strong father figure the weaker traits of Daisy's character were thus left to flourish unchecked.

At the age of twelve Daisy met the beautiful nineteen year old Emile Charlotte Le Breton, otherwise known as Lily Langtry, at the Chelsea studio of the artist Frank Miles and was immediately struck by her beauty:

I found the loveliest woman I have ever seen... She had dewy violet eyes, a complexion like a peach, and a mass of lovely hair drawn back in a knot at the nape of her classic head. But how can words convey the vitality, the glow, the amazing charm, which made this fascinating woman the centre of any group she entered.

She made such an impression upon Lord Rosslyn that he immediately invited her to dine with the family at their Grafton Street house in London. Accompanied by her husband she was radiant in her 'signature back dress' and from then onwards was frequently invited to the family home at Easton in Essex until she caught the eye of the Prince of Wales and became his mistress.

The encounter with Lily, left an indelible impression on Daisy who would eventually follow in her footsteps and become a royal mistress but before that momentous occasion her mother determined that she should be wed. As the co-heiress of her father Daisy was a considerable catch but fate had definitely decided that royalty would feature in her life one way or another. At the age of eighteen two suitors appeared in her life, the first Prince Leopold, was the youngest son of Queen Victoria and the second, Lord Brooke, son and heir of the Earl of Warwick.

Leopold who as a child had displayed an 'incorrigibly wilful nature' nevertheless had grown up to be an 'intelligent and affectionate son' who reminded the Queen very much of her dear deceased husband Prince Albert. Unfortunately Leopold was a haemophiliac but despite this he 'had spirit, intellect, considerable book learning and a vivid interest in politics'. Rather belatedly the Queen eventually created him Duke of Albany but it was only after he threatened to stand for a Parliamentary Borough 'in which interest' asked his equerry 'Extreme Radical' he replied!

Lady Rosslyn was flattered beyond measure by the prospect of her daughter marrying a Royal Prince and did everything she could to progress the match but the situation was complicated by the fact that Daisy had clearly taken a strong fancy to Lord Brooke, much to her mother's annoyance. Despite this added complication Queen Victoria invited Daisy to Windsor Castle and pronounced herself very satisfied with the young lady. For his part Leopold made the expected moves but even he was unaware that Daisy was in fact smitten by the charms of his equerry Lord Brooke. When Victoria continued to press for a decision

Daisy wrote and declined the great honour that had been offered her and then secretly became engaged to Lord Brooke. The Queen was furious at the rejection and 'did not hid her annoyance' but was anxious that 'no word of what she regarded as a humiliating refusal should leak out'.

Francis (Greville), Lord Brooke, known to his more intimate friends as 'Brookie', was a dashing twenty six year old army officer and aide de camp to Lord Lytton, Viceroy of India, whose 'ease of manner' and 'droll sense of humour' appears to have captivated Daisy. Lady Rosslyn strongly disapproved of him but when 'Brookie' formally asked for her hand in marriage, Lord Rosslyn immediately gave his consent. To his friend Lord Beaconsfield he wrote: 'He is a steady and domestic young man, who is not tarred with the brush that so often disfigures the golden youth of this century but so far as we can see he gives promise of making a true and loving husband'. It was a remarkably accurate assessment of his character and one that he truly lived up to.

Unfortunately, however, Lord and Lady Rosslyn's demands over Daisy's marriage settlement almost prevented the marriage from taking place. Lord Rosslyn's proposal that Daisy should be responsible for the huge debt he had incurred of £50,000 for extensive building at Easton, without the permission of the other trustees of Daisy's estate or the Chancery Court and a jointure of £5,000 for Lady Rosslyn immediately caste him in the role of wicked stepfather and drew forth from 'Brookie' the comment that Lord Rosslyn was clearly 'inordinately fond of money'. But when all of these problems were resolved the marriage did take place and Daisy was blissfully happy until shortly after the birth of her first child, known affectionately as 'Guido'.

The sudden realisation that she and her husband were sexually incompatible must have come as a great shock to Daisy. Clearly the remarkable sexual prowess for 'Brookie's' ancestor, the celebrated John (Wilmot), Earl of Rochester had not been transmitted to his descendant but the speed with which she sought satisfaction elsewhere was bewildering and totally unexpected. Within a year she had begun a passionate affair with Lord Charles Beresford 'a volatile, charismatic Irishman' and , former equerry to the Prince of Wales. Like Daisy, Beresford's ancestry was replete with royal mistresses, including Anne,

Lady Stanhope, mistress of Edward, Duke of York; Sarah, Countess of Tyrconnel, mistress of Frederick, Duke of York and Lady Almeria Carpenter, mistress of William, Duke of Gloucester.

Most society wives would have accepted their situation but Daisy was not one of them and unfortunately for her much abused husband, she began to display all of the wilfulness and lack of sensitivity that was such a hallmark of her ancestor Barbara Villiers. Indeed this unbridled wilfulness and passion for her lover eventually drove him away but not until she had borne him two children, the younger of whom a son named Charles died as an infant. The affair lasted from early 1884 to 1886 and when the end came it was sudden and very dramatic. During a visit to Easton as a guest of Daisy and her husband, Lady Beresford was informed very abruptly by Daisy that she was divorcing Lord Brooke and eloping with Lord Beresford. The shock reverberated throughout polite society and the Beresfords who were shaken by Daisy's outburst never again appeared as guests at Easton. Several years later Daisy tried to win her lover back but her attempts to do so only caused further problems. Finally Lady Beresford was forced to employ the services of George Lewis, a solicitor with a reputation of dealing with such delicate affairs but the outcome was not at all as she had planned.

On receiving Lady Beresford's letter threatening legal action Daisy went straight to the Prince of Wales and pleaded with him to help her. The approach could not have been better timed. Since the end of his affair with the beautiful Lily Langtry in 1880, the prince had gone thorough a succession of mistresses including the 'elegant and very beautiful' Comtesse de Boutourline (born Countess Ludmila Pavlova Bobrinsky), a great-granddaughter of Catherine the Great of Russia, whom he would visit at the Hotel de Calais in Paris, during his frequent trips to that city. But his main passion between 1886 and 1889 was the beautiful and fascinating Lady Randolph Churchill, otherwise known as 'Jennie Jerome', the mother of Winston Churchill. In addition to the Prince, Lady Randolph also had other romantic and sexual attachments including Count Charles Kinsky but her connection with the Prince eventually ended because her husband was unable to endure the continual stigma of being thought a cuckold. On the death of her husband Lady Randolph subsequently married George Frederick Myddleton Cornwallis-West, who was widely believed to be the Prince's son by Mrs William Cornwallis-West. George a much younger man than his bride by some twenty years was advised by the Prince against 'the inadvisability of marrying a woman so much his senior' but still chose to ignore the warning. The marriage lasted just fourteen years.

When Daisy arrived on the scene the Prince received her with open arms and before long she had established a complete ascendancy over him and his affections. Meanwhile the Beresford affair was eventually resolved but Lord Charles and his wife were banished from the royal circle and for many years thereafter never received another invitation to Marlborough House. But still Daisy was not satisfied. Something was missing from her life but she was unable to articulate what it was. Her restlessness found a brief outlet in a whirl of social gatherings and balls, the most memorable being in 1895 to celebrate her husband's succession to the Earldom of Warwick. But the event drew much criticism from the press who contrasted the gaiety and ornament of the occasion with the state of the dispossessed in society and condemned the 'Thousands of pounds spent on a few hours silly masquerade; men and women strutting before each other's envious eyes in a mad rivalry of wanton dissipation... a vulgar saturnalia of gaudy pride...'. The criticism would mark a major turning point in Daisy's life.

Like Daisy, the Prince of Wales appeared to the outside world to be a 'a hedonist down to the soles of his royal feet and no leash could have been fashioned strong enough to hold him back entirely from the pursuit of pleasure' but it was apparent from an early stage in his life that he was deeply interested in Foreign Affairs and had the Queen, his mother, given him the opportunity to indulge his interest, he may not have pursued the role of 'irresponsible playboy' with such gusto.

By 1896 the affair had lasted seven years but it was soon apparent that Daisy had once again fallen in love and was about to produce very visible proofs of her indiscretion. Whilst the Prince had been 'a very perfect and gentle lover' the affair lacked that vital ingredient 'passion'. Daisy's new lover was Joseph Frederick Laycock, six years her junior and the heir to a considerable fortune. Whilst not from the same aristocratic background as Daisy, he was destined to be her one and only true 'Grand Passion' but he proved to be feckless and weak. The affair produced two children but when Joe tired of her he began an affair with the Marchioness of Downshire. When Daisy discovered the Marchioness's letters to Joe she immediately sent them to the Marquess, who promptly sued for divorce citing Joe. The Prince was not amused! Once again Daisy's lack of judgement in choosing her lovers was apparent to all.

Joe went on to become Brigadier General Sir Joseph Frederick Laycock, (1867-1952) and eventually married his new love Kitty, Marchioness of Downshire and their eldest surviving son when on to marry the younger daughter of Freda Dudley Ward, the longstanding mistress of the Prince of Wales, later King Edward VIII.

Despite his reputation the Prince of Wales throughout all of his major relationships with Lily Langtry, Daisy and Alice Keppel, remained on excellent terms with all of his ex-mistresses. It was a quality he shared with Charles II and time and again we see 'a true element of companionship' replacing the sexual element in their relationships when the physical passion had died. The Princess of Wales for her part continued to love her husband despite his many amorous escapades and affectionately described him as 'my naughty little man'. But for Daisy her days as the Prince's principal love interest were effectively over by 1897 and she retired to concentrate on her doomed relationship with Joe Laycock. Her dominance over the Prince was effectively compromised when he discovered that she was bearing her lover's child. Had the child been her husband's it would not have mattered so much but the Prince's pride was clearly wounded by her perceived betrayal of his friendship and love.

What then were the qualities that had enthralled and enchanted the Prince for some many years. Her physical beauty and the breathtaking shape and grace of her form was undeniable but it was her intelligence that helped her to retain her ascendancy over the Prince for so many years. As the architect Philip Tilden wrote many years later after her death 'All people forgave her everything, for they loved her so very much. Her human instincts and interests were many and marvellous, her sense of humour and infectious laugh tied one to her for life…' Also her seemingly open, honest and childlike nature and captivating charm created an illusive and indefinable charisma which coupled with her socialist leanings and determination to always help the underdog in society portrayed a very unusual, complex and interesting woman.

Mrs Alice Keppel

Alice Edmonstone, was the ninth and youngest child of Admiral Sir William Edmonstone of Duntreath, 4th Bart and his wife Mary Elizabeth Parsons. Her arrival twenty-eight years after her parents marriage finally brought Lady Edmonstone's childbearing days to a very welcome end. But providing dowries for so many daughters placed an incredible strain on Sir William's finances and threatened the prospects of his youngest daughter ever finding a rich and noble born husband.

The only post of importance that Sir William held was ADC to Queen Victoria and as a result he was able to move in the highest royal circles. However, Sir William's record of finding suitable husbands for his elder daughters was not impressive but for his youngest and one assumes his favourite he made a considerable effort. His choice, the Honorable George Keppel, 3rd surviving son of the 4th Earl of Albemarle, was a considerable step up in social rank for Alice and was greatly facilitated by his daughter's obvious beauty and the fact that the Earl of Albemarle was also an ADC to the Queen and thus a close colleague.

The Keppels were, of course, descended from Arnold Joost van Keppel, the protege and favourite of William III, whose youth and good looks made such an impression on the Dutchman that many believed they were lovers. But Keppel was a notorious womaniser and nearly caused one international scandal 'by trying to seduce the mistress of the Elector of Bavaria and who did cause another by having a child by Mme de Richelieu, the latter, a daughter of Hortense Mancini was renowned for her beauty and later went on to become the mistress of Henri Jules, Prince de Conde, son of 'La Grande' Conde.

Apart from the 2nd Earl, succeeding generations of the Keppel family did not seek their brides from the higher eschelons of aristocratic society, quite the reverse in fact but the marriage of the 2nd Earl more than made up for this lapse when he took the grand-daughter of Charles II and his French mistress Louise de Queroulle, Duchess of Portsmouth, as his bride. The Duchess was descended from many of the ancient noble families of France including the princely de Rohans, She was also a cousin of Renee de Rieux, a mistress of the bi-sexual Henri II of France and the Duchess de Etampes, mistress of Francois I of France. Another cousin was the notorious Marquis de Sade.

The marriage also brought connections with the celebrated Dukes of Richmond, owners of Goodwood House in Sussex, who were renowned for their whiggish principles. The 2nd Duke of Richmond, his brother-in-law the 2nd Earl of Albemarle and the latter's eldest son were all staunch supporters of George II and very active in helping to suppress the Jacobite Rebellion of 1745/6. The Edmonstones also supported the status quo. Despite her lack of social status however, Alice also had some very interesting family connections with other royal mistresses most notably, Anne Vane, mistress of Frederick, Prince of Wales; Mary, Countess of Deloraine, mistress of George II, and Elizabeth, Duchess of Rutland, mistress of Frederick, Duke of York.

At the time of Alice's marriage London was experiencing an:

> era of the greatest refinement of aristocratic society, with the nobility – not excluding the nouveau riche – bringing gracious living to a fine art with their balls and parties, yachting and racing, expending for one day's pleasures sums that would have kept a street of slum-dwellers in comfort for a year. Country House parties were the rage, with dancing, sports, flirtation and practical jokes the order of the day.

The reigning belle of the ball in the 1890s was, of course, Daisy, Countess of Warwick, mistress of the Prince of Wales, the finest practitioner of the maxim 'that only married women might indulge in extra marital liaisons'. The result was five children of whom only the first belonged to her husband!

Once she was launched on to the London Season in the wake of her marriage, Alice became a very popular addition to any Country House party and her undoubted beauty attracted a great deal of comment from the gentlemen attending these occasions. She was in fact far more beautiful than Daisy Warwick, as her portraits can testify, but she did not possess the former's keen intellect or have any pretentions to a social conscience. What she did possess was all the qualities needed to capture and sustain a lover's interest eg. beauty, a natural gaiety, charm, artistic sensibility, good humour, tact, discretion and an innate ability to understand and manipulate her lover's mood. Sadly all of these qualities were lost on her husband who very early on in the marriage realised that his wife's nature did not allow her to be faithful to just one man, he therefore sensibly retired to the background and left the field clear for his wife to climb higher on the social ladder by bedding various lovers, the first of whom was William (Beckett), 2nd Baron Grimthorpe, a renowned banker.

The greatest exponent of the maxim that 'discreet unfaithfulness in marriage was acceptable' was Lady Melbourne, mistress of George IV, who in the words of a contemporary historian 'managed to have her children all safely under her husband's name'. She belonged to 'the Devonshire House set' which set great store on the rejection of contemporary morals but still insisted on maintaining an outward propriety. Alice it would seem took these principles to heart and within a several years of her marriage produced a daughter who to all intents and purposes was her husband's but in reality was the product of the affair with her lover; the child was named Violet after Lord Grimthorpe's sister.

The following year the marriage of Alice's brother Sir Archibald Edmonstone to Ida Agnes Stewart-Forbes, niece of the Ladies Forbes and Mordaunt, brought her an unexpected connection with royalty. Each of these ladies was in turn a mistress of the Prince of Wales, later Edward VII. Although they were brief affairs the result in Lady Forbes's case was a daughter Evelyn Elizabeth, who has a very strong claim to being considered the Prince's bastard daughter.

Such an entree into the magic royal circle was all that Alice needed and when the opportunity arose following the retirement of Daisy Warwick, she was able to capitalise on this connection to engineer a meeting with the Prince himself. When and where they met is a matter of conjecture but most accounts agree that it was at an intimate dinner arranged by Alice with her husband also present.

By the time Daisy Warwick had relinquished her role as royal mistress the relationship between her and the Prince was just platonic but the transition had not been plain sailing. As her interests took up more of her time the prince was forced to ask her:

> has it been my fault that we have not met so often lately as of yor? Especially in the evenings?… It is ten years since we became the great friends which I hope we were still… Time and circumstances have doubtless produced changes, but they should be faced and not change a friendship, may I say a devotion, which should last till 'death do us part'.

However, when it came to telling her about his new 'friendship' with Mrs Keppel he wrote: 'Though I should hate more than anything in this world to have any disagreeable discussion with you, still I cannot shrink from it now, and hope an opportunity in the autumn may enable me to have a good long talk with you'.

Eventually Daisy seems to have accepted the situation and so began the prince's last and most well known liaison which lasted until his death in 1910. When the Prince met Alice he was fifty-seven years old:

> a portly man with a closely cropped grey beard and a head from which much of the natural covering had receded' who 'if he was already gorged by life's pleasures, he was not satisfied by them. And now, he had found a woman who was to help him make the evening of his life the most radiant and rewarding time of all.

Not everyone accepted Mrs Keppel's new position as the Prince's mistress. A number of the great country houses firmly closed their doors to her including Hatfield House, home to the Marquess of Salisbury that 'pillar of Conservative tradition and of Victorian morality', who was 'her most powerful social enemy'. Her contemporaries were also just as severe with her husband, one anonymous commentator observing that 'Had Keppel been put up for membership at some London clubs, the black balls would have come rolling out like caviere'. Indeed there were many who condemned him for being so philosophical about his wife's new position and for being so much the 'mari complaisant'. However, Alice won many admirers by her tact, common sense and absolute discretion when dealing with the Prince's affairs but she never used her position to further the interests of her family or friends.

Two years after their first meeting Alice produced a daughter Sonia Rosemary who according to one historian was 'widely believed to have been the Prince's child although never acknowledged as such' but according to another 'was almost certainly the daughter of George Keppel whom she resembled'. If she was the Prince's child the truth will probably never be known but her arrival did nothing to upset the devotion that he clearly felt for Alice.

The Keppels lack of income, however, would always be a problem and one that seemed incapable of being resolved. George had never been a rich man and his affairs reached such a point after his wife's success that he was finally reduced to seek relief by going 'into trade' with Sir Thomas Lipton, the grocer millionaire and yachting friend of the prince. As one historian so aptly put it 'For an Earl's son to be a salesman in Edwardian England was bad enough. For a salesman to be the husband of the King's official mistress was an added humiliation'. Clearly whether mistress of the Prince or the King, Mrs Keppel did not benefit financially from her association at all!

When the Prince succeeded his mother Queen Victoria in 1901, Alice took the very sensible view that in order to succeed in her new role she would have to adopt a very pragmatic approach to her enemies, of which there were a good number. Indeed 'It is said by one who knew Mrs Keppel well that she always refused to take revenge for any of the deliberate snubs to which she was subjected. The King would often breathe fire and brimstone on her behalf and threaten counter-measures against the offender. But she would always calm him down and persuade him to do nothing'. There were, of course, other ways of obtaining redress such as the occasion in June 1909 when barred from Hatfield House, she took up residence at Knebworth House a short distance away, the home of Lord Lytton and promptly invited all of Lord Salisbury's guests to tea, including the King and Queen, which they did minus of course Lord and Lady Salisbury!

On another occasion Alice was seated next to the Kaiser, the King's nephew, at a special dinner and despite his well known abhorrence for his uncle's mistresses he appears to have been charmed by her. Neither her husband or the King was present but Count Mensdorff, the Austro-Hungarian Ambassador felt the event was worthy of recording: 'It was amusing to see how, at table, in disregard of all rules of precedence, the 'Favorita' was seated next to the Kaiser, so she might have the opportunity of talking to him. I would love to know what sort of a report she sent back to Sandringham'.

Alice's special abilities also enabled her on occasions to touch upon the most delicate political situations without any unfortunate repercussions. This ability was fully recognised by Lord Hardinge, later Viceroy to India in a memorandum he drew up after the King's death viz:

Everyone knew of the friendship that existed between King Edward and Mrs George Keppel, which was intelligible in view of the lady's good looks, vivacity and cleverness... 'I would like her to pay tribute to her wonderful discretion, and to the excellent influence which she always exercised upon the King. She never utilized her knowledge to her own advantage, or to that of her friends; and I never heard her repeat an unkind word of anybody. There were one or two occasions when the King was in disagreement with the Foreign Office and I was able, through her to advise the King with a view to the policy of Government being accepted. She was very loyal to the King, and patriotic at the same time. It would have been difficult to find any other lady who would have filled the part of friend to King Edward with the same loyalty and discretion'.

During her reign as the King's favourite the later would pay annual visits to two of the most popular spa's on the continent Marienbad and Biarritz but Alice would only accompany him to Biarritz. Prior to his succession the King paid only two visits to Marienbad, each time as a guest of Prince Metternich once in 1897 and again in 1899. Why Alice never went to Marienbad is unclear but a possible explanation is that 'King Edward was, after all, an honoured guest... of the Emperor Franz Josef... it would not have done for the King of England to parade his famous mistress each day and every summer...' Everything at Biarritz was so much more informal than at Marienbad where he was surrounded by Grand Dukes, Archdukes, statesmen and diplomats and he was able to relax and enjoy his visits. It was during his visit to Marienbad in 1899 that Sonia Keppel was conceived but Alice was not with him.

As her reign as the royal favourite continued unchecked the King made generous financial provision for Alice with the help of Sir Ernest Cassel, in order to ensure that she should 'get peace and quiet and to escape her creditors'. She then invested the money in Canadian stocks and went on to make a fortune. It was a generous gesture and one that was very welcome to the Keppels and it came at just the right time because in the May of 1910 the King suddenly died. Within a short time Alice was forced to move out of her Portman Square House and lamented to friends 'How people can do anything, I do not know, for life with all its joys have come to a full stop, at least for me...'. The realisation that she would no longer be a central figure in society had clearly hit home. All that remained to her now was her family and close friends.

6

THE HOUSE OF WINDSOR

THE DUKE OF WINDSOR

King Edward VIII, like his grandfather Edward VII had a reputation as a great womaniser. His first attempt, however, at a serious affair was with the Hon Sybil Cadogan, the daughter of Viscount Chelsea, whom he saw 'most days and nights' in 1916/7 but it ended abruptly when he began to discuss matrimony. Sybil, or Portia as she was known to her friends, was a close friend of Princess Mary, Edward's sister and later married Lord Derby an old friend of the Prince's from his days at Oxford University. During the period of the Prince's interest in her she was an extra Maid of Honour to Queen Mary, thus close to hand.

Despite the abrupt termination of their relationship, the Prince remained friends for a short time afterwards and there are several references to Sybil and her husband in Edward's letters to his mistress Freda Dudley-Ward. Although Edward and his father did not have a good relationship, the question of Edward's marriage was always something that they could converse about but the prince seemed very indifferent to the idea and apart from Princess May of Schleswig-Holstein whom the Prince had met shortly before the 1st World War he displayed no real interest in marrying a foreign royal. The idea of finding a well born English wife had not occurred to him because he thought his parents would not agree to it. Sybil was in many ways eminently suited to fill the role and in addition was also descended from Charles II and his french mistress, thus adding an extra twist to her appeal. Many years later her nephew Andrew Parker-Bowles would become a very good friend of Princess Anne, Edward's neice, and the husband of Camilla Shand, who later married Prince Charles.

The first major love of the Prince's life was Marion, Viscountess Coke, 4th daughter of Colonel the Hon. Walter Trefusis and his wife Lady Charlotte Montagu Douglas Scott, thus a descendant of Lucy Walter, mistress of Charles II and Louise von Dagenfeld, mistress of Charles Louis, Elector Palatine, Prince Rupert's brother. She was twelve years the Prince's senior and also cousin of Denys Trefusis who later married Violet Keppel, daughter of Alice. The affair with the Prince is alleged to have begun in 1917 when she was already the mother of four children, one of whom David Arthur, born 1915, was the Prince's godson. During their time together 'He saw much of her when he was in England and when he was away poured out his love in letters to her… ' She was '*small, lively, with an individual humour*' but the affair had ended by the spring of 1918 and the Prince had moved on to his next major romance, Lady Rosemary Leveson-Gower whom he met at an army hospital in France in 1917, where she was working as a Red Cross nurse.

As the Prince was godfather to Lady Coke's second son questions have inevitably been raised about his paternity but there is no proof one way or the other. But it is perhaps well to remember that a serious attack of mumps in 1911 may have made him sterile.

Rosemary Leveson-Gower was the neice of Daisy, Countess of Warwick, mistress of Edward VII, the Prince's grandfather. The Prince was captivated by her and later told Freda Dudley Ward that 'she was the only girl I felt I ever could marry'. The King was not keen on his heir apparent marrying into such a family and there the matter died. Nevertheless Lord Loughborough, the Earl of Rosslyn's son and heir became a very good friend of the Prince but like his father he 'was addicted to gambling and alcohol' and ended his life by committing suicide in 1929. Lady Rosemary also had her share of tragedy when her seven year old son was killed in a motoring accident in the same year whilst she was killed in a plane crash the following year!

Lady Rosemary was succeeded in the prince's affections by Freda Dudley Ward; Freda's husband, William Dudley Ward, who was seventeen years her senior, and Lady Rosemary's husband the 2nd Earl Dudley, were cousins. William was a great nephew of the 1st Earl of Dudley whose wife Georgina and two of her sisters had brief but torrid affairs with Edward VII when he was Prince of Wales.

Freda first met the Prince in early March 1918 when she was caught up in a Zeppelin raid on London. Taking refuge in the door way of a house in Belgravia Sqyuare, the home of a friend, Maud Kerr-Smiley, (the sister of Ernest Simpson, who was destined to marry Wallis Warfield) she found a party in progress, attended by the Prince of Wales, no less, and was immediately invited to join them. On meeting the Prince, he was immediately attracted to her and they danced together all evening. When the Prince was posted to Italy shortly afterwards he continued the intimacy with dozens of letters from the front where he remained until mid-August. Whilst he was away Freda met Captain, later Major, Reginald Seymour, cousin of the Marquess of Hertford, and as their letters to each other testify they had a brief but intense affair which lasted until the Prince's return. Unable, at first, to contemplate losing her, he wrote chiding her about abandoning him 'How was your young man ? Do you like him making love to you better than me?... I can't forget how divine you were to me last Thursday, only 6 days ago... I fully accept my position of No 2... '

It was a heated affair at first but conducted with 'complete discretion', although the Prince was still seeing Rosemary Leveson Gower when they met. Although at the beginning the relationship was 'all consuming' and he dearly wanted a child by her, it had run into trouble by 1923 when he had a brief affair with Mrs Audrey Coats, a far cry from the time when he declared that 'I swear I'll never marry any other woman but you'. Initially she was pursued by Lord Mountbatten who was besotted with her. The Prince became involved when 'Dickie' asked him if he should marry her but she turned him down and married instead a wealthy cotton magnate.

Mrs Coats, with whom the Prince had a brief affair in 1923, was the daughter of Evie James, alleged bastard daughter of Edward VII by Lady Forbes and thereby quite possibly the Prince's first cousin. 'As the prettiest debutante of her season with £4,000 a year and a fast reputation, she had earlier been courted by an enraptured Lord Louis Mountbatten' and before her marriage in 1922 'had played havoc with a wide swathe of London Society'. But the affair did not last and before long the Prince had returned to Freda and it would be another six years before he became involved with another woman.

The affair with Audrey Coats prove to be a watershed in his relationship with Freda, because from then on he remained faithful until the appearance of Lady Furness in 1929. However, it has been alleged that he also had a brief affair with Freda's sister, Vera, the wife of Major (Frank) James Wriothesley Seely, Major Seely was very well connected and brought with him two descents from Charles II through his mistresses Barbara Villiers and Louise de Queroualle and kinship to the Duchess of Rutland, the 'Grand Amour' of Frederick, Duke of York, brother of George IV plus Lady Sarah Wilson an alleged mistress of Edward VII; he was also a cousin of Diana, Princess of Wales. At one point before her marriage, Freda and the Prince had discussed the possibility of Vera becoming his wife but nothing came of the idea, 'You will remember our discussing her as a possible wife for me', he wrote on one occasion.

Although Tim Seely, Vera's son, declared in public on a TV 'Talk Show' in 1988 that he was the illegitimate son of the Prince of Wales, the Prince was in the Mediterraean with Mrs Simpson at the time of his conception thus making it impossible for the claim to be taken seriously. In addition, as Mr Seely already has 'Royal Blood' flowing through his veins, his claim that he was the prince's son is rather pointless.

The Seely and Birkin families are relatively undistinguished, the royal connections coming from the maternal lines. But, Major Seely was also kin to the Duchesses of Richmond and Manchester, sisters of his great-great-grandmother, the Duchess of Bedford, both of whom were ardently pursued by George IV. Neither Duchess had a good reputation, the first according to a contemporary being 'excessively proud, and distainful of persons of inferior rank'. The Duke of Gordon, father to the Duchesses was also descended from Mary Carey, mistress of Henry VIII and Esme (Stewart), Duke of Lennox, the favourite of James I. Mr Seely should be proud of such royal connections!

In 1922, Freida embarked upon another intense relationship with Michael Herbert, a cousin of the Earl of Pembroke. The couple had known each other for some time much to the annoyance of the Prince.

When there was talk that Freida and her husband were to be divorced, he feared that she might even marry him! But significantly after this date her feelings for the Prince did change and she devised ways and means to see less of him than before in order to preserve the reputation of her children. Thereafter she became just his confidante.

As the letters to Freda Dudley-Ward show, in private the prince was a self obsessed individual, prone to depression and who did not always treat the women in his life with the respect that was their due. He clearly felt a deep affection for Freda which unfortunately was not returned in equal measure. The letters also reveal his constant insecurity and immaturity, self pity and unhappiness and the major part that Freda played in supporting him and allaying most of his fears.

ELIZABETH, THE QUEEN MOTHER

The Royal Family's predilection for choosing to marry non-royal partners has become so common that there is a real possibility that they will soon cease to be royal in the strict sense of the word. The trend that was begun by Edward IV and made acceptable by Henry VIII has now become almost the norm. Whether this is a good thing or a bad one is open to debate but it does have a direct bearing upon the major theme of this book. But the debate on whether the Royal family should only marry people of equal rank or not as the case maybe has now been overtaken by events.

What ever the merits of marrying someone of equal rank and there are some, marriage with persons of a lesser rank does present the monarchy in a more modern light but at the same time it loses much of its mystique and appeal. However, perhaps we should bear in mind the thoughts of Lord Folkestone on the 'supposed dishonour of the crown from an alliance with a subject' when it was raised in Parliament during the passing of the Royal Marriage Act in 1772 viz: 'I will never persuade myself that any British King, much less one who publicly gloried in 'being born and educated a Briton', could so far forget the natural equality of all mankind, the boasted independence of every individual in this nation, as to think dishonourable a stream of British blood in the royal veins'.

In more recent times the trend once again has taken on a new lease of life, of the five sons of King George V, only the Duke of Kent, chose to marry another royal i.e. Princess Marina of Greece. The eldest son, Edward VIII married an American divorcee and as a result was effectively excluded from the family whilst the younger sons the Dukes of York and Gloucester took partners from the British Aristocracy i.e. the Lady Elizabeth Bowes-Lyon and the Lady Alice Montagu-Douglas-Scott.

The choice of partners was instructive as both were direct descendants of King Charles II, Lady Elizabeth from his mistress Louise de Queroualle and Lady Alice from Lucy Walter and Louise de Queroualle. Lady Elizabeth, who later married King George VI, was also descended from Lady Chesterfield, a mistress of King James II and in addition was a cousin of Mary Venetia James, who was reputed to have been a mistress of King Edward VII; Sarah Ferguson who later married her grandson Andrew, Duke of York was also a relative. The 1st Earl of Portland, a favourite of William III, and his wife Anne Villiers, cousin of Barbara and Elizabeth Villiers, mistresses of Charles II and William III, are also direct ancestors. Oswald Mosley, the famous fascist was also a cousin. But her most notorious ancestor was Mary Eleanor Bowes, wife of the 9th Earl of Strathmore and Kinghorne.

Lady Alice for her part was descended from the 2nd Duke of Buccleuch, a notorious womaniser who had ten bastard children in addition to his legitimate issue, all of whom were mentioned in his will. As a great-grandson of King Charles II this type of behaviour is not unexpected. Lady Mordaunt and Lady Forbes both mistresses of King Edward VII were also cousins of Lady Alice and Sarah Ferguson, late Duchess of York is a close relative.

The Lady Elizabeth, the mother of our present Queen, was given the standard education for a young lady of her times in French and German plus domestic science, painting, dancing and music. But from a very early age she astonished some of her contemporaries with her precociousness and instinctive grasp of knowing when to say the right thing; according to one visitor to Glamis Castle 'had she been consciously rehearsing for her future she could scarcely have practised her manners more assiduously'. Allied with a strong desire to please she also possessed a strong sense of duty and a steely determination to succeed in anything that she set her mind on. She could also be a formidable enemy as the Duchess of Windsor would find to her cost.

Finding a suitable husband for such a beautiful and charming daughter as Lady Elizabeth, was a problem for her father, Lord Strathmore. His desire to see her suitably wed was understandable but the Strathmores close connections with King George V virtually ensured that the two families saw a great deal of each other and eventually the inevitable happened. The first official record of a meeting between the Lady Elizabeth and her future husband was at a birthday party given by the Duke of Buccleuch when she was just five years old and he was nine. Many years later they met at another party and the young Prince George was immediately smitten by Elizabeth and remarked to his parents on her kindness to him, so much so that he proposed marriage but she declined.

Her first serious suitor was James Stuart, the third son of the Earl of Moray, who was for a short time an equerry to the Duke of York, her future husband. The Earls of Moray were descended from James, Earl of Moray, the bastard half-brother of Mary, Queen of Scots and a marriage with such a noble family would have been very acceptable to the Earl of Strathmore but it was not to be! Lady Elizabeth was in no hurry to wed, preferring to play the field and enjoy life. Another of her suitors was Prince Paul of Serbia, later Yugoslavia, who was six years her senior. The Prince had a very colourful ancestry and was related to the celebrated Anatoly Demidoff, Prince of San Donato, husband of Mathilde Bonaparte, niece of the Emperor Napoleon. Such a match would have been a considerable step up in social rank but again she refused to commit herself. The Prince, who later went onto become Regent of Yugoslavia during the 2nd World War, eventually married the sister of Princess Marina of Kent and thus became Elizabeth's brother-in-law.

Although she refused his offer of marriage on two previous occasions, she accepted Prince George's third proposal when he made it in person and they were duly married on the 26 April 1923 at Westminster Abbey.

But the Lady Elizabeth did have misgivings including the fact that she was 'afraid (she would) never, never again.. be free to think, speak and act as I feel I really ought to'. Initially she did not love him commenting that 'I felt it was my duty to marry Bertie' but then qualifying it with another comment saying 'I fell in love with him afterwards'.

The marriage took place just ten days after the anniversary of the fateful Battle of Culloden in 1746, an event that will always be etched in the memory of the Scottish nation because of the savage repression of the Highlands that followed and the final destruction of all hope for a Stuart Restoration. Although Lady Elizabeth's ancestor, the 8th Earl of Strathmore did not support the pretensions of Bonnie Prince Charlie or raise his tenants to support him in 1745, his brothers, the 5th, 6th and 7th Earls were all strong supporters of the 'Stuart Cause'. Indeed the 5th Earl was killed at the Battle of Sheriffmuir fighting for the Prince's father, the Old Pretender. When the latter came to Scotland in 1716, he was royally housed at Glamis Castle by the 6th Earl before moving on to stay at another seat of the Strathmore's, Castle Lyon. Although his expedition to Scotland eventually failed the 6th Earl remembered him as 'a very fine gentleman, very punctual, very religious... modest, chaste and of a great and unusual understanding' and the memory of his visit remained with the Strathmore family for generations to come. Indeed it is possible that the choice of the name Charles for her grandson was a direct consequence of Lady Elizabeth's inherited affection and regard for the Royal House of Stuart. What the young prince thought of the Earl is not on record but the Duke of Liria, the prince's nephew judged him very harshly and thought he was 'inconceivably stupid'.

HM THE QUEEN & PRINCE PHILIP

HM the Queen has only two passions in life, horses and her husband Philip. Educated at home in a very sheltered environment her school curriculum included lessons on the British Constitution, Art, music and languages plus the more physical pursuits of riding and swimming. As a youngster she was described by her cousin Margaret Rhodes as 'a jolly little girl, but fundamentally sensible and well behaved' and her stable and happy home life within a caring and loving family equipped her with a great inner strength and quiet dignity that appealed immensely to Prince Philip, who was brought up in a completely different way.

Philip was greatly attracted to the idea of a loving and stable family environment, having never had one himself. As the youngest child and only son he was effectively an only child, his eldest sister was fourteen years his senior, and he grew up in a variety of different countries, most notably Greece and France before ending up in England. Whilst living in Paris Philip attended a day school at St Cloud but by 1931 all of his sisters had found German husbands. Shortly afterwards when his mother Princess Alice became ill, the family sold their home and she retreated to a sanitarium in order to regain her health. Philip meanwhile was sent to England to finish his education at Gordonstoun in the care of his uncle Lord Milford Haven with frequent visits to his grandmother and Lord Mountbatten another uncle.

His unorthodox upbringing was a source of great concern to the British Establishment who 'feared he might be like his father (Prince Andrew of Greece), a gambler, & womaniser who ended his days as a playboy in the South of France' but Philip clearly grew up with a strong respect for family values and a great longing to settle down to a secure home life. When his uncle Lord Milford Haven died in 1938, Prince Andrew asked Lord Mountbatten to take over the supervision of his education which he duly did and in that same year he entered the Royal Naval College as a cadet. The following year he met his future wife for the first time and made an instant impression, he was eighteen and Elizabeth just thirteen. They would not meet again for another six years during which time he was able to sew some wild oats.

If Prince Philip did have any affairs and the rumours are that he did, then they would almost certainly have taken place before he married the Queen. Although he is rumoured to have had extra-marital affairs there is no firm evidence. Nevertheless his name has been linked to a number of very beautiful and attractive women both before and after his marriage. Before he married his cousin, Alexandra of Yugoslavia recalled that 'blondes, brunettes & redheads, Philip gallantly & I think quite impartially squired them all' indeed at the end of the war it is alleged that he had two special girl friends, Sue Other-Gee and Sandra Jacques; with the latter he is alleged to have had 'a terrific and very full love affair'. Philip's need for the company of witty and beautiful women was duly acknowledged even by Lady Mountbatten who very sensibly summed up the situation thus 'Prince Philip is a man who enjoys the company of attractive, intelligent, younger women. Nothing wrong in that!'.

Another alleged affair with Helen Cordet, a Greek cabaret star, gave rise to the rumour that Philip was the father of her two sons but the truth of the matter was that he had apparently known her since childhood and he was simply godfather to her children. Other names included Princess Alexandra (Philip's cousin), Merle Oberon, the film star, Susan Barrantes, mother of Sarah Ferguson, Pat Kirkwood, the star of stage and screen, the Duchess of Abercorn (another cousin), the Countess of Westmorland and Lady Romsey. His appeal was obvious, he was quick witted, amusing, tall and good looking with blond hair and a quick temper but regardless of whether the rumours were true when they came to the Queen's attention she was predictably very upset. The result was 'blazing rows' but according to one friend she eventually 'accepted that she married a man who takes a lot of amusing' and that she 'accepted the occasional fling as unimportant because she understands that some men have certain needs & that doesn't mean they love their wives any less'.

Of the ladies he is alleged to have pursued only Lady Abercorn and Pat Kirkwood have spoken about him in public. Lady Abercorn duly acknowledges that there was 'a highly charged chemistry' between them but 'the passion was in the ideas' what ever that means. When asked by a reporter about his alleged extra-marital affairs Philip snapped back 'Good god woman, I don't know what company you keep, have you ever stopped to think that for the past forty years I have never moved anywhere without a policeman accompanying me? So how the hell could I get away with anything like that?

The Prince met Pat Kirkwood for the first time in 1948, when the Queen, then Princess Elizabeth was eight months pregnant with Prince Charles. After her act she was informed much to her surprise by her then boyfriend that Philip, would be joining them for dinner. When they arrived at *Les Ambassadeurs* a very fashionable restaurant in Mayfair, the other diners fell silent and you could hear a pin drop. Afterwards Philip attempted to drive them home but kept bumping into the back of other cars and the next morning they had breakfast together. The furore in the press the next day was remarkable and the King was said to be extremely angry at his antics. The incident immediately gave rise to the rumour that Philip and Miss Kirkwood were intimately involved. Unfortunately such wilful and impetuous behaviour had unfortunate repercussions for Miss Kirkwood and did her a great deal of harm. Indeed many years later when the press revived the details of the incident and beat a path to her door, she wrote to Philip in some distress asking for advice on how to kill the rumours. In reply he wrote:

I am very sorry indeed to hear you have been pestered about that ridiculous 'rumour'. The trouble is that certain things seem to get into journalist 'folklore' and it is virtually impossible to get it out of the system. Much as I would like to put a stop to this, and many other similar stories, about other members of the family, we have found that, short of starting libel proceedings, there is absolutely nothing to be done. Invasion of privacy, invention, and false quotations are the bane of our existence… I feel the best bet is to put the facts squarely in your book. It may not make any difference to what the 'evil-minded' may think but I am sure that most reasonable people would accept what you say, and it would then be on record. Philip.

In an attempt to scotch the rumours the Prince took the Queen to one of Miss Kirkwood's performances but they still persisted.

Philip's need for excitement and the company of beautiful or attractive women is a common characteristic in most men but he also had many male friends and he was particularly attached to Michael Parker whose disregard for Philip's rank and general good nature endeared him greatly to the Prince.

The Queen's reaction to her husband's rumoured infidelities was to maintain a dignified silence but in private rumours circulated of 'blazing rows at times & in racing circles tongues have wagged for years speculating that she may have 'got her own back' on Philip by having an affair with her late racing manager Lord Porchester'. 'Porchie', the Queen's nickname for Lord Carnarvon, had been a friend since she was a teenager and it was their common interest in horses that brought them together. Rumours of long romantic walks around the palace grounds were probably nothing more than just two friends engaging in equine conversation with perhaps the odd request for advice and help in understanding and dealing with some of her husband's more outrageous outbursts and frequent use of the 'f' word!

The rumour that Lord Porchester was the father of Prince Andrew, the Queen's third child, arose because of an alleged physical likeness between the two and it was given some substance by the knowledge that Prince Philip was away on a sea voyage in the yacht 'Britannia' for three months in early 1959, shortly before Prince Andrew was conceived. However, Andrew, was born 19 February 1960, thus conceived around the second week in May 1959, after Prince Philip had returned. 'Porchie' was a gifted man 'with an agile brain and a sharp eye' who according to his obituary had 'an intuitive knack of sending mares to the right stallions and a fantastic memory for bloodlines'. It is easy to see, therefore, why the Queen valued his advice and why they became such close friends. He also had some very interesting family connections; his stepmother was the former dancer Tilly Losch (a one time mistress of Prince Serge Obolensky), who was previously married to Edward James, grandson of Lady Forbes, mistress of Edward VII and he was a cousin of the writer Auberon Waugh.

PRINCESS MARGARET

When Princess Margaret was approaching marriageable age, the Queen Mother drew up a list of suitable candidates which included the Dukes of Buccleuch and Rutland. 'Johnny' Dalkeith, as he was then known, was the eldest son of the 8th Duke of Buccleuch and his wife Vreda Lascelles, granddaughter of the 10th Duke of St Albans. Johnny was Scotland's premier nobleman and an excellent choice as a husband for the princess. As a descendant of Charles II by two of his mistresses, Lucy Walter and Nell Gwyn, thus of royal blood, he was emminently preferable to a foreign prince. The Princess, however, had other ideas and although Johnny was a member of her social set the marriage never materialised.

Charles John Manners, 10th Duke of Rutland was ten years older than the princess and was descended from that very colourful character Nell Gwyn. He was also a descendant of Elizabeth Howard, wife of the 5th Duke of Rutland, who became romantically involved with Frederick, Duke of York, brother of George IV, the godfather to her eldest son. At the time the Duke was sixty two years old and the Duchess just forty four but they acted as if they were just seventeen and fifteen. But within three years the Duchess was dead of a burst appendix and the Duke 'never having been the same since her death' followed two years later. But like Johnny' Dalkeith, the Duke of Rutland fared no better in the marriage stakes and eventually went on to become the son-in-law of Margaret, Duchess of Argyll, of the 'headless man fame'. But the Duke did have some consolation when his daughter Lady Charlotte became a girl friend of the present Prince of Wales an honour she shared with her cousin Elizabeth Manners. It was perhaps just as well as Margaret preferred partners from a more bohemian or unorthodox background, a characteristic which was very much in the spirit of her ancestor Mary Eleanor Bowes.

Mary Eleanor Bowes was orphaned at the age of eleven and inherited a fortune estimated between £600,000 and one million pounds but the lack of adequate moral and spiritual guidance from a strong father figure during the crucial years in her development had unfortunate consequences. Extremely intelligent she embraced many of the ideals of the later Romantic Movement i.e. intuition and emotion over rationalism, before they were fashionable and in consequence found herself repeatedly at odds with conventional society. After encouraging several suitors such as the younger brother of the 3rd Duke of Buccleuch and Lord John Stuart, later Lord Mount Stuart, she married John Lyon, Earl of Strathmore, dutifully producing five children in as many years. Whilst continually bearing children there was obviously very little opportunity for her to allow her passions and emotions full expression but as her husband's increasing dependence on drink became more pronounced she inevitably looked elsewhere for diversion.

When Lord Strathmore suddenly died in 1776, Mary immediately regained control of her fortune and took a lover Charles Gray and within a short space of time had three abortions before being seduced by Andrew Robinson Stoney, an Anglo-Irish adventurer. The latter on discovering that she had made a pre-nuptial agreement retaining control of her fortune, force her to recant and then subjected her to eight years of mental and physical abuse before she was finally able to escape from his control and petition for a divorce. Undaunted he then proceeded to abduct her until he was arrested and sent to prison for three years. Her story is indeed a sad one and unfortunately some of her children inherited her more wayward characteristics.

The eldest son John, 10th Earl of Strathmore, was a notorious womaniser, one of his mistresses being Sarah, Lady Tyrconnel, former lover of Frederick, Duke of York, brother of George IV and 'the wildest of her race' the famous Delavals. The affair followed on from that of the Duke of York and lasted from 1791 until her death in 1800. Sadly her reputation was such that she was 'famed for disdain of virtue... which she learnt in her pupillage from the lessons of her father'. When the lady died the Earl took up with the daughter of a local gardener who bore him a son and whom he later married. Scandal and notoriety are commonplace in most noble families and the Queen Mother's family is no exception but perhaps the most notorious connection was with Sir Oswald Mosley, the Neo-Nazi fascist.

Despite what she perceived as her lack of a proper education Princess Margaret did have intellectual leanings and enjoyed reading and discussing serious topics. Had her mother followed Queen Mary's advice, the princess would probably not have turned to more bohemian pursuits. Indeed when Queen Mary insisted that such an education was good for them the Queen Mother replied 'I don't know what she meant. After all I and my sisters only had governesses and we all married well, one of us very well!' Instead Margaret was encouraged to develop her musical skills and consequently she became very proficient at playing the piano and singing. The Queen Mother's attitude to her daughter's education was summed up quite well by Randolph Churchill who said 'the Queen Mother never aimed at bringing her daughters up to be more than nicely behaved young ladies'. Although Queen Mary clearly recognized the need for a good education and was loathe to encourage her more frivolous side even she was amused by the princess's mad cap and humorous outbursts and remarked to a friend that the princess was 'so outrageously funny that one can't help encouraging her'.

When it came to the choice of a husband Princess Margaret was most unfortunate. Her first choice Group Captain Peter Townsend, her father's equerry, was a divorcee and when he proposed in 1953, the whole of the British Cabinet vetoed the idea and Parliament would only agree if she renounced her rights to the succession. The storm of controversy that blew up over the affair was completely out of proportion to the situation but did not dampen the Princess's determination to marry for love. Many years later Townsend wrote about the affair and painted a very romantic picture of their relationship declaring that 'their love took no heed of wealth and rank and all other worldly, conventional barriers which separated us.' An arranged marriage with the likes of Johnny Dalkeith or the Duke of Rutland would have been more acceptable but the Princess was drawn more and more to the attractions of a bohemian existence which found it's fullest expression during her subsequent marriage to Anthony Armstrong-Jones.

'Tony' Armstrong-Jones was a totally bohemian character who whilst engaged to the princess also carried on an affair with another woman. His fondness for the opposite sex was a byword in London's social scene and was one of the major reasons why the princess found him so attractive. Indeed to use the words of a contemporary he displayed a relentless and 'undisguised sexual promiscuity' that was truly astonishing, perhaps a reaction to the commonly held belief that he was 'gay'. When asked if it was true he replied 'I didn't fall in love with boys – but a few men have been in love with me'. As the nephew of Oliver Messel with whom he had frequent contact, the belief that he was gay is understandable especially as he is alleged to have picked up some of his uncle's mannerisms and always addressed Princess Margaret as 'Ducky' in private, a term she disliked intensely.

Inevitably, however, Tony found the whole royal thing just too much and slowly they drifted apart, he to concentrate on his work and indulge in other affairs and she to look for comfort elsewhere. Rumours of the princess taking Anthony Barton, her daughter's godfather, as her lover in 1966 were soon picked up by the press and this was followed by reports of him being replaced by Robin Douglas-Home, a cousin of Lady Diana Spencer, who on breaking up with the princess committed suicide in 1967. Prior to his affair with Margaret he had proposed marriage to the Princess Margaretha of Sweden, later Mrs Ambler, but her parents refused to sanction the match. Margaret's next love interest 'Roddy' Llewellyn, now Sir Roderick Llewellyn, 5th Bt, was considerably younger but the affair brought her marriage to an end with Tony playing the outraged husband.

PRINCESS ANNE

With her aunt's example before her, Princess Anne was adamant that she also would not marry into the 'cousinhood', i.e. the descendants of Queen Victoria or marry any other foreign royal. As a result when Dom Duarte of Portugal, the pretender of the throne of Portugal, expressed an interest in her, she refused to entertain the idea preferring the company of Andrew Parker-Bowles, who also came from a catholic background. At the same time Camilla Shand, his future wife and great-granddaughter of Alice Keppel, Edward VII's mistress, was being pursued by her brother the Prince of Wales.

The social caché that was conferred on Andrew by his association with Princess Anne was very similar to that enjoyed by his great-aunt the Honourable Sibyl Cadogan, a Maid of Honour to Queen Mary, who was romantically linked with the Duke of Windsor, formerly Edward VIII, the princess's great-uncle. The romance began in the spring of 1915, when the prince was just twenty one and Sybil just a year older. By early 1916 the affair had progressed to the point where he saw her 'most days and nights' but when he discussed marriage the family stepped in and hastily arranged her marriage to Lord Stanley. Sybil had also attracted the attention of the Duke of York, the prince's younger brother but of course nothing came of his interest.

Andrew also had other very interesting connections most notably with Charles II and his French mistress Louise de Queroualle; Lady Craven, subsequently Margravine of Brandenburg-Anspach; the actress Louisa Brunton, who married the 1st Earl Craven, son of Lady Craven and Henrietta, Countess Grosvenor, mistress of Henry Frederick, Duke of Cumberland. The Berkeley family, of which Lady Craven was a member, were renowned for their profligacy and waywardness and she was no exception. In character she was very much like her great-grandmother Louise de Queroualle, who bewitched and fascinated Charles II until the day he died, the only difference being that Lady Craven had innumerable lovers, including the Duc de Guines, French Ambassador to the Court of St James, thereby fully justifying Ninon de l'Enclos's famous epigram 'the virtue of women is the finest invention of man'. Louisa Brunton, was an actress of great beauty who during her short career specialised in 'genteel comedy' a role that she inherited from the far more famous Eliza Farren, who subsequently went on to marry the 12th Earl of Derby. She first appeared on the stage as 'Lady Townley' in the production of 'The Provoked Husband' a role that her descendant Andrew Parker-Bowles was forced to played many generations later but for a different reason.

Richard, Earl Grosvenor was a close friend and racing companion of the Duke of Cumberland, and renowned for his sexual escapades which badly damaged his health and eventually resulted in 'serial bouts of venereal disease'. 'Tall, thin, of a black complexion, with a long nose and heavily marked by smallpox' he was far from handsome but nevertheless one of the richest men in London. His twin passions were street girls and horse racing and he was a frequent visitor to the flesh pots and brothels of Piccadilly and Covent Garden. The duke 'a vulgar, noisy, indelicate but intrepid and gay little man' also visited the same haunts and was known to be partial to the charms of Nancy Dawson, a well known dancer and singer at the Drury Lane Theatre. Lady Grosvenor, for her part was very unhappy at her husband's behaviour and sought consolation elsewhere. She did not have to look far and before long had established a very close intimacy with the Duke. Neither she or her husband behaved with any discretion or honour in the subsequent proceedings with the result that she gave birth to a son who died the following year. When the Duke and Lady Grosvenor were caught in compromising circumstances, Earl Grosvenor sued for divorce and she was abandoned by her lover.

Prince Charles was just twenty-five years old when he met Camilla and the attraction was instant but not powerful enough for him to make a proposal of marriage. Disappointed Camilla transferred her affections to Mr Parker-Bowles who had also just lost out in the marriage stakes with Princess Anne. Andrew and Camilla were married in July 1973, whilst Charles was away on duty with his ship and Princess Anne married Mark Phillips in November 1973, on his return.

Despite his relatively humble background on his father's side, Mr Phillips does have an interesting maternal ancestry with descents from Sir John Perrott, allegedly a bastard son of Henry VIII and Sir Rhys ap Thomas, that famous Celtic warrior who helped Henry VII win the battle of Bosworth in 1485. But the most interesting is his connection with Lucy Walter, mistress of Charles II and mother of the Duke of Monmouth, ancestor of 'Johnny' Dalkeith; he is also a cousin of the present Duchess of Bedford. The only other ancestor to perform anything of note was Sir Arthur Owen, 4th Bart, who 'by a rapid ride from Wales, reached Westminster in time to vote for the Act of Settlement in 1701, thereby securing the Hanoverian Succession, which was secured by one vote'.

No doubt completely unaware of the contribution her husband's ancestor had made to English History, Princess Anne eventually found that they did not have many qualities in common apart from a passion for equine pursuits which sadly was insufficient to keep them together. As a result after nine years of marriage they were divorced in 1992 and she immediately married one of her mother's equerries, Timothy Laurence. The trend for seeking partners from amongst the royal equerries began with the daughters of George III, in particular the princesses Augusta, Elizabeth and Amelia. Divorce in the Royal Family was now gathering greater momentum and when Prince Andrew divorced his wife Sarah in 1996, the Monarchy reeled under the impact.

PRINCE ANDREW

Like all of the Queen's children, Andrew, popularly known as 'Randy Andy', has never had a properly defined role in life and as a consequence has enjoyed a relatively privileged and pampered lifestyle. Despite his commendable service in the Falklands War and his studious attendance to his official duties he has pursued a singularly wilful path in his attempt to find some meaning to his life. With so little outlet for the Royal Family to engage in politics or any other contentious activity he has followed the path taken by so many princes before him and acquired a considerable reputation as a ladies man.

His girlfriends have all come from very diverse backgrounds and included 'Koo' Stark, of 'The Awakening of Emily' fame, the US actress Angie Everheart, Denise Martell, former Playboy model from LA plus PR girls Aurelia Cecil, Caroline Stanbury, a former girl friend of Hugh Grant, the actor and Ryan Giggs, the footballer and business woman Harriet Staveley. At one point Koo was tipped to become Andrew's wife but her past caught up with her and they split after he returned from the Falklands War. She then went on to marry Tim Jefferies, grandson of Richard Tompkins, the founder of the 'Green Shield Stamp' Empire, before she was diagnosed in 2002 with breast cancer and sadly was forced to have a double mastectomy.

The unremitting publicity that the prince was subjected to throughout his life ensured that very few of his girl friends stayed with him for long. The most interesting was Aurelia Cecil, daughter of Lord Amherst of Hackney, a distant cousin of Princess Diana; the relationship lasted just ten months, who founded her PR company 'Aurelia Public Relations' in 1990, aged twenty-three, with just £7,000, which she then sold in 1997 to Abbott Mead Vickers for £4.25 million. Specialising in upmarket promotions her clients included such luxury brand names as Versace, Jaguar, Krug Champagne and Gieves and Hawkes.

The Cecils rose to fame when William Cecil, Lord Burghley, became Elizabeth I's chief minister; his son Robert, Earl of Salisbury was also chief minister to James I. Aurelia also descends from John (Wilmot), Earl of Rochester, the famous Restoration Rake, Mary Boleyn, the mistress of Henry VIII and Mrs Poyntz, who was romantically linked with Edward Augustus, Duke of York, brother of George III; the latter descent provides a connection with Camilla, Duchess of Cornwall. Her Cecil descent also gives her connections to Barbara and Elizabeth Villiers, mistresses of Charles II and William III, the Countess of Deloraine, mistress of George II, Anne Vane, mistress of Frederick, Prince of Wales and Maria Waldegrave, wife of William Henry, Duke of Gloucester. Aurelia is now married to Old Etonian Rupert Stephenson and has three children.

In terms of noble descents Aurelia had much to recommend her but the same could not be said for Caroline Stanbury, who is now married to Turkish financier Gem Habib. According to newspaper reports she met Prince Andrew at a posh dinner party in 2000 and was introduced to him by her then boy friend Michael Edwards-Hammond who commented that she was a 'gorgeous, fantastic, sexy lover' with 'an insatiable appetite for sex' Although not invited to the party she insisted on attending dressed in a very tight mini skirt once she heard that Prince Andrew would be there and then spent the whole evening flirting with him. Unknown to her boy friend she then accepted Andrew's invitation to return to his apartment at Buckingham Palace on a number of occasions for secret dates. Andrew was captivated by her but they were intimate for only a few months before he moved on to his next conquest.

PRINCE EDWARD

The marriage in 1999, of Prince Edward and Sophie Rhys-Jones was a welcome change to the prevailing trend of divorce in the Royal Family but like all of the partners of the Queen's children, despite the lack of royal blood they brought many interesting connections with former royal mistresses and Sophie was no exception. Sophie, a distant cousin of Andrew Parker-Bowles, is also related to Henrietta Vernon, Countess Grosvenor, the mistress of Henry Frederick, Duke of Cumberland. Another connection is the Lady Almeria Carpenter, mistress of William Henry, Duke of Gloucester, and Sarah, Countess of Tyrconnell, mistress of (1) Frederick, Duke of York, brother of George IV and (2) John Bowes-Lyon, 10th Earl of Strathmore & Kinghorne, a great-uncle of the Queen Mother.

Edward had also had a number of girlfriends before his marriage viz: Eleanor Wightman, during his days at Cambridge, Georgia May, whom he met at Cowes in August 1986, Anastasia Cook, the TV journalist, Rhian-Anwen Roberts, Gail Greenough, the Canadian Sportswoman, the model Romy Adlinton, again when he was at Cambridge; his interest lasted just eighteen months, briefly Ulrika Jonsson, the grand daughter of Folke Jonsson, the Swedish Opera Singer and the actress/singer Ruthie Henshall. None, however, came with a title. The only occasion that his name was ever linked to another royal was when he spent some time in the company of his cousin Martha Louise, of Norway, who would have been an excellent bride for him but he showed no interest at all in marrying into the 'cousinhood', i.e. descendants of Queen Victoria.

Ruthie Henshall, the daughter of David Henshall, a former editor of the *East Anglia Daily Times*, was the prince's main interest for at least two years but she continued to see him over a period of five years before she became engaged to John Gordon Sinclair. She eventually married Tim Hower, a former lead singer with the band *Van Tramp* and by him had two children. But the most interesting of his love interests was Georgia May, the daughter of David May, the yachting tycoon. The affair lasted for just two years but twenty years later her father hit the headlines when he announced that he was going to marry another man twenty years his junior!

Interestingly neither Prince William or Prince Harry have taken girlfriends from amongst Britain's more distinguished families. Are we perhaps witnessing another stage in the dumbing down of the monarchy?

PRINCE CHARLES

King Edward VIII or the Duke of Windsor as he became paid a high price for his determination to marry the woman he loved and it was a scenerio that would be repeated with his great nephew Prince Charles. Charles was expected to chose a royal bride and despite much speculation that he would marry Princess Marie Astrid of Luxembourg', albeit a catholic, he chose instead to marry the Lady Diana Spencer, daughter of Earl Spencer. However, the match was not greeted with universal approval indeed his German relatives considered it to be a 'mesalliance' in the grandest manner and were very pointed in their disapproval to Prince Philip. Untrained in the ways of royalty Diana immediately charmed all who came into contact with her including the press and media but from the outset of the marriage there was another woman, Camilla Parker Bowles.

Like the Countess of Dorchester, mistress of James II, Camilla did not rate highly in the beauty stakes but like the Countess she more than made up for this with a strong independent personality, coupled with great charm, a very keen sense of humour and a great inner self confidence. They met for the first time in August 1971 at a polo match at Windsor castle where Camilla complimented him on his mount and his skill with horses and again several weeks later when they were formally introduced to each other by Lucia Santa Cruz a former flame of the Prince's. At the first meeting Camilla is alleged to have reminded Charles that her great-grandmother had been the mistress of the Prince's great-great-grandfather Edward VII but this has been denied by those that know her well. However, she was reputedly very interested in her grandmother's role as Edward VII's mistress. Charles was smitten by the frankness and the ease with which they were able to converse and the fact that she was never overawed by his rank, a breath of fresh air to him. Later she would recall to a friend that '… I never felt intimidated in his presence… I felt from the beginning that we were two peas in a pod. We talked as if we had always known each other'.

Camilla's first boyfriend was Kevin Burke, son of Sir Aubrey Burke, Deputy Chairman of the Hawker Siddeley Group, a self made man who like so may of his ilk married into the lower ranks of the peerage. Many years later Kevin reminisced about their relationship and recalled that 'Every night we went to two or three cocktail parties and then a dance. It was the best time and I had the best partner you could wish for.

She was never bad tempered. She knew how to have fun. I remained with her all that year (1965). I suppose we were in love... then she ditched me'. Her next boyfriend was Rupert Hambro from the famous banking family whose only recommentation appeared to be his money and a descent from the Earl of Bute, who was briefly Prime Minister and a great favourite of George III and his mother the Princess Augusta.

But Hambro was soon forgotten when her future husband Andrew Parker-Bowles, a former escort of Princess Anne's, came on the scene. Camilla's attraction to Andrew has never been fully explained but his reputation as a ladies man was clearly a major draw. Indeed as one ex-girlfriend recalled 'his greatest gift to women was the knowledge that sexuality was healthy – something to be explored. She was very innocent when they met but they spent many, many nights together. He schooled her in the ways of the world'. Princess Anne still enjoys his company despite being on her second husband and whenever he is away on duty, they can often be seen in each other's company. However, despite telling Camilla that he loved her, by the time Charles had returned Camilla had married Andrew Parker Bowles.

Camilla was born on 17 July 1947, the daughter of Major Bruce Middleton Hope Shand and his wife the Hon Rosalind Maud Cubit, the grand daughter of Alice Keppel, mistress of Edward VII. In addition to being descended from Louise de Queroualle, the French mistress of King Charles II, who was cousin of the notorious Marquis de Sade, Camilla also descends from Mary Carey, the mistress of Henry VIII and Sir William Villiers, brother of the 1st Duke of Buckingham, the favourite of James I; she is also related to the Hon. Anne Vane, the fair 'Vanella' mistress of Frederick, Prince of Wales. But her most interesting forebears were the 1st Marquess of Argyll and his son the 9th Earl of Argyll, both of whom were beheaded in 1661 and 1685, but for different reasons.

Archibald Campbell, 1st Marquess of Argyll, so created by Letters Patent, 15 November 1641, was both the saviour and the jailer of Charles II during his brief time in Scotland. A covenanter and the acknowledged master of Scotland whilst Charles was in exile, he was according to Edward Hyde, 'A man of craft, subtlety and falsehood who wanted nothing but honesty and courage to be a very extraordinary man, having all the talents in a great degree'. However, his shameful treatment of Charles during that period was never forgotten by that monarch and when he arrived in London shortly after the Restoration to congratulate the King he was immediately arrested, imprisoned and then summarily beheaded. His son the 9th Earl, sort to repay the Stuart family by supporting the Duke of Monmouth during his ill fated attempt to dethrone James II in 1685 but he suffered the same fate as his father.

The list of the Prince's ex-girlfriends is almost endless therefore only those who fit into the criteria of this book will be mentioned, in particular Lady Sarah Spencer, Diana's older sister; Lady Jane Wellesley, daughter of the Duke of Wellington and a relative of the seriously wealthy Catherine Tynley-Long, to whom William IV proposed marriage but was rejected; Lady Leonora and Lady Jane Grosvenor, daughters of the Duke of Westminster and both since married and divorced, descendants of Lady Grosvenor, mistress of Henry Frederick, Duke of Cumberland and relatives of the late Princess of Wales. In addition, there was Lady Caroline Percy, eldest daughter of the Duke of Northumberland and a descendant of Charles II by his mistresses Lucy Walter and Louise de Queroualle; she is also a descendant of the celebrated beauty Elizabeth Gunning, the actress Louisa Brunton and the notorious Lady Craven and a relative of Mrs Fitzherbert, mistress of George IV; Lady Henrietta FitzRoy, eldest daughter of the Duke of Grafton and a descendant of Charles II and Barbara Villiers, is also related to the above mentioned Lady Craven.

Of course some of the above mentioned ladies only had to appear with the prince at an official function for the press to immediately assume that they were having an affair. But it is very interesting to note how a good number of them were related to each other and the late Princess of Wales in particular. However, of all the above only Lady Jane Wellesley has remained unmarried. Nevertheless she has sought comfort in a number of relationships in particular with the novelist and TV presenter Melvyn Bragg, Andrew Holden, the poet Mick Imhal and more recently the TV personality Lloyd Grossman.

Lady Jane has a colourful ancestry including a descent from the famous Arthur Wellesley, 1st Duke of Wellington, who defeated

Napoleon at the Battle of Waterloo in 1815. But the most interesting member of her family is her late grandmother Dorothy Violet Ashton, who after producing two children by her husband, abandoned them to become the lover of Vita Sackville-West and later Hilda Matheson, a prominent TV producer.

Lady Leonora and Lady Jane Grosvenor, the former widow of the Queen's cousin Lord Lichfeld, and the latter formerly wife of the Duke of Roxburghe but now the wife of Edward Dawnay, were also considered by the press as possible consorts for Prince Charles. Lady Jane, a very attractive brunette, with a vivacious and bubbly personality divorced her first husband and then married her cousin Edward Dawnay but her sister has not remarried and thus retains her title. The sisters have a number of descents from Royal Favourites including Henrietta, Lady Grosvenor, mistress of Henry Frederick, Duke of Cumberland, brother of George III; Robert Carr, Earl of Somerset, the favourite of James I and also Elizabeth, Lady Orkney, the mistress of William III. In addition they are related to George Villiers, 1st Duke of Buckingham, favourite of James I and Augusta Murray, mistress/wife of Augustus, Duke of Sussex, younger brother of George IV.

Lady Augusta, first met the Duke in London in 1785 but he did not become romantically involved with her until January 1793, during a visit to Rome. Several months later they were married in contravention of the Royal Marriage Act, without witnesses at the home of her mother and again later in the year in London. After giving birth to a son, the prince was ordered to return to Italy minus his wife (?) and child and remained there until 1799. On his return they were reunited and lived as husband and wife until December 1800 when he was sent to Portugal. After the birth of another child, this time a daughter, they never saw each other again. Lady Grosvenor's story, which has already been recounted, was a very sad one indeed.

Neither Lady Leonora or Lady Jane were serious contenders for the position of wife to Prince Charles and the same could be said for all of the other candidates that have been singled out by the press but once again it is interesting to see how many are directly related to previous royal mistresses. Lady Henrietta FitzRoy, who has known Prince Charles from childhood, they took dancing lessons together, is a close friend of the Queen. Like Diana, the later Princess of Wales, she was trained as a kindergarten teacher and later a children's nurse and has been a tireless advocate of childrens welfare in the Bahamas where she lives. Despite the suggestion that she might make a suitable bride for Prince Charles, Lady Henrietta quickly married the twice widowed Maltese nobleman, Edward Zimmerman-Barbaro, Count St George and set up home in the Bahaman islands. As a fourth cousin of the prince, she was more closely related to him than any other the other candidates. Part of her appeal appears to have been her royal descents from Charles II and James II but like Lady Jane and Lady Leonora Grovenor, she has some very colourful ancestors including the celebrated Lady Craven and the Duchess of Gloucester.

Lady Craven, who was 'a more likeable edition of Charles II's French mistress' and 'freed from the anger and jealousy which were the Duchess of Portsmouth's besetting sins' was according to Horace Walpole 'very pretty, has parts and is good-natured to the greatest degree', with 'magnificent chestnut hair, glorious eyes and white skin marred only by a few freckles'. Unfortunately she also resembled her royal ancestor when it came to matters of the heart. Within six years of her marriage she conducted a very passionate affair with the Duc de Guines, the French Ambassador to the Court of St James, who was renowned for his good looks, courtly manners and fascinating appearance. The result was almost certainly a daughter Georgiana, born in 1773, but as Lady Craven was also receiving the attentions of 'half a dozen or more 'gentlemen of pleasure' at the same time including Sir William Hamilton, later British Ambassador at Naples who was the husband of Nelson's mistress Emma Hart, her paternity must remain in some doubt.

But Lady Craven was more than just a pretty face, she was also very vain! Indeed she exhibited a positive addiction to being the centre of attention and to that end developed a 'craze for authorship, play writing and acting' in order to keep herself in the public eye. However, with the advent of a second husband, a German princeling no less who had renounced all his rights to his sovereign the King of Prussia, the widowed Lady Craven, quickly set about finding another lover, her choice falling on the royalist emigre Count Alexander Tilly. The story of the Duchess of Gloucester, has already been recounted.

Lady Caroline Percy, allegedly a former love interest of Andrew Parker-Bowles, is a descendant of Charles II and three of his mistresses, Lucy Walter, Nell Gwynn and Louise de Queroualle plus Lady Craven, mentioned above, Elizabeth Gunning and Mary Bellenden. Elizabeth Gunning a celebrated beauty at the Court of George III, was greatly admired by that monarch but chose instead to marry the Duke of Argyll, whose mother Mary Bellenden, the previous Duchess of Argyll, was pursued by George II, when Prince of Wales.

No breath of scandal appears to have sullied the name of Elizabeth Gunning but her mother-in-law was not so lucky. Mary Bellenden first attracted the attention of George II 'immediately upon his first coming over... ' to England, when she was appointed maid of honour to his wife Caroline. According to Lord Hervey she was 'the most likeable woman of her time' who was 'celebrated for her wit, vivacity and beauty'. However, she never became his mistress despite his best efforts but Lord Hervey recalled that 'her situation was only having the scandal of being the Prince's mistress without the pleasure and the confinement without the profit'. Lady Suffolk, who did become the Prince's official mistress, later recalled that Mary 'by no means felt a reciprocal passion' adding for good measure that 'The prince's gallantry was by no means delicate & his avarice disgusted her... in fact her heart was engaged & so the prince, finding his love fruitless suspected'.

These are just a few examples of potential consorts or companions for Prince Charles and as you can see most if not all had connections with previous Royal Mistresses. The Prince's second wife, the Duchess of Cornwall, is no exception but in her case the connection is more recent. It is now time to recount the story of the Princess of Wales, his first wife.

Diana 'The People's Princess'

When the Prince of Wales chose a bride it was not from amongst the

Royal Families of Europe but from the British Aristocracy. Lady Diana Spencer was not of equal rank to her husband but royal blood still flowed in her veins. She was descended from six royal mistresses, Barbara Villiers, Louise de Queroualle, Nell Gwynn, Arabella Churchill, Clara von Meisenburg and Lady Jersey. Among her non-royal ancestors she could also count the formidable Sarah, Duchess of Marlborough who tried unsuccessfully to marry her grand daughter, another Lady Diana Spencer, to Frederick, Prince of Wales, the father of George III; the famous John Churchill, Duke of Marlborough and the infamous Robert Spencer, Earl of Sunderland, chief minister to James II.

The Spencer family fortunes were founded on the successful achievements of Sir Robert Spencer who in 1603 was *reputed to have by him the most money of any person in the kingdom*. The source of this wealth was sheep farming and by the early seventeenth century the family's yearly income was between £6,500 and £8,000, a very princely sum in those days. But the family's entry onto the political stage came when Robert Spencer, 1st Earl of Sunderland was appointed one of James II's Secretaries of State. A man of bewitching charm he was 'one of the key men of the age' but 'so utterly unprincipled, so doubly and trebly proved a turncoat, so enriched by his tergiversations, that he never really received his due for the outstanding gifts of intellect he possessed'. Charles II a very shrewd judge of character 'kept him at arm's length' but he was able to dominate James II completely.

The next generation of the family to hit the headlines were the daughters of the 1st Earl Spencer, the fascinating and tragic Georgiana, Duchess of Devonshire and Harriet, Countess of Bessborough, both of whom bore illegitimate children by their respective lovers, Charles, 1st Earl Grey, whose son the 2nd Earl piloted through the Great Reform Bill in 1832 and Lord Granville Leveson Gower. Lady Bessborough, previously the mistress of Charles Wyndham and Richard Brinsley Sheridan was Lord Granville's mistress for seventeen years and on one occasion the recipient of the unwelcome attentions of George IV no less! Many years later Lady Bessborough was forced to endure the unfortunate spectacle of her own niece marrying her ex-lover! The origin of this wayward behaviour in the daughters of Earl Spencer can be traced to Henrietta and Mary, daughters of Sarah, Duchess of Marlborough, both of whom had several lovers and in the case of Henrietta at least one illegitimate child. Chastity was clearly not a premium that was held in high regard by the Spencer family!

For a brief period of time Mrs Stephen Poyntz, mother-in-law of the 1st Earl Spencer, was also rumoured to be having an affair with Edward Augustus, Duke of York, the brother of George III and this was hardly surprising given that she was the grand daughter of Carey Frazier, Countess of Peterborough, a one time candidate for the position of mistress to Charles II, whose eccentric husband subsequently married the celebrated actress Anastasia Robinson; the Earl was also a descendant of Mary Carcy, mistress of Henry VIII. These are just a few of the very colourful characters that appear in Lady Diana's ancestry. Among her more recent relatives are, Humphrey Bogart, JP Morgan, General Patton, Orson Welles and Patrick, Earl of Lichfield, the photographer. She also has connections with eight American Presidents.

Diana also had royal connections from other branches of her ancestry. among them Lady Archibald Hamilton (*nee* Lady Jane Hamilton, daughter of the 6th Earl of Abercorn). Lady Jane was unfortunate enough to be singled out for special attention by Frederick, Prince of Wales but historians are divided on whether she was actually the Prince's mistress or just a royal favourite. Horace Walpole certainly thought that she was the former 'stronger symptoms of an affaire faite never appeared on any pair than were to be seen between this couple' he declared. But at the time she was a married woman with ten children! Nevertheless she retained his interest for ten years 'finding her company congenial and her experience useful'. When she fell from favour it was suddenly and without any regrets with a pension of £1,200 per annum. Many years later in 1779 Lady Jane's granddaughter Mary Hamilton was briefly the object of George IV's passion but she resisted all of his attempts to make her his mistress.

Several generations later Lady Jane's great-nephew the 1st Marquess of Abercorn took as his second wife Lady Anne Hatton, previously the mistress of Lord Hervey and later Augustus Frederick, Duke of Sussex, sixth son of George III. The relationship was very brief, it lasted just a few months in late 1791 and early 1792 whilst on a visit to Naples. Many years later the prince took as his companion Lady Cecilia Buggin, Lady Hatton's much younger sister and they lived together until the Duke died in 1843 but there were no children from these affairs. David Cameron, the present Leader of the Conservative Party, is a descendant of Sir Charles Gore, brother of Lady Hatton.

Another of Diana's direct ancestors the 1st Earl Howe, is chiefly remembered for his excessive devotion to Queen Adelaide, wife of William IV. As her Lord chamberlain from 1830 to 1831 and again from 1834 to 1849 Earl Howe had unlimited access to the Queen which soon gave rise to the belief that they had become lovers! Although described by a modern historian as 'fatuous, foppish and ineffably vain', he was according to the diarist Greville 'like an ardent young lover' in her presence. The Earl a distant relative of the Queen was also a near kinsman of William IV, being the great-grandson of the Countess of Darlington, bastard sister of George I.

Lady Graves, the sister of Diana's direct ancestor Henry William (Paget), 1st Marquess of Anglesey, was also the unfortunate recipient of the attentions the Duke of Cumberland, later to become King of Hanover after the death of his brother William IV in 1837. His visits began in 1829, although they were rumoured to have been old friends, she was also the mother of fifteen children, the last born in 1825! The duke never attempted to conceal his regard for the lady and before long it became common knowledge. Poor Lord Graves was so upset by the rumours about his wife's relationship with the Prince that he committed suicide drawing from Mrs Fitzherbert the observation that 'I dare say his yielding to the solicitations of the King and the Duke to make it up with his wife to prevent an exposure, was more than his mind under such distressing circumstances could bear'. Undaunted by the whole experience and in complete disregard of the feelings of Lady Graves, the duke continued to visit her until the continuing unwelcome attention they received from the press forced him to terminate their association.

Elizabeth, Duchess of Rutland, another of Diana's ancestors and a recipient of the royal favour, was the daughter of the 5th Earl of Carlisle and a member of the powerful Howard clan. But exactly when she struck up an intimacy with the Duke of York, the 2nd son of George III is unclear. The Prince who was godfather to the duchesses second son in 1814 had previously been romantically involved with the duchesses mother-in-law, Mary, widow of the 4th Duke of Rutland! Indeed it was reported by Lady Elizabeth Foster, mistress and subsequently wife of the Duke of Devonshire that in 1790 'The Duke of York was very near marrying the Duchess of Rutland . She has long aimed at it, and this year at Brighthelmstone, after receiving Colonel St Leger as a favoured lover, she took the advantage of his absence to renew her attack on the Duke of York. The Prince of Wales is very uneasy at it, and urged his brother, even for his friend Colonel St Leger's sake to desist'.

The Prince whose preference was for ladies of much lower social rank had recently become a widower and was a very lonely man. The Duchess was the perfect antidote to his depression being good natured and 'of the most perfect grace and beauty' but it was not her physical beauty that attracted him but the 'vigour of her understanding and clearness of intellect seldom equalled in either sex' that held him enthralled. When she died suddenly in 1825 the Duke was heartbroken and two years later he also died.

Similar illicit connections with other members of the royal family amongst the relatives of Diana's direct ancestors are also alleged for Lady Sarah Lennox, daughter of the 2nd Duke of Richmond, with George III, the 3rd Duchess of Richmond with Edward Augustus, Duke of York, brother of George III and the 9th Duchess of Richmond with George IV.

According to the author of 'Who Owns Britain', the present Earl Spencer is the second largest land owner in Northamptonshire with a total acreage of 13,000 and a land value of £96 million. In addition to their wealth the Spencer family also had numerous close connections with the present Royal Family. Lady Fermoy, formerly Ruth Sylvia Gill, and Diana's grandmother was a lady in waiting to the Queen Mother and two of her Spencer great-aunts were also members of her household whilst Lady Fermoy's husband was a close shooting companion of George VI.

The Spencers and the Royal Family met on a fairly regular basis but initially the Prince of Wales interest was in Lady Sarah Spencer, Diana's elder sister. In the marriage stakes the only foreign royal ever linked with the prince was Princess Marie Astrid of Luxemburg but he showed no interest in her at all. Indeed the Queen does not appear to offered her son any advice on who would make a suitable bride. It was Lord Mountbatten who took the lead in selecting his future consort. His choice of Amanda Knatchbull, was singularly instructive because she was his own granddaughter (the daughter of Lady Brabourne) and also the Prince's second cousin. Such a union would have been in the best of royal traditions but although he proposed to her, the assassination of Lord Mountbatten in August 1979 effectively destroyed all hope of her becoming his wife.

Charles's romantic interest in Diana began in the summer of 1980. The prince still in shock over the death of his uncle found her a very willing and sympathetic listener when he talked of his grief and sadness at the tragic turn of events. Eventually he asked her to marry him and much to the surprise of the Brabourne family she accepted his proposal. The press immediately fell in love with her, one newspaper columnist even calling her 'the epitome of a fairy tale princess' who was 'beloved for her gentle and loving nature'. In time they noted her 'natural affinity with children and the sick', natural charm and gaeity and her robust sense of humour. During her brief life she also 'achieved an unrivalled glamour and respect' in the fashion world as a result of her 'fresh, attractive and original' ideas.

The name Diana was taken from the Roman 'Goddess of the Hunt' who was renowned as an emblem of chastity, the principal quality for which the Princess of Wales was chosen. But it was not a quality that the Prince Charles possessed in any abundance because at the time of his engagement he decided to renew his relationship with an old flame Camilla Parker-Bowles. The immense pressures placed upon Diana as a new member of the Royal Family and her husband's flagrant infidelity would eventually prove too great a burden. A much stronger character would have accepted the situation and made the best of it. But this was not in Diana's nature, revenge was sweeter and here again we once see those double standards at work that have always been applied to men and women over the conduct of their love affairs. She quickly learnt that the opportunities for her to indulge in extra marital affairs were severely restricted whilst her husband on the other hand had no qualms about embarking on an affair provided he did it discreetly.

Diana's reaction to the discovery that Charles was unfaithful was unexpected but once she had determined that this was her only course of action she pursed it with commendable vigour and single mindedness. When the marriage ended she resorted to the time honoured aristocratic tradition of seeking some consolation from the company of a variety of different dashing and good looking men but was unable to keep them out of the public eye.

Her interests included James Gilbey, a member of the famous 'Gin' making family, James Hewitt, a Captain in the Life Guards, Oliver Hoare, an art dealer, Will Carling, the rugby player and also Dodi Al Fayed. None could claim descent from the upper classes but James Hewitt and Oliver Hoare were very ambitious and had social pretensions. Gilbey, of 'Squidgygate' fame and a PR executive for Lotus cars was quickly superceded by others including Hewitt, who taught her sons to ride and Hoare with whom she had a four year affair.

Oliver Hoare, a close friend of Prince Charles and Diana, first met the royal couple at a Royal Ascot party at Windsor Castle in 1984. Described by a friend as 'an old fashioned gentleman' with 'a very scholarly background & a retiring even vulnerable manner that is very appealing to women', he was educated at Eton and later studied at the Sorbonne. Although the son of a civil servant Hoare, was not connected to the well known banking family of that name. Acutely conscious of his lack of social credibility he sought to overcome the problem by marrying the very wealthy and well connected Diana de Waldner, whose mother Baroness Louise was a good friend of Queen Elizabeth the Queen Mother.

The marriage produced three children and considerably increased the size of his bank balance but also brought him an interesting connection with Napoleon Bonaparte, whose brother Joseph had two illegitimate daughters by Diana de Waldner von Freudenstein, Countess von Pappenheim. Oliver and his wife live in a £3.5 million house in

Chelsea's Tregunter Road and he runs an Art gallery in Eccleston Street. Amongst his clients are the Sultan of Brunei and Queen Noor of Jordan. At the time he met Diana he was thirty-nine, with a reputation as a compulsive charmer; in his youth he was described as 'An extravagantly pretty young man, who would turn the heads of both men and women'. Diana was immediately smitten but they did not become really close until 1990. Many years later in 2005 Hoare became embroiled in an official inquiry into the financial dealings of Sheikh Saud Al Thani of Qatar when it was discovered that his company had issued invoices totally £20 million for pieces of art that were only worth a fraction of that on the open market.

Like Oliver Hoare, James Hewitt did not come from a gentry or aristocratic background. Although his full name is James Lifford Hewitt, he has no connection with Edward James Wingfield Hewitt, the present Viscount Lifford. Hewitt allegedly met Diana for the first time at a party organised in 1986 by Hazel West, Diana's Lady in Waiting, although he later claimed that he first met her officially in 1981 at a polo match at Tidworth, shortly before her marriage to Prince Charles; Prince Harry was born in 1984. Hewitt has declared publicly that he is not the father of Prince Harry but some of his friends have said that he did met privately with Diana before Harry's birth despite his protestations.

Hewitt was perhaps the least likeable of all Diana's love interests and he has certainly not been shy about capitalising on their affair. Indeed he was reputedly paid £1 million pounds for selling his story to the newspapers in 1994. Diana allegedly sent him some sixty plus love letters, ten of which he offered for sale for the sum of £10 million! Although he was educated at Millfield and then Sandhurst Royal Military College, he never managed to rise above the rank of Captain, however, when he retired after serving seventeen years in the army he was awarded the honorary rank of Major. His association with Diana lasted from 1987 to 1992 and he presently lives in Spain.

Unfortunately Diana's search for happiness was never to be satisfied and her tragic death in Paris at the age of thirty-six was a great shock to her family and the whole nation. However, if there are any lessons to be learnt from her short life it is that perhaps the Queen and Prince

Philip should have adopted a more hands on approach to the choice of suitable partners for their children.

Prince William

What then of Prince William and Prince Harry? Diana's belief that they should live a normal life is commendable but it does have disadvantages. Both clearly enjoy expensive clubbing and wild parties as one would expect of the youth of today but it is hardly the best preparation for the very public roles that they will assume in later life. So far they have been remarkably monogamous in their relationships but have shown a marked reluctance to chose girlfriends from the upper echelons of society. At first glance William's long term relationship with Kate Middleton, would appear to support the belief that to have a working class partner is a good thing and certainly her innate good sense, remarkable self assurance, pleasant manners and classic good looks, make her a very agreeable one.

Like most young people Prince William likes to have fun and if this element is missing from any of his relationships he simply moves on. His first girlfriend of any note was Arabella Musgrave, daughter of Major Nicholas Musgrave, whom he met just before going to University. Unfortunately the relationship did not last long due to the strains of university life and he had soon moved on to a more serious affair with Kate Middleton. Arabella subsequently became Head of PR at Gucci's and had a five year long relationship with James Tollemache, a close friend of William's, and heir to a brewery fortune. Although he originally went to St Andrews to study the history of art William soon realized it was not his subject and he switched instead to geography. Initially he had some difficulty adjusting to university life and even contemplated abandoning his courses but with Kate's timely help and advice he soon buckled down and began to enjoy himself. At this period in his life Kate's support was vital and he re-paid her by forming a very strong attachment with her which, despite a few rocky patches, has lasted.

Although Kate does come from a long line of Durham miners with an ancestor, Edward Thomas Glassborrow, who spent some time in Holloway prison, the perception of her origins as one hundred percent working class is misleading. She is in fact descended from two royal mistresses, Mary Boleyn, mistress of Henry VIII and Catherine Swynford, mistress and later wife of John of Gaunt, Duke of Lancaster. In addition she is related to Lady Hertford, mistress/companion of George IV and Maria Waldegrave, wife of William Henry, Duke of Gloucester, brother of George III plus Guy Ritchie, late husband of Madonna. The debate over whether Catherine Carey was Henry VIII's bastard daughter by Mary Boleyn continues unabated even today and in the event that it could be proven, Kate could boast of a truly royal descent indeed!

William arrived at St Andrews with 12 GCSE's and 3 A-levels and at Eton had excelled at sports, particularly swimming. Kate on the other hand was more artistic and a former pupil of Marlborough College. Both however, shared 'a love of the countryside and enjoyment of London's night life' but their relationship was not all plain sailing. During his studies he developed a passion for several other young ladies including the beautiful Isabella Calthorpe, a model and actress, who had appeared on the covers of the *Tatler* magazine, *Harpers & Queen* plus *Country Life*.

Isabella Anstruther-Gough-Calthorpe, to give her full name, is a young woman who has it all. Beauty, wealth plus impeccable aristocratic connections, she seemed to be an ideal partner for William in the absence of any potential royal brides. Through her mother she was descended from the Dukes of Marlborough, Earls of Lichfield and Earls of Cardigan and in addition is descended from Sophie, Countess of Darlington, bastard half sister of King George I. On her father's side she descends from a long line of Scottish baronets and also the ducal houses of Grafton, Hamilton and Brandon plus the Earls of Mar and Kellie. As a result of the Grafton link she is a descendant of King Charles II and Barbara Villiers. In addition to the aforementioned it appears that William and Isabella are also fourth cousins. They first met in 1999 but they did not socialize on a regular basis until they were at university where she studied classics. William, who at the time was in a relationship with Kate, was deeply smitten with her and during the summer of 2004 proposed several times but she rejected him claiming that it would be too damaging to her career.

William is probably unaware of the acute irony of the situation over his choice of girlfriends and the public's obsessive interest in their different backgrounds and there is no reason why he should be given that we were all unaware of the finer details of Kate's ancestry. Seemingly from an ordinary working class background she nevertheless has several royal descents and is also descended from two royal mistresses. None of this information was available to the public until research was commissioned into her ancestry. On the other hand details of Isabella's ancestry with it's obvious royal connections have always been in the public domain. The discovery of Kate's royal connections has now clearly raised her profile and possibly made her much more acceptable as a suitable spouse for William but of course this still does not resolve the issue of why the younger members the Royal Family no longer seek partners from amongst the other royal houses of Europe.

William and Katherine were finally married on 29 April 2011 at Westminster Abbey thus bringing to an end the years of speculation about whether their relationship would last. The Monarchy now has a third generation of the royal line in place with the prospect of another to be born shortly. To celebrate the Queen issued orders that Prince William should henceforth be called HRH The Duke of Cambridge and Kate HRH The Duchess of Cambridge. The title has an interesting and unfortunate history.

William's predecessor as Duke of Cambridge was HRH Prince George, eldest son of HRH Prince Adolphus, the 1st Duke, 7th son of King George III, who married his mistress Sarah Fairbrother (Mrs FitzGeorge); prior to this union she bore him two sons and after it another son. Prince George was at one point a suitor to Queen Victoria but she preferred another cousin Prince Albert of Saxe-Coburg-Gotha. The first creation was in 1661 and this was followed by others in 1663, 1667, 1677 & 1706, the first four for short lived sons of King James II by his two wives and the 1706 creation for George II, prior to his father becoming King in 1714.

The announcement that the royal couple are now expecting their first child is obviously good news for the survival of the monarchy but the present attempt to change the rules of succession to allow the first born if it is a girl to succeed is a controversial move and many fear that this may lead to titles of nobility being included in the same legislation. But what title will they give to this royal child? If it is true that she is carrying a daughter will she be called Countess of Strathearn, her father's secondary title?

PRINCE HARRY

Prince Harry's determination to experience life to the full and enjoy himself at all costs has unfortunately come at a great cost to his public image. Whilst some allowances can be made for him because of his age and royal status he should not forget the very privileged position he holds in our society and the respect in which it is held by many of the people of this country. Prince Charles is a very loving father but has been very indulgent over the behaviour of his sons. A quiet word in their ear about their wilder antics and the choice of suitable partners would not come amiss.

Harry's first girlfriend of note was Chelsy Davy, the daughter of Charles Davy, a millionaire safari operator and his wife, who was a former model and Miss Rhodesia. Educated at the very prestigious Cheltenham Ladies College and then Stowe, she met Prince Harry in the spring of 2004. But like all of her predecessors the media pressure was very intense and did nothing to help the relationship. Like Prince Andrew, Prince Harry's frequent absences on duty in the Armed Forces put considerable strain on the relationship as did his marked preference for a night out with his army chums. As a result they split up for a short time despite having spent quality time abroad on holiday in Mozambique and Botswana. The relationship, however, lasted until the early part of 2009 and within a few months Harry was seen in the company of Astrid Harbord, a close friend of Kate Middleton. The twenty seven year old Miss Harbord, a former student of Bristol University is the daughter of Charles Harbord, a relative of Lord Suffield and cousin of the musician Mike d'Arbo. She is also a close friend of Lord Freddie Windsor, son of

Prince Michael of Kent. Miss Harbord was educated at Tudor Hall a very exclusive boarding school near Banbury but would seem to have very little to recommend herself as a suitable partner for Harry; because of her addiction to partying and drinking, she and her sister are generally known as the 'Hardcore Sisters'.

Finally, the rumours that Prince Harry was in fact the son of Major James Hewitt, a one time boy friend of Princess Diana, persist to this day but as Major Hewitt himself has said 'There really is no possibility whatsoever that I am Harry's father. I can absolutely assure you that I am not'. However he was Diana's secret love interest for five years but the relationship did not begin until Prince Harry was 'already walking'.

Prince Harry's role as a younger 'Royal' has many advantages but also some disadvantages. and in his search for a suitable bride he is clearly set to follow the example of his elder brother and choose a non-royal. Surprisingly, his present girlfriend Cressida Bonas, is the younger half sister of Isabella Gough-Calthorpe, once a girlfriend of Prince William, a lady who gave Kate much cause for concern prior to her marriage. Cressida, like her sister Isabella, is also descended from Sophia, Countess of Darlington the bastard half sister of George I. The two sisters are daughters of Lady Mary Curzon a renowned socialite from the nineteen sixties who is the daughter of the well known World War II racing driver Earl Howe. Cressida takes the place of Florence Brudenell-Bruce, who first met Harry in 2008 and is now due to marry Henry St George, a grandson of the late Duke of Grafton; Henrietta FitzRoy, Henry St George's mother, was once counted amongst the girl friends of Prince Charles.

Harry is now twenty eight years old, the same age as his brother William when he married Kate Middleton. Will he marry Cressida? The present indications are that he will as he is very eager to settle down. What title will he be given? The only titles available are the Dukedoms of Clarence or Sussex last given to William and Augustus the 3rd and 6th sons of George III. The present Earl of Wessex is the only Royal to depart from family tradition when accepting the title of Earl, all royals prior to that have borne the title of Duke.

BIBLIOGRAPHY

1. The Tudor Period: The Howard & Boleyn Families & the English Succession

Marie Louise Bruce, *The Making of Henry VIII* (London, 1977)
Anne Duffin, *Edward Fiennes de Clinton, Earl of Lincoln*, Oxford Dictionary of National Biography (OUP 2004-9)
Charles Ferguson, *Naked to Mine Enemies, The Life of Cardinal Wolsey* (London, 1958)
Anthony Hoskins, *Mary Boleyn's Children – Offspring of King Henry VIII?, Genealogists Magazine* (March Issue 1997, Vol 25, No 9)
Jonathan Hughes, *Mary Stafford (c 1499-1543)*, ODN (OUP 2004-9)
Jonathan Hughes, *Thomas Boleyn, Earl of Wiltshire (1475/6-1539)* ODNB (OUP 2004-9)
E.W. Ives, *Anne Boleyn, Queen of England (c 1500-1536)* ODNB (OUP 2004-9)
Stanford Lehmberg, *Sir Nicholas Carew*, ODNB (OUP, 2004-9)
Beverley A Murphy, *Bastard Prince, Henry VIII's Lost Son* (Stroud, 2001)
Beverley A. Murphy, *Elizabeth Blount* ODNB (OUP 2004-9)
H.F.M. Prescott, *Mary Tudor* (London, 1953)
Michael Riordan, *William Carey, Courtier (c1496-1528)* ODNB (OUP 2004-9)
Desmond Seward, *Prince of the Renaissance, The Life of Francois I,* (London, 1973)
Neville Williams, *The Royal Residences of Great Britain* (London, 1960)

2. The Jacobean Period

Dulcie M. Ashdown, *Royal Paramours* (London, 1979)
Maurice Ashley, *The Stuarts in Love* (London, 1963)
Sir Bernard Burke, *Burke's Dormant and Extinct Peerages* (Baltimore, 1978)
Eileen Cassavetti, *The Lion & the Lilies 'The Stuarts and France'* (London, 1977)
Barry Coward, *The Stuart Age* (London, 1980)
G.M.D. Howat, *Stuart & Cromwellian Foreign Policy* (London, 1974)
Lawrence Stone, *The Crisis of the Aristocracy* (London, 1967)

3. The Stuart Period

Allen Andrews, *The Royal Whore* (London, 1971)
Rosemary Baird, *Mistress of the House: Great Ladies and Grand Houses* (London, 2003)
Olive Baldwin & Thelma Wilson, *Mary Davis,* ODNB (OUP 2004-9)
Andrew Barclay, *Catherine Sedley, Countess of Dorchester*, DNB (OUP 2004-9)
Bryan Bevan, *Charles II's French Mistress, A Biography of Louise de Keroualle, Duchess of Portsmouth* (London, 1972)

Bibliography

Bryan Bevan, *James, Duke of Monmouth* (London, 1973)

Hester W. Chapman, *Four Fine Gentlemen* (London, 1977)

Hester W Chapman, *Privileged Persons: Four Seventeenth Century Studies* (London, 1966),

Hester W. Chapman, *The Tragedy of Charles II* (London, 1964)

John Childs, *The Army of Charles II* (London, 1976)

Peter Cunningham, *The Story of Nell Gwyn* (Edinburgh, 1908)

Peter B. Dewar & Roger S. Powell, *Royal Bastards* (Stroud, 2008)

Bernard Falk, *The Way of the Montagues* (London)

Bernard Falk, *The Royal Fitz Roys* (London, 1950)

Allan Fea, *Some Beauties of the Seventeenth Century* (London, 1906),

Brian Fothergill, *Mrs Jordan, Portrait of an Actress* (London 1965)

Antonia Fraser, *Cromwell, Our Chief of Men* (St Albans, 1976)

David Green, *Queen Anne* (London, 1970)

Geoffrey F. Hall, *Moths Round the Flame, Studies of Charmers & Intriguers* (London 1935)

F.E. Halliday, *A Shakespeare Companion 1564-1964* (Baltimore, 1964).

Hugo Albert Rennert, *The Spanish Stage in the Time of Lope de Vega* (Hispanic Society of America, 1909).

Anthony Hamilton, *Memoirs of the Comte de Gramont* (London, 1930)

Elizabeth Hamilton, *The Illustrious Lady* (Newton Abbot, 1980)

Elizabeth Hamilton, *William's Mary* (London, 1972)

John B. Hattendorf, *Richard Savage, 4th Earl Rivers*, DNB (OUP 2004-9)

Ragnhild Hatton, *George I, Elector & King* (London 1978)

T.F. Henderson, *David Colyear, 1st Earl of Portmore*, DNB (OUP 2004-9)

Philip H. Highfill, *A Biographical Dictionary of Actors, Actresses, Musicians etc (1660-1800)*, 16 vols (Southern Illinois Press, 1973-93)

Mary Hopkirk, *Queen Over the Water, Mary Beatrice of Modena, Queen of James II* (London, 1953)

Maria Kroll, *Sophie, Electress of Hanover* (London 1973)

David Lasocki, *James Paisible*, ODNB (OUP 2004-9)

Robert Latham and William Matthews (editors), *The Diary of Samuel Pepys*, 11 Vols (London, 1970-83)

Harold Love, *Sir Charles Sedley, 5th Bart*, DNB (OUP 2004-9)

Rosalind K. Marshall, *The Days of Duchess Anne* (London, 1973)

Patrick Morrah, *Prince Rupert of the Rhine* (London, 1976),

Patrick Morrah, *A Royal Family, Charles I & His Family* (London)

Antoine E. Murphy, *John Law, Economic Theorist & Policy-Maker* (Oxford, 1997)

Lucy Norton (ed), *Duc de Saint-Simon, Historical Memoirs, Vol 1 1691-1709, Vol 2 1710-1715* (London 1967, 1968)

Richard Ollard, *Clarendon & His Friends* (Oxford, 1987),

Carola Oman, *Mary of Modena* (London, 1962)

Sir Charles Petrie, *The Marshal Duke of Berwick* (London, 1953)

Prince Michael of Greece, *Louis XIV* (London, 1983)

Nesca A. Robb, *William of Orange* (London, 1962)

A.L. Rowse, *The Early Churchills, An English Family* (London, 1956)

Joan Sanders, *The Devoted Mistress, A Life of Louise de la Valliere* (London, 1959)

Lord George Scott, *Lucy Walter, Wife of Mistress* (London, 1947)

The Works of Sir Charles Sedley in Prose and Verse (1778).

V. de Sola Pinto (ed), *The Poetical and Dramatic Works of Sir Charles Sedley*, 2 vols., (London, 1928; repr. New York, 1969)

Francis Steegmuller, *La Grand Mademoiselle* (London, 1955)

Lawrence Stone, *Broken Lives* (Oxford, 1993),

Lawrence Stone, *The Crisis of the Aristocracy*, (Oxford, 1967),

G.M. Thomson, *The First Churchill* (London, 1979)

Peter Thomson, et al., *The Cambridge History of British Drama*, eds. 3 Vols (Cambridge, 2004).

Claire Tomalin, *Mrs Jordan's Profession; the Actress & the Prince* (New York, 1995)

Henri & Barbara van der Zee, *William & Mary* (London, 1973)

H. Noel Williams, *The Love Affairs of the Condes* (London, 1912)

H. Noel Williams, *A Rose of Savoy: Marie Adelaide of Savoy Duchesse de Bourdoogne, Mother of Louis XV* (London, 1909)

John Harold Wilson, *Court Satires of the Restoration* (Ohio, 1976)

John Harold Wilson, *Nell Gwyn, Royal Mistress* (London 1952)

John Harold Wilson, *All the King's Ladies: Actress of the Restoration* (Chicago, 1958).

Philip Ziegler, *King William IV* (London 1971)

4. THE HANOVERIAN PERIOD

Mark Bence-Jones, *The Catholic Families* (London, 1992)

Tracy Borman, *Henrietta Howard 'King's Mistress, Queen's Servant'* (London, 2007)

E.J. Burford, *Wits, Wenchers and Wantons: London's Lowlife Covent Garden in the Eighteenth Century* (London, 1986)

Anthony Camp, *Royal Mistresses and Bastards, Fact and Fiction 1714-1936* (London 2007)

Bernard Falk, *The Berkeleys of Berkeley Square* (London, 1944)

Bernard Falk, *The Royal Fitz Roys* (London, 1950)

P.M. Geoghegan *Frederick Howard, 5th Earl of Carlisle*, ODNB (OUP 2004-9)

Jonathan David Gross, *Elizabeth Lamb, Viscountess Melbourne* ODNB (OUP 2004-9)

Anthony Hamilton, *Memoirs of the Comte de Gramont* (London, 1930)

Christopher Hibbert, *George IV* ODNB (OUP 2004-9)

Maria Kroll, *Sophie, Electress of Hanover* (London, 1973)

Martin J Levy, *Frances Villiers, Countess of Jersey*, ODNB (OUP 2004-9)

Steven Parissien, *George IV, Inspiration of the Regency* (New York, 2001)

Sir Charles Petrie, *The Jacobite Movement* (London, 1959)

Christopher Rowell, *George O'Brien Wyndham, 3rd Earl of Egremont*, ODNB (OUP 2004-9)

Lawrence Stone, *Broken Lives, Separation & Divorce in England 1660-1857* (Oxford, 1993)

Stella Tillyard, *A Royal Affair, George III & His Scandalous Siblings* (London, 2006)

H. Noel Williams, *The Love Affairs of the Condes* (London, 1912)

5. THE EDWARDIAN ERA

Sushila Anand, *Daisy, The Life and Loves of the Countess of Warwick* (London 2008)

Theo Aronson, *The King in Love, Edward VII's Mistresses* (London 1988)

Theo Aronson, *Alice Frederica Keppel*, ODNB (OUP, 2004-9)

Stephen B Baxter, *William III* (London, 1966)

Laura Beatty, *Lillie Langtry* (London, 1999)

Bryan Bevan, *Charles II's French Mistress, A Biography of Louise de Keroualle, Duchess of Portsmouth* (London, 1972)

James Brough, *The Prince & the Lily* (London 1975)

Gordon Brook-Shepherd, *Uncle of Europe, The Social and Diplomatic Life of Edward VII* (London, 1975)

Anthony Camp, *Royal Mistresses and Bastards, Fact and Fiction 1714-1936* (London, 2007)

James Falkner, *Arnold Joost van Keppel, 1st Earl of Albemarle*, ODNB (OUP 2004-9)

Alan Hardy, *The King's Mistresses*, (London, 1980)

Raymond Lamont-Brown, *Edward VII's Last Loves, Alice Keppel and Agnes Keyser*, (London, 1998)

Elizabeth Longford, *Victoria RI* (London, 1966)

6. The House of Windsor

E.J. Burford, *Wits, Wenchers & Wantons, London's Low Life: Covent Garden in the Eighteenth Century* (London, 1986)

Anthony Camp, *Royal Mistress & Bastards, Fact & Fiction 1714-1936* (London, 2007)

P.B. Dewar & Roger S. Powell, *Royal Bastards* (Stroud, 2008)

John Ezard, 'A Life of Legend, Duty & Devotion', *The Guardian*, 1 April 2002

Frances Donaldson, *Edward VIII* (London, 1974)

Bernard Falk, *The Berkeleys of Berkeley Square* (London 1944)

Rupert Godfrey (ed), *Letters From a Prince: Edward, Prince of Wales to Mrs Freda Dudley Ward* (London, 1998)

Alan Hamilton, 'Girl Interrupted', *Times Online*, 17 April 2001

Hello Magazine, 'Profile on Prince William'

Peter Hunt, 'Prince William Splits from Kate', *BBC News*, 14 April 2007

Peggy Miller, *James* (London 1971)

Charles Higham, *Mrs Simpson; Secret Lives of the Duchess of Windsor* (London, 2004)

Stella Tillyard, *A Royal Affair, George III & His Scandalous Siblings* (New York, 2006)

Christopher Warwick, *Princess Margaret* (Carlton, 2002)

The Duchess of Windsor, *The Heart has its Reasons* (London, 1956)

Philip Ziegler, *Edward VIII; the Official Biography* (London, 1990)

'Obituaries, Queen Elizabeth, The Queen Mother', *The Independent*, 1 April 2002

John Ezard, 'Obituaries, Queen Elizabeth, The Queen Mother', *The Guardian*, 30 March 2002

Charles Nevin, 'Obituaries, Princess Margaret', *The Guardian*, 9 February 2002

'Weddings of the Past', *BBC News*, 11 June 1999

'A Very Modern Wedding', *The Daily Mail*, 20 December 2005

The Telegraph, 28 September 2005

Consuela B., *Right Celebrity*, 8 March 2009

John Bingham, *The Telegraph*, 10 March 2009

Shaun Milne, 'Prince is a Love Rat', *The People*, 14 September 2001

Ryan Sabey & Robert Jobson, 'Your Palace or Mine', *News of the World*, 8 March 2009

Julian Wilson, 'Obituaries, Lord Carnarvon', *The Guardian*, 22 November 2001

Geoffrey Levy & Richard Kay, 'His Royal Grumpiness', *The Mail Online*, 11 November 2007

Michael Thornton, 'Prince Philip's Secret Letters to the Showgirl', *The Mail Online*, 20 December 2008

'Portrait of a Marriage', *The Telegraph*, 5 September 2004

BBC News, 21 September 2002

The Telegraph, 25 January 2009

INDEX

Also available from Amberley Publishing

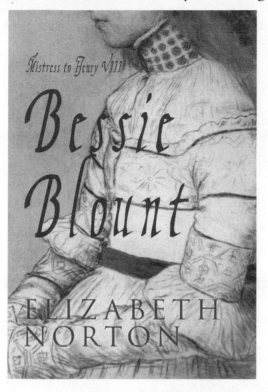

Beautiful, young, exuberant, the amazing life of Elizabeth Blount, Henry VIII's mistress and mother to his first son who came tantalizingly close to succeeding him as King Henry IX

Sidelined by historians until now, Bessie and the son she had by the king are one of the great 'what ifs' of English history. If Jane Seymour had not produced a male heir and Bessie's son had not died young aged 17, in all likelihood Henry Fitzroy could have followed his father as King Henry IX and Bessie propelled to the status of mother of the king.

£25 Hardback
77 colour illustrations
384 pages
978-1-84868-870-4

Available from all good bookshops or to order direct
Please call **01453–847–800**
www.amberleybooks.com

Also available from Amberley Publishing

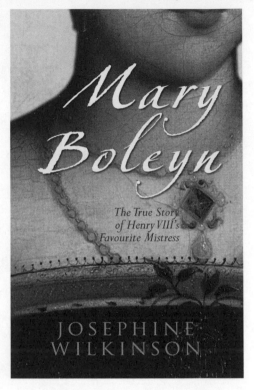

The scandalous true story of Mary Boleyn, infamous sister of Anne, and mistress of Henry VIII

Mary Boleyn, 'the infamous other Boleyn girl', began her court career as the mistress of the king of France. François I of France would later call her 'The Great Prostitute' and the slur stuck. The bête-noir of her family, Mary was married off to a minor courtier but it was not long before she caught the eye of Henry VIII and a new affair began.

Mary would emerge the sole survivor of a family torn apart by lust and ambition, and it is in Mary and her progeny that the Boleyn legacy rests.